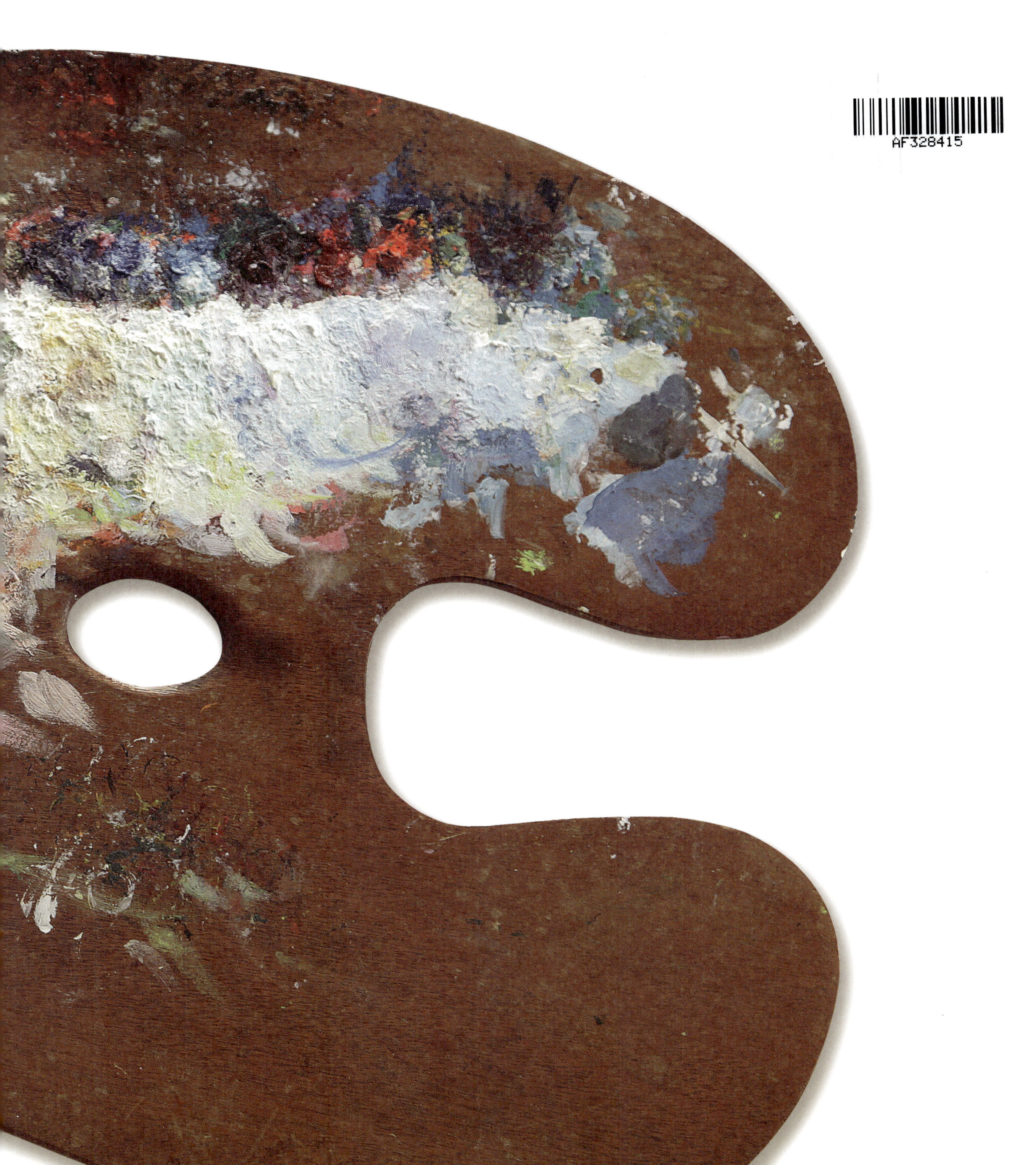
AF328415

WILLIAM WILKINS

DAVID FRASER JENKINS

GRAFFEG

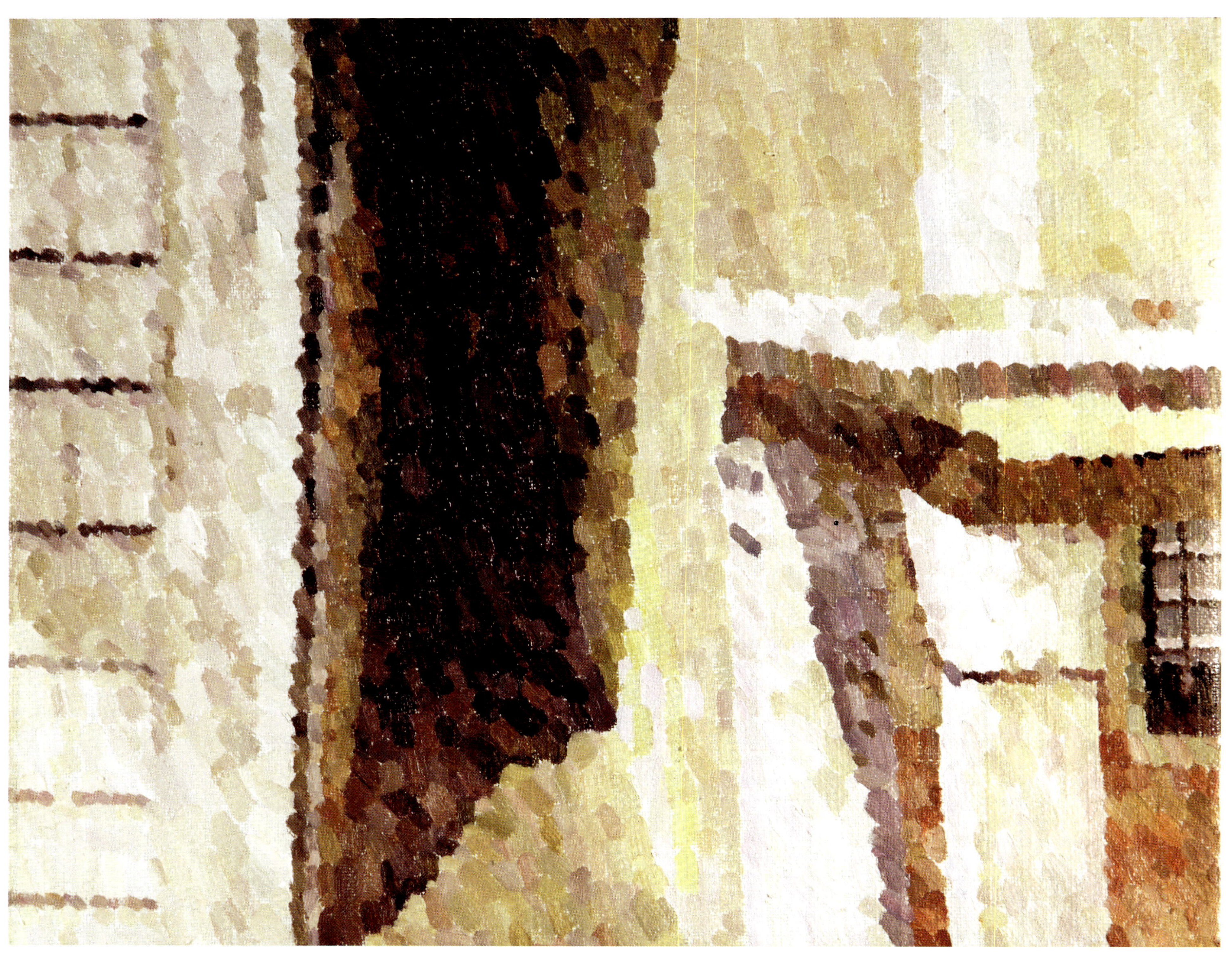

Calle Widmann, Venice, 2013, oil on canvas, 25 x 32cm, Courtesy of the artist.

CONTENTS

Cover image: Sunlight, Cornus Florida, 2014, oil on canvas, 86 x 92cm, Courtesy of the artist.

INTRODUCTION

GERAINT TALFAN DAVIES

In the late 1990s a lean man in a pin-stripe suit came to my office at the BBC in Cardiff to sell the idea of 'a visual equivalent of the BBC's Cardiff Singer of the World competition', and to see whether we would help him develop it. At once imaginative, persuasive and practical, William Wilkins is a man not easily denied. That morning he did not get quite as much as he had hoped, but within a few days he had been equally persuasive at the Wales Tourist Board. The Artes Mundi Visual Arts Prize was on its way.

Through a potent mix of vision, old-fashioned courtesy and steely fixity of purpose William Wilkins has, in less than two decades, bestowed on his own small country a personal legacy that even the grand patrons of old would be hard-pressed to match: a new national institution, the National Botanic Garden of Wales; the peeling away of centuries-old layers to reveal the exquisite intimacy of Aberglasney and its gardens; the rescue of Llanelly House from the unseeing neglect of officialdom; a biennial visual arts prize that both rewards a focus on the human condition and connects his home patch purposefully with the rest of the globe – both aims another measure of the man.

It is this extraordinary accumulation of civic achievement that has led people to exclaim misleadingly, "And he paints as well!" Misleading, because William Wilkins is a painter first and foremost. It is the painter's eye and sensibility that have informed everything he has done, an artist's seriousness of intent that is so striking in his own self-portraits.

In this sense, this volume is an overdue corrective to the widely-held impression of William Wilkins as cultural entrepreneur first and painter second, reminding us of the chronology of his developing interests, as well as the content of his art. Words that imply discipline and intensity recur throughout: 'long and self-imposed period of disciplined studies', the 'intense period of drawing', 'prolonged and copious study', 'the compromise between disciplined touch and emotional sympathy', 'his long training in observation'.

His public projects, meticulous in both conception and execution, have been another expression of the discipline that underlies his painting, to an extent that it comes as no surprise that his chosen style, pointillism, is so painstaking and time-consuming. It is almost as if, in the Celtic tradition, he has felt the need to impose a challenging technical discipline upon his work, against which to struggle and conquer. But, as one reviewer of his first New York exhibition remarked, "There is a uniform quality – a delicacy of feeling that elevates a very fastidious technique to the level of poetry." The same might be said today of Aberglasney.

In William Wilkins the personal and the public have run in parallel – the artist/citizen - exemplified in the combination of his painting and his deep knowledge of architecture, gained in the energetic architecture department of the former Greater London Council. Anyone whose family home overlooks the most spectacularly sited of Welsh castles, Carreg Cennen, cannot but have a regard for the past, for the landscape and for the impact of buildings. Welsh weather will have imprinted those infinite variations of light that are so central to his painting.

Wales has much cause to be grateful to William Wilkins for allowing himself to be distracted from his painting to enrich our public realm so profusely. We can repay our debt to him by not allowing those achievements to eclipse his equally rich art that, inevitably, takes us even more directly to the heart of the man.

Geraint Talfan Davies, March 2014

THE PAINTINGS OF WILLIAM WILKINS

DAVID FRASER JENKINS

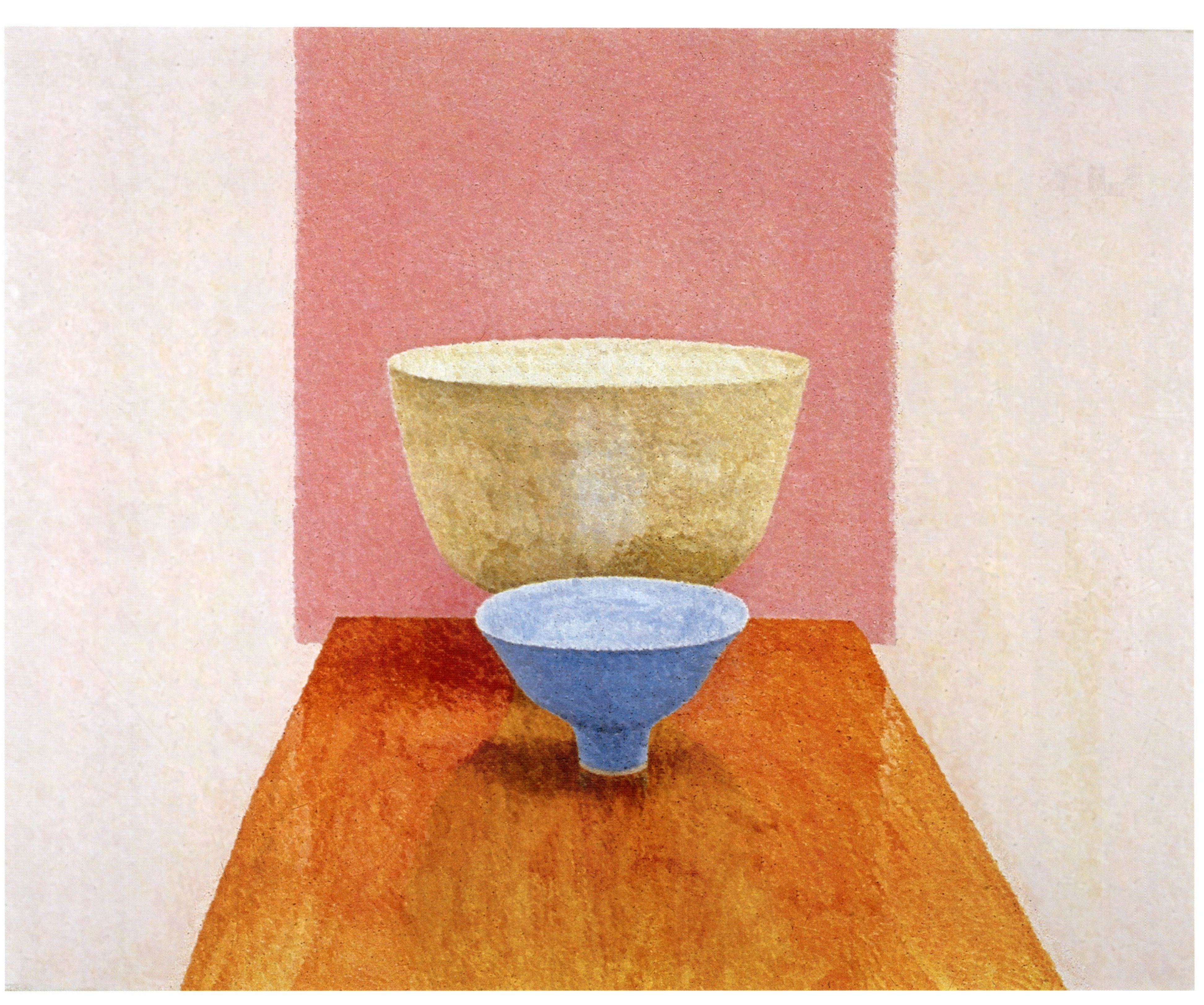

Still Life: Magenta Field, 1984, oil on canvas, 60 x 76cm, Private collection.

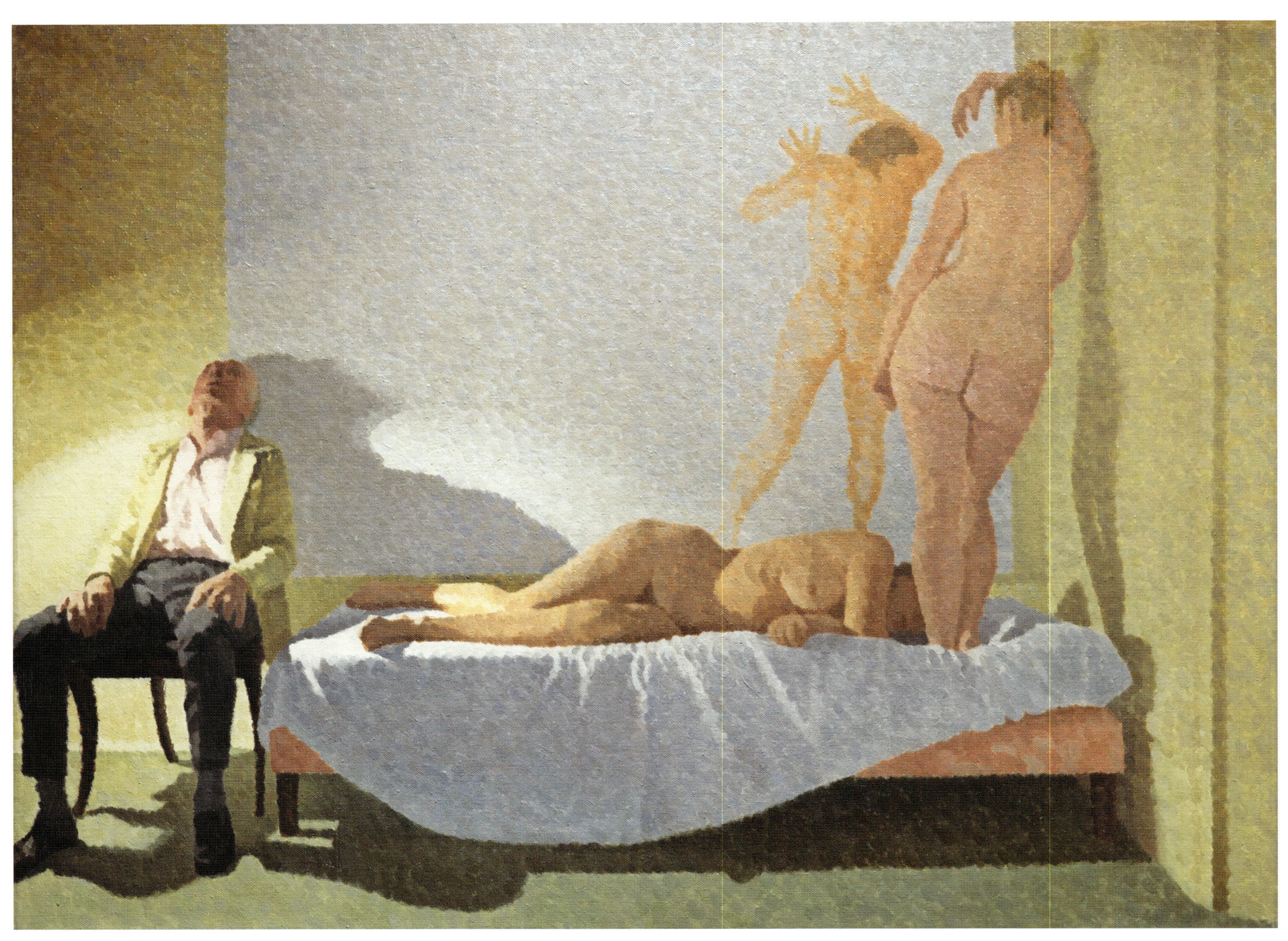

Figures in a Studio, 1977, oil on canvas, 40 x 55cm, Private collection.

Figures in a Studio

'Figures in a Studio' was shown in Wilkins' first ever exhibition of paintings. He was aged thirty-nine at the time in 1977, and had often exhibited drawings, but had purposely delayed embarking on making his first paintings for display. The picture is of a size to fit a usual room, but is monumental in appearance, with four figures seen quite close-to who look huge, as well as strange, all of them arranged and posed, as the title says, 'in a studio'. They are artist's models, paid to stand and lie there while being watched and painted, sometimes all of them together and otherwise in ones and twos, in this enigmatic scene carefully arranged by the artist.

The picture is strange enough to demand our searching look, and it becomes clear that one of the figures is only there in the form of a painting on a background canvas, hung down the far wall beyond the group, and she is smaller than the scale of the others. She appears as a painting of a painting, and unlike them she makes a dramatic and artificial pose, with both hands splayed open into the air and her head buried in her elbow. The artificial lighting is arranged so that the two figures at the left are in strong contrasts of light and dark shadow, but the other two are held in half-light. The group separates into two pairs, one asleep, the man clothed and the woman relaxed naked on the bed in a sleeping position, the other pair both naked, standing, their faces completely hidden. The eyes of the first couple are obscured.

The clothed and every-day looking sleeping man casts a striking double shadow of his face and chest in profile, lying across the corner of the painted backdrop. There is a suppressed narrative that runs around these people, quite insistently, as if to query how much can be known from appearances alone, without speech or explanation, or as if everything were a dream. The picture makes the artifice very evident, yet at the same time also stays within the strict rules of what the artist could see. But the painted woman is clawing at a cloth in front of her, as if not only is she a painting, but she is attacking the surface of another painting at one stage even further removed from us. Everything is visually clear, but all their eyes are hidden, and there is a marked disjunction between our attention and the withdrawal of their power of sight.

The painting itself is made without lines or drawing of any kind on the canvas. It was begun, as are all Wilkins' paintings, touch by touch of small patches of colour on the white ground. It was designed in the first place with all the models assembled together in front of the painted backdrop, like a theatre peep-show, and the whole thing adjusted with a complicated array of spotlights, ceiling lights and Anglepoises on tables and on the floor. The poses and the lighting were tuned to each other, all to the position of the artist's eye. For these complex paintings Wilkins always makes a large diagram on paper to record the set-up, with outlines in sweeps of pencil lines. Then, on a blank canvas marked to the decided proportions within its rectangle, in this case 16 x 22 inches, the colour is gradually applied in touches, at first in the larger background areas that set the tone and harmonic contrast, and establish the space.

The narrative is not really a story, but more of a provocation, or a definition of levels of meaning. The base level is given in this painting by the only figure in a rhetorical pose, the painted female nude in the background, looking like an Eve in the 'Expulsion from Paradise' or some such lamentation. If she has the status of a continuity from the Old Masters, then the living set-up is contemporary, of mere people, professionals paid to be able to work with an artist, posed and then watched by him. The painted scene depends on their appearance, and this tableau is a collaboration with these models, who became companions of the artist over the long hours of work. The sexual compulsion that is visible to the eye in these handsome bodies without clothes is frustrated by their sleepiness, as well as by their involvement in this unknown drama that keeps their attention separate.

When Wilkins began to paint in oils in 1974, at first he posed naked models individually. The studio groups, three of which were in his first exhibition, load further visual meaning into the notion of how to make a valid painting of the nude. 'Figures in a Studio' is exemplary. What is bizarre about this procedure is the double act of creation: first the setting up of the tableau for his own private vision; then the making of a painting of it, in touches of coloured oil paints. The first, the set-up, must always have seemed rather clunking, like an arranged still life, a deliberate contrivance, with arty elements of shadows and the cunning outline shadow of a hand on the floor. But all the while the artist was thinking of the process that would turn this into sense.

A model for this process which I cannot escape is Vermeer's painting of 'The Artist's Studio', since this shows two artists, one seen there painting away, the other implied, who is making the painting we look at. We never hesitate to believe that they are the same person, as we are invited to look at the momentary pose of the model both as a contrivance in the studio and as a painting, so that here again is a confrontation of art and reality. In this Vermeer, made at the end of his life, and by a Catholic in a Protestant country, everything is metaphorical, even 'the sun's illumination stealing like a tide across a map to his girl solid with yearning' (Robert Lowell, in his last published poem). This is easy to feel, and (luckily) beyond my brief to account for. But move forward to 1977, and skill in

representation itself accounted for very much less. The first function of Wilkins' beautiful painting was to prise apart these levels of meaning that had been intact, and then to go further on beyond the now sadly meaningless rhetoric of the Old Masters.

Vermeer's figures, like all in the old galleries, are trapped within their outlines. Drawing gives rhythm to the design, and it marks off as separate, finite, and knowable all that it contains, and which it necessarily restrains as well. But boundaries made of painted colour, like a fuzzy molecular border, allow each object-touch its own space, with no subservience to the hand moving at right angles to the sight. The shadow of Wilkins' sleeping man shares a space on the canvas with the painted figure, as if to say that lines are not to be trusted, they are invented or are mere shadow, and they could never be argued back single mindedly to their original figure. They are all like the myth of the 'Corinthian Maid' who outlines the shadow of her departing lover, and records something that was real, but that marks an absence.

A Programme of study

It is mighty peculiar that an artist in 1974 should choose to start to paint by imitating the technique of the Pointillists, not only taking up something of the 1880s that had been achieved for long-lost purposes, but also in itself such a laborious and expensive practice. But Wilkins came of age as an artist at a time when the herd of new painters disbanded. His near contemporaries amongst British painters and sculptors include Paul Huxley, John Walker, Allen Jones, John Byrne, Ivor Abrahams, Anthony Green, William Tillyer, Patrick Caulfield, Terry Atkinson, Terry Setch, Tom Phillips and Barry Flanagan, all of whom have a striking fact in common, that their work is as diverse as are the animals in the zoo. Wilkins' position was chosen with knowing deliberation, after an extraordinarily long and self-imposed period of disciplined studies.

The breakthrough came when, amongst other things, he realised that he could master a Seurat-like style without any of the aesthetics, politics or attitudinising of the great Post-Impressionist. The British artists listed above made individual choices, and so far as I am aware no one else anywhere had chosen to paint in the manner of the Pointillists, but that can be said in principle of each of them in turn, so unlike the others. Not that no one else used dots of paint, on the contrary, the practice of Ian Stephenson and Andrew Forge, and Tom Phillips at times, and probably others, was also dependent on dots of colour, but in their cases on the surface, as abstraction in a shallow space. And of course Wilkins sought to revive not just a certain discipline of painting, but the classic vernacular subjects as well, the nude, still life, landscape and architecture.

Wilkins more or less trained himself as a painter. At the Royal College of Art he studied the design and manufacture of stained glass, working with the former masters of the new Coventry Cathedral slightly after that event. The making of stained glass, notably for his future, worked for architecture, and with the separation of individual colours, and with the separation of colour from drawing – three habits that persisted. At the same time he studied drawing intensely at evening classes. On leaving the Royal College, he then launched into eight years of experimental painting, abstract sometimes, and realist, a bit neo-romantic, even minimalist.

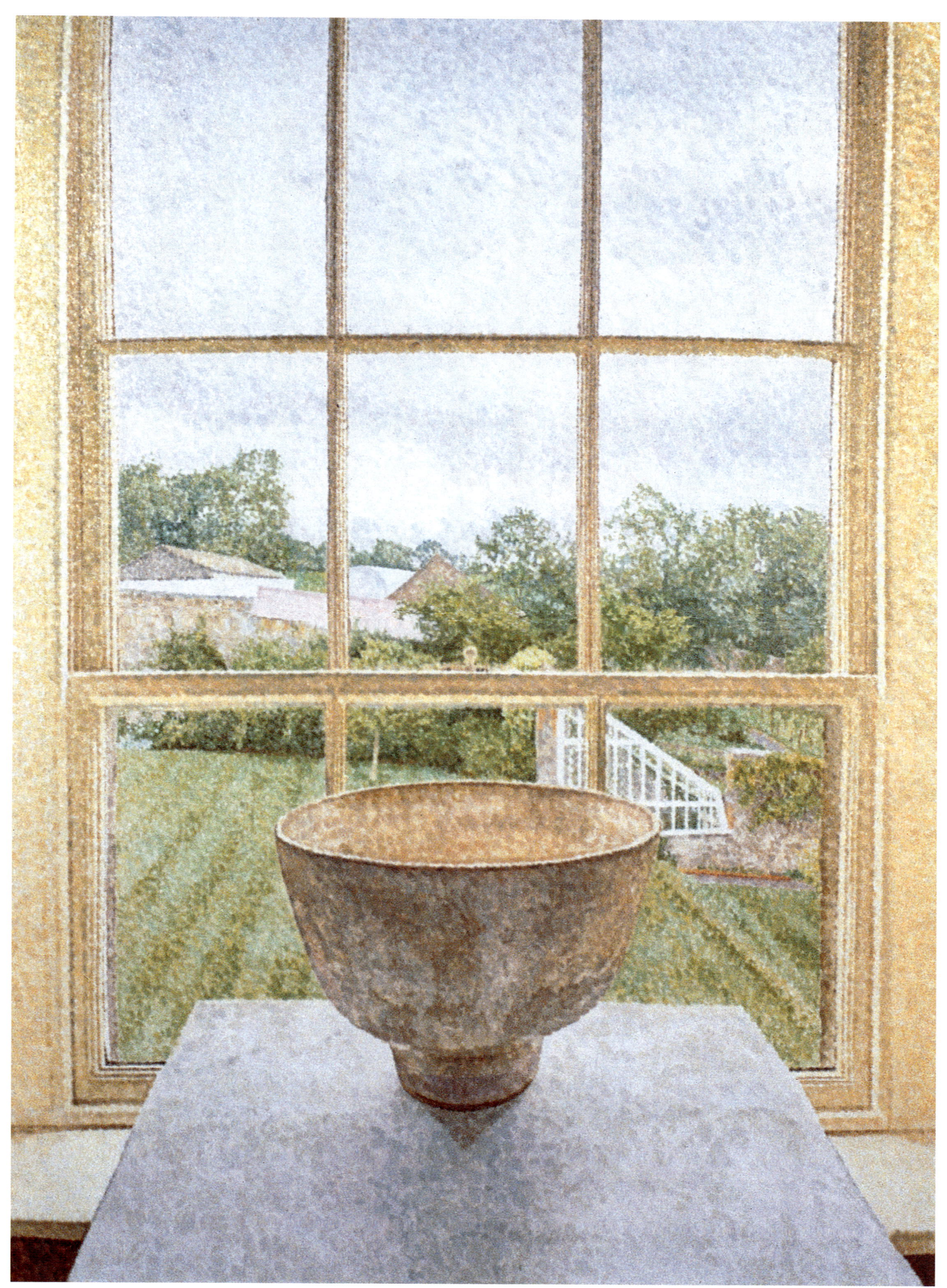

Bowl before window, 1984, oil on canvas, 101 x 76cm, Private collection.

At the same time he was teaching art and the history of architecture at a boys' school, reviving the pupils' interest in the arts and setting up a pottery.

In the midst of this period Wilkins bought at great extravagance (which now seems the opposite) a particularly massive ceramic bowl by Lucie Rie, which he had seen in an exhibition. It seems that this bowl became his talisman, although his own art could not catch up with it for a further ten years. The simple shape, whose structure, texture and colour unite to make it as it is, no more nor less, with nothing extraneous, no symbolism, yet with touchable implications of the slow time of its manufacture, and its turning to solid stone in the kiln, anticipate his own art.

Then from the time of around his thirtieth birthday in 1968 he threw in all his practice and prejudices to begin a period of back-to-basics practice of drawing. He destroyed all the experimental paintings, so that almost none survive. Just then the example of Seurat's career was well known and was cited sometimes as a model in that he had deliberately undertaken a period of drawing alone. Wilkins' first new drawings were a bit like Seurat's in their reticence, and realism of light and shade. And he did have a model for his way of drawing, but it was not Seurat but the etchings of Morandi. Morandi's etched still lifes are miracles of the making of shape by cross-hatching alone, and seem to award presence and ghostly mass to his congregations of pots and cans.

This was an intense period of drawing for Wilkins, lasting as much as six years, crammed into long evenings and weekends after work in the architectural department of the Greater London Council. The range of his inspiration was minute and yet enormous, excluding everything but the persistent survivors of the art of the past. He drew the greatest of old architecture, and the simplest (and most easily held) poses of the body – buildings and nudes. From this distance it seems like a process of understanding, comparable to his admiration of modern ceramics. The drawings were all done on the spot with a pad of paper on an easel or propped against him. And at first they were on architects' graph paper, as if to make the announcement 'Here is the structure' in the perceived appearance of stone and body, before he moved on to use heavyweight Arches paper for the bigger landscapes.

'Plans, as the key to the space of a building, and the organisation of windows, as the key to the lighting, are the two factors that most interest me in architecture', he wrote of a relentless survey he made in the summer of 1971 of the churches of Brittany, visiting and recording several hundred of them, with a grant from the Welsh Arts Council. But all the same, he followed a Cotman-like love of the way light falls on the weathered stone when he chose to draw the churches. The presence of the printed squares in the graph paper becomes a modern screen, as does the accumulation of sheer information in the survey. The features of some of the drawings are strung out in a horizontal line, and the buildings appear as if along the fold between a vast flat and undefined foreground and the vertical backdrop of sky, with a narrow band where geometry gives way to intricacy, pushing against perspective. The sheer manual skill shows itself not just in the sensitivity of

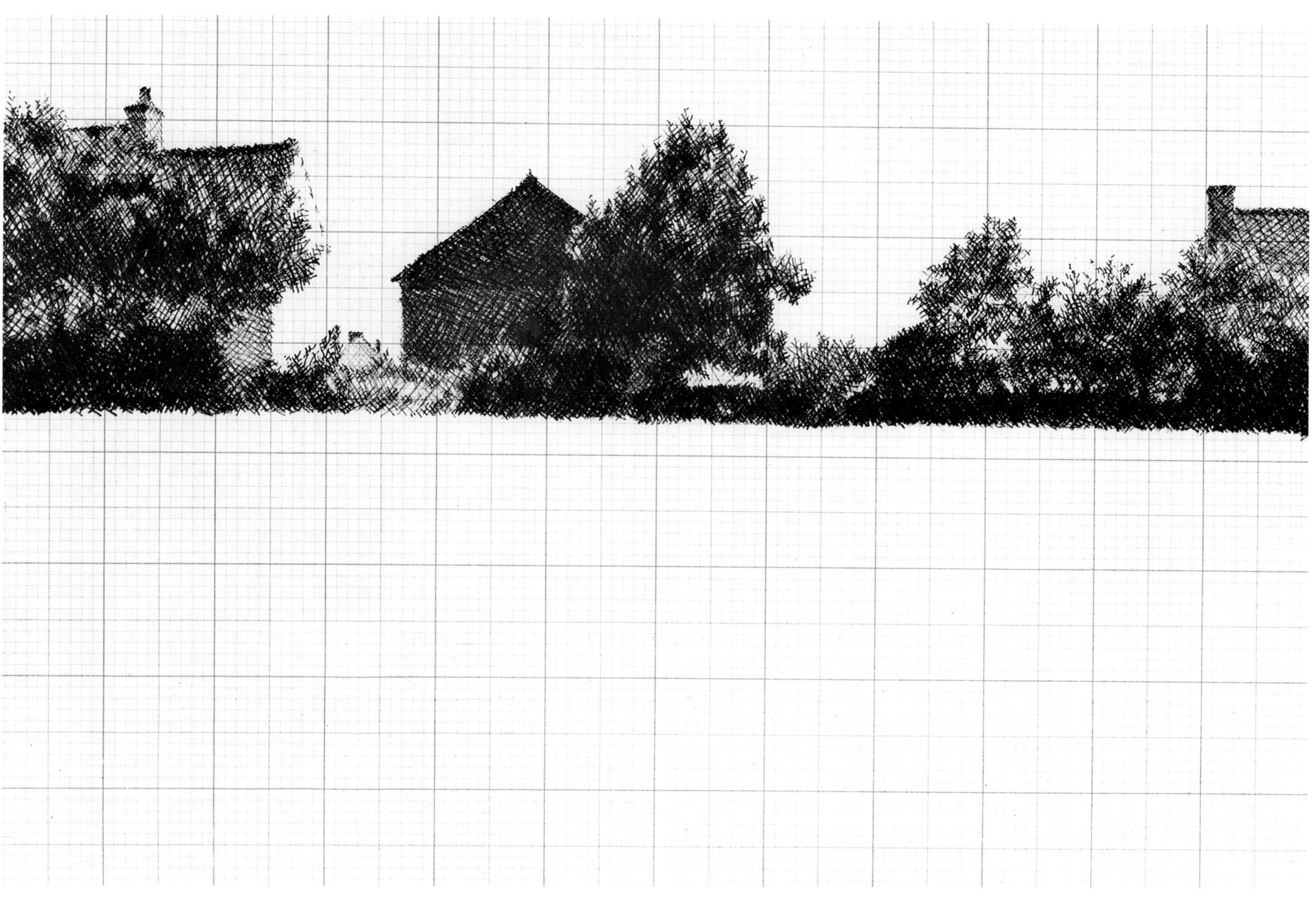

Near Ezer, 1971, pencil on graph paper, 20 x 30cm, Private collection.

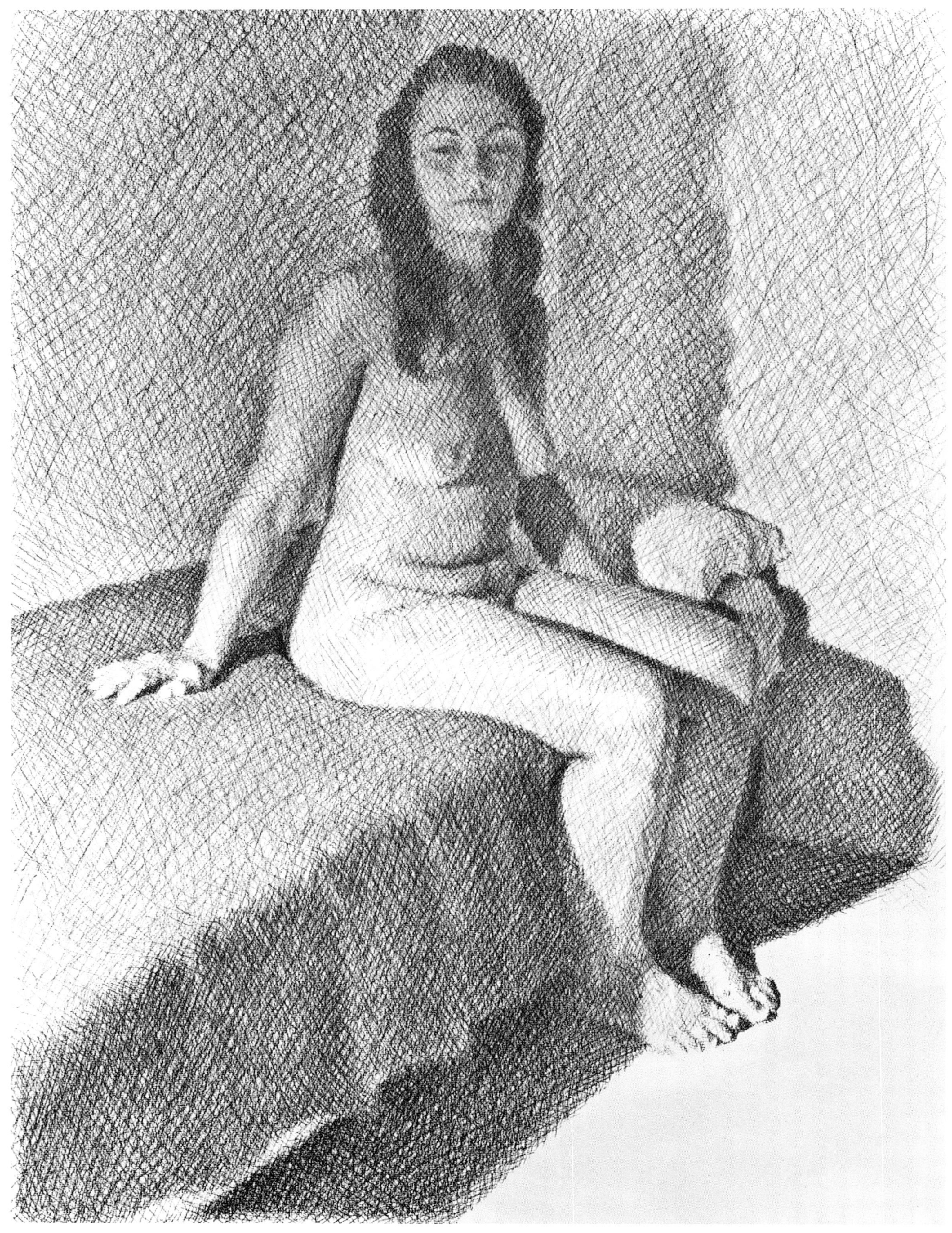

Seated Nude, pencil on paper, 35 x 25cm, Private collection.

cross-hatching, but in the restraint of omissions, allowing unsuspected shapes simply to appear. This process is selective, not photographic, as the eye chooses what and how to caress of the vast higgledy-piggledy of land and buildings as seen.

In this prolonged and copious study Wilkins learned a habit of eye and mind that seemed to work without prejudice or given thought. But that is not quite the case, and the appeal of these Brittany drawings lies in the compromise between disciplined touch and emotional sympathy. Architecture is shown locally, in situ, as it is, yet adjusted to focus on the most significant, as for the knowing eyesight. The village on the cover of his Brittany exhibition catalogue is not part of his survey, but registers his vision square by square, checked off by the artist's spider-like weaving of tangents, coming to show an amazing church belfry concealed between two telegraph poles.

The most persistent subject of his drawings in this period of 1968-74 was the single female nude, of a model posing, relaxed and close to his eye. The skill of these tender drawings in making an illusion disguises for a moment the special way in which information in them is discovered by the viewer, and not dictated by the preferences of the artist. It is not a question of what detail he chose to include, but of how much can be seen within the shadowy lights, as the vision of the viewer steps in to share the subject with the drawn paper. The line varies in direction, heaviness, length, but can only make the darks, so the process becomes one of seeking the intervals and spaces between things, like carving directly into marble, and significance is given according to the degree that the surface is left alone. Wilkins set figures in doorways, on the floor, in one room seen from another, in both casual and old masterly poses, but always with this strange sense of revelation by touch. The figures have a strong erotic appeal yet are not taken away from their own self possession.

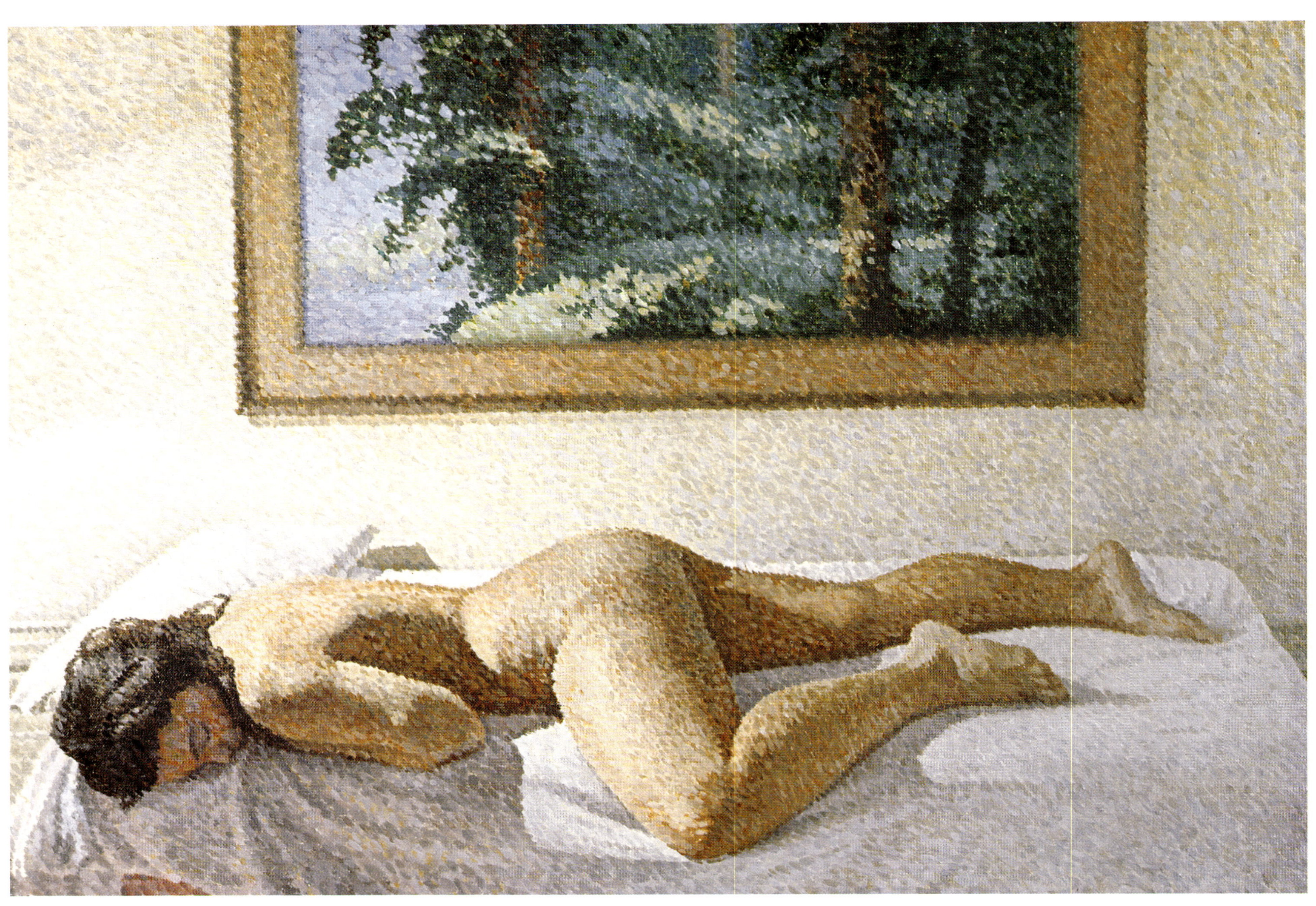

Nude with Landscape, 1974, oil on canvas, 30 x 45cm, Private collection.

Oil paintings

Colour is the real thing. Wilkins' jump to oil painting in 1974 was at first an extension from the drawings of his vision as tonal study, and he seems to have chosen the early Corot as one at least of his inspirations, for the colouring, for his choice of model (or, perhaps it was his sight of the model that suggested Corot) and for the detachment of his approach. Corot was a challenge, because his early nudes are a landmark of modesty in painting, with a unique grey-ochre palette, and introduced a restrained but compelling sensuousness. Desire is more overt in these first oil paintings by Wilkins than ever again later in his painting, especially in two of the first, one of a woman lying naked on her front with one knee raised. This was his Opus 1, re-commencing his self-respect as an artist, but he had to make do with a fictive landscape framed on the wall above her, as he had not yet begun to paint outside the studio. The other painting was of an elongated figure reading on a bed seen from behind, again as if in the fold of space between flatness and verticals, traversed by the eye horizontally left and right. They are a tease, as if the hand did not know what it was making.

Even more remarkable than performing a pointillist technique was Wilkins' continuity from these first oils, and the consistency of his development afterwards, as if this were a predestined change, like a coloured butterfly shaking itself out of the chrysalis of drawing. It is apparent now that in fact these paintings have little to do with Seurat, and the links now seem to be to the Euston Road School (which he hated), Lucien Pissarro, Derain, Corot as remarked, the backgrounds of David (perhaps) and Lucian Freud, as well as to a feeling of contrariness to most high-profile art being done at the time, which was not painting. His own beacon for painterly behaviour was Morandi. At first there was little evidence of engagement with the models as individuals, and there is a perceptible strain in later examples as the poses incrementally turn to face the viewer, who gradually is asked to confront the character of the face.

Making a painting with touches of colour is not straightforward. To transcribe the nude in colour is a wonderful task, with the flesh of a smallish but vital range of colour. Wilkins' painting was also in character deliberately anti-Coldstream. The latter's 'Reclining Nude' of 1974-6, for example, even apart from the savagery of measuring marks and the lack of finish, and reek of disegno, shows a flesh without warmth, fragmented by changes of tint that are neither modelled nor brushed in terms of the tensions of surface. It is a large painting that took Coldstream fifteen months, and it has other ambitions, but Wilkins' tiny nudes, taking just as long to paint, retain unity and an apparent realism with no overt artiness. Perhaps without Coldstream and his disciples Wilkins would not have felt this need for a purer painting. His restriction of touch to accumulated pats of colour is not like dot-matrix printing, it forces a summary of detail, a loss of surface blemish and shine, but gives an overall evenness and allows a procedure of touch and modification. It is rather misleading to call these paintings 'realist' (as they were known by critics in America), since their basis is totally artificial and within the enclosed world of the studio. The untenability of the position of the observer is emphasised in Wilkins' only narrative painting 'Interior with Man Dressing' 1976, of a man doing up his trousers while turning his back to a crumpled nude on a bed. This is a reprise of a favourite theme of Sickert's, and of Dutch genre, of paid sex, here with a mood of sadness and emptiness. It is unreal, as a performance of a scene from a play which cannot have had a real observer.

But these little nudes are varied in pose and light, seemingly to match the bodily character of the models, all waiting in repose (as they have to be), frozen in reflection, in dialogue between their personalities and the weight of the artist's stare at their body. They avert their eyes, and this discontinuity is played up in a series of paintings of two figures, a clothed man and a nude woman in ignorance of each other, but often with the man singing or playing music, a contemporary miniscule re-staging of the great Giorgiones and Titians. Clearly the male becomes an alter-ego for the painter and viewer (male or female), waiting, still waiting, for a means into the centre of this key to the great art of the past. The men are often dressed in cornflower blue, and there is a match of colour as well as music. The female nude, if partly clothed, was usually in red. In the interior with a man dressing, his blue trousers and a blue cloth at the foot of her bed begin to orchestrate a balance of the genders by colours, to match an enriching and a calming of an overall harmony. In all the hesitancy and potential of these early paintings there is an element of abstraction in the way of a late Kandinsky painting that provokes and resolves a risky balance.

But most of the paintings in Wilkins' first two exhibitions in New York in 1977 and 1979 were landscapes of western France. All these were painted out of doors in the summer, depending on particular light and time of day, and were done more quickly than the nudes. His first few landscapes were painted on another trip to Brittany in 1975, but he realised he needed to find a countryside to work where the weather was less changeable. In 1977 and the following year he went further south, at first near Uzes in Languedoc, and then at Loches on the Loire, in both places borrowing rooms to live. He took his

easel, palette, paints and brushes, sometimes a stool, off into the fields to paint the out-of-the-way places where he could work and not be disturbed.

These are ambitious paintings of complex views that mostly lacked much structure, so that all depended on slight varieties in pitch of colour, although sometimes they were pegged to a lane turning around into a distance. They were also a test of his endurance, spending hours alone in remote corners of fields and woods, returning day after day while the weather held, with all at risk till the last. An accumulation of leaves is already a fragmented sight and more accessible to Pointillism, and some of these landscapes look like paintings by Camille Pissarro and Sisley of about 1870. But more exactly they add to the long tradition of plein-air studies from throughout the nineteenth century. Wilkins in effect was doing Impressionism again from Nature. He favoured most often a grey light in these first painted landscapes, allowing a dominant subdued green. The success of these paintings is a question of skill and his long training in observation, matching touch from the palette to the structure of paint on the canvas. It was applied with a soft, sable brush, and modified during progress with a richer oil medium. They are paintings without people, of ordinary and un-picturesque places, with none of the Impressionists' interests in vacations or rural activity, merely staring at an indifferent nature. Together with the nudes painted in the studio these two groups of pictures, inside and outside, seem to grab and hold the small areas of individual perception that are real – an artificial contrivance with people, an accumulation of gestures within an isolated and foreign nature.

The exhibitions in New York, in the Robert Schoelkopf Gallery, were a critical and commercial triumph, giving Wilkins the re-assurance to continue, and confirming that this idiosyncratic choice of style, which he had pursued alone since his extraordinary gamble in re-starting in 1968, was justified and financially possible. His practice was set, even though still almost totally unique apart from a few naturalist painters also showing at Schoelkopf, notably William Bailey, the American painter of nudes and still lifes.

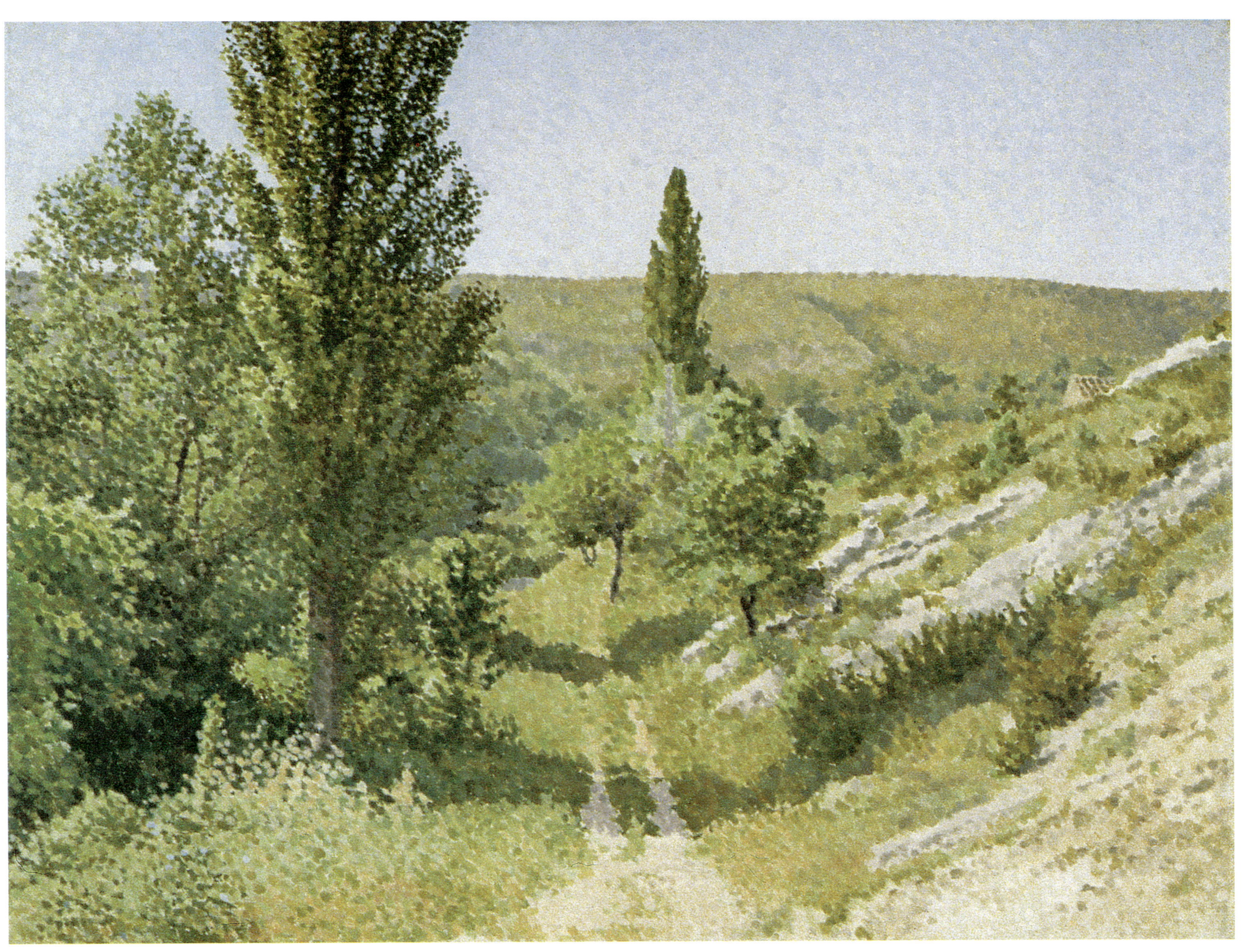

Morning Languedoc, 1977, oil on canvas, 30 x 40cm, Private collection.

Possibilities of paint

In the years around 1980 Wilkins was supported both financially and in his confidence by the exhibitions in America, and possessed a language of painting, or at least an alphabet, that was poised to take on more. He was recently married, and living in Brook Green in west London with their two young children – and he had a Folly (at first in both senses), for he had bought the wreck of his family's house in Carmarthenshire, a neo-classical villa, in sight of Carreg Cennen castle, which he planned to restore and to re-plant the four acres of garden.

But what can oil painting do, painting that looked something like an art of a hundred years earlier, and which took so long to do that it could not incorporate anything that moved, yet had to have its subject before the eyes? Wilkins made this query the basis of his series of still-theatre paintings, some in acknowledgement of the most memorable of the Old Masters. His position at the time seemed quite out-of-the-usual, but the artists of his generation in London were generally idiosyncratic, many looking also to New York. His isolated stance and regard for the past are not so different in principle to that of his contemporaries listed above, for instance

again Huxley, Walker and Abrahams, whose output is so unlike each others, but all of whom at times revived older images.

To make a new painting of objects assembled is like casting a spell. There are unusual things to be gathered together, odd actions of the body to repeat, a place to perform with unusual markings on the floor, nothing to chant admittedly but lights to arrange, and when all is ready, coloured minerals are stirred with a wand, and placed in order on a flat surface; and then, if all was done well, a lively spirit will move into this surface, to reside and to be felt by others. De Chirico, aware of all this, kept a charm over his easel to ensure only a good influence. Wilkins with his studio theatre set a task for himself to cast such a spell with his painting, to make something that would come alive under enchantment, within the routines of the necromancy validated by the power of old paintings.

The art of the galleries is no longer something of our own visual experience, and yet in Wilkins' time the accepted alternative practice had simply deteriorated into an action without meaning, the painting he almost came to

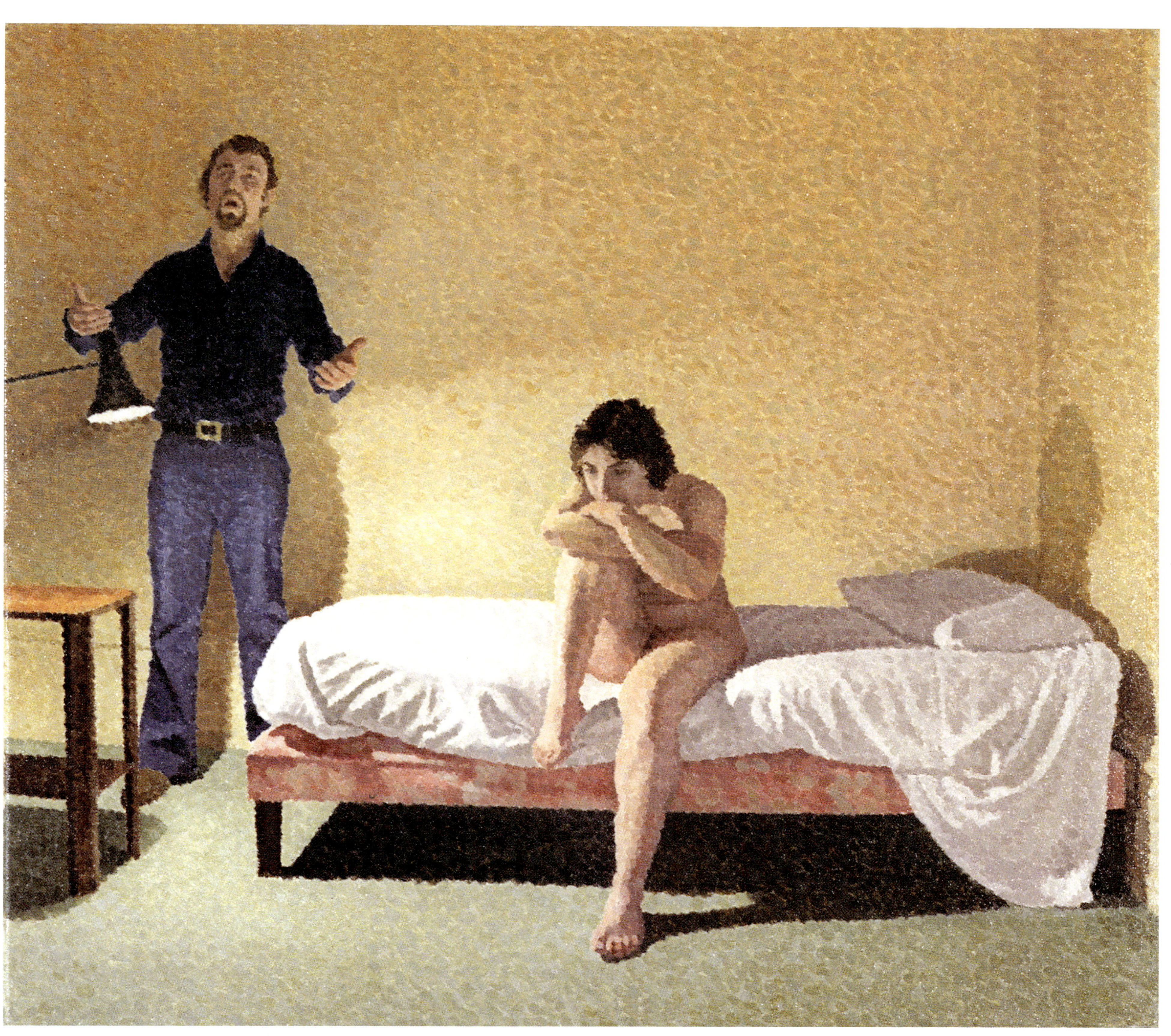

Two Figures, the Man Singing, 1978, oil on canvas, 40 x 48cm, Private collection.

do himself, of 'white on white'. This was
a modernist cul-de-sac, but art is just as
decisively cut off from the bourgeois art of
nineteenth century France. The studio is a
laboratory, where to be modern is to be honest
– a simple demand, but of near impossibility.
But the continued ethical practice of the art of
painting depends on a triangulation, to bridge
from the past to our own activity and onwards to
an outlook for the future. It was this rationale for
painting from the past to the future that Wilkins
pursued, constructing tableaux to paint like the
'Figures in a Studio', making some ten of them
in his London studio.

The idea of 'Picnic' (1981) came from a winter
landscape that Wilkins noticed and drawn when
briefly he was artist in residence at Walpack,
New Jersey in 1980-1, which reminded him of
the place of the figures beside a pond in a wood
in the 'Dejeuner sur l'Herbe'. His 1981 version
of the Manet looks rather different, and is a
good deal smaller, although seen by him in the
studio as life size. He enlarged a sketch of the
wood to become a painted backcloth, he painted
a flecked green and blue floor covering, set

up the lights at high and low levels and hired
these models. He also rummaged to find some
plastic picnic stuff in dense colours, which
he arranged to sit on the floor as if trying to
make a shape, a bit like Tony Cragg's 'Axehead'
sculpture of 1982. There is an interaction of
pose and plastic. A pair of hesitant lovers, he
looking and she touching, share their studio
picnic with a middle-aged, balding man opening
a bottle of beer. At the right, a woman who looks
a bit young for him is putting on her clothes
before departing. This is just on the edge of
absurdity, as it seems this charade could never
become that famous painting. Manet's situation,
famously echoing a Renaissance print, cannot
become contemporary, although the disjunction
here between studio props and real woodland
point to the lack of reality in the Manet itself.
This great subject, Wilkins' painting exclaims,
is no longer valid, and the artifice is here
made plain, but look, the palette of blue
cups and plates, with a bit of red and yellow,
might sometime enable this conjunction of
colour patches to come to life, in tune with
reciprocated desire.

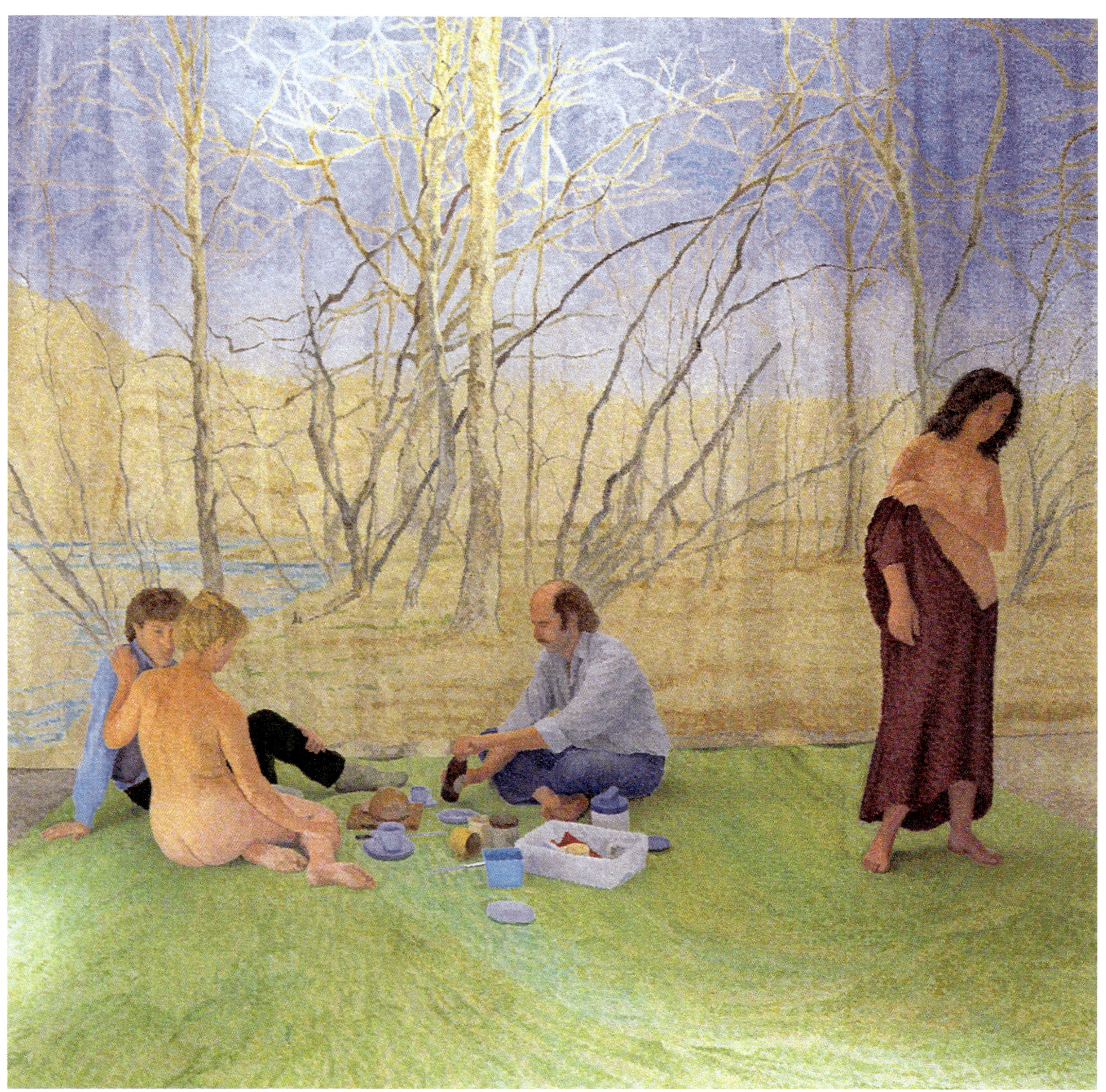

Picnic, 1981, oil on canvas, 71 x 78cm, Private collection.

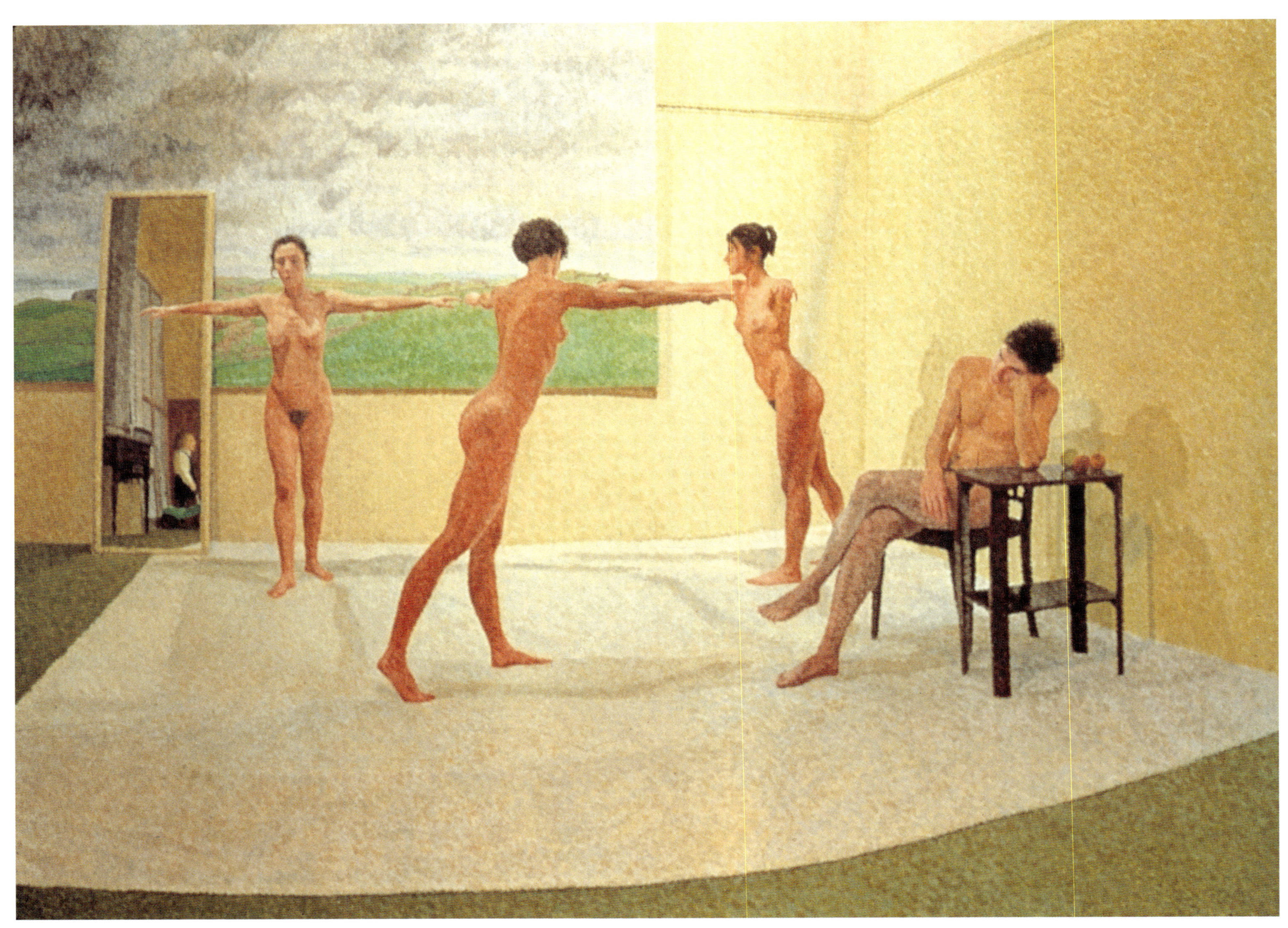

A Dance, 1983, oil on canvas, 78 x 109cm, Glynn Vivian Art Gallery, Swansea.

'A Dance' (1983), a truly difficult scene to enact, keeps aloft the whole critical basis of Wilkins' painting. He himself looks at the tall mirror in the background where his young daughter is beside him watching him at work; a geometrical square appears on the floor covering; there is a cloudy panorama of South Wales hills; the figure of a man may be dreaming, but at least he too is naked, and shares a place with the dancers, to whom he pointedly is not awarding apples; the three barefoot nudes pose as if in a ballet at the briefest pause before movement, to form a straight line of hands and arms, and a striking foreshortening. The whole scene re-enacts Poussin's 'Dance to the Music of Time' in the Wallace Collection, London. The symbolism of that painting is both instantly understandable to the eye, and yet has the look of a mystery. Any metaphorical meaning in Wilkins' 'A Dance' is withdrawn and concealed within the figures who are preoccupied with their absorbing stance. In some visual way the elements of his art are present and silent: the geometry, the imagination, the separation of the everyday from the essential depths of life. The artist is at ease with his family and with the models who are dancers (in fact, only one of them was a professional dancer) who lock their minds completely into their performance. The colouring is integrated into bodies and space. There is an equivalence between dream and pose, as the dreamer feels the power of their dance, and the dancers inspire the dream.

Wilkins made about three of these large painted backdrops for such groups, but began also to use painted rectangles of colour on the studio walls behind his subjects, of various reds, yellows, blues and greens. Their colour implied its own space and light in an abstract sense, and the staging of old-masterly groups became unnecessary, as the painting itself, with space, colour and light integrated, implied its own rationale. The last of these groups, in effect, although without figures, was a painting of 1989 'Still Life: Fallen Chair', of his London studio with the painted backgrounds, and with a chair knocked over on its side, to say that everything to do with that kind of sitting was over.

Space

From the early 1980s Wilkins' painting has stuck its course, becoming apparently simpler as more and more elements are brought directly into the act of painting in colour touches. His rate of output varied, in part for practical reasons. His market in New York suffered in 1989-90 when his new dealer went out of business, and as his experience in cultural organisation, particularly with architecture and garden design, was more in demand, he for a time transferred his activity to front line work in public taste in Wales. These positions cut into his studio and painting time, but were also of a kind that tested his aesthetic eye, and the popular face of art appreciation. In particular his two massive projects with gardens and revivals at Middleton Hall and Aberglasney, which paralleled his re-creation of his own house and garden, were another kind of landscape making. And the foundation in 2001 of Artes Mundi was a view on the largest scale of new art. His painting was consistent, but what had begun so privately was tested even within the tiresomeness of fund-raising and committees, since to paint a landscape is to be aware of its third-party appreciation.

The elements of Wilkins' mature art are described here separately, but all different kinds of his art progressed together, still life, nudes, buildings, landscape and gardens.

He painted a series of stunning still lifes of his ceramic bowls by Lucie Rie between 1980 and 1986. Yet he had acquired the large bowl in about 1964, and later he had met the ceramicist and asked her to make him two new bowls in particular colours. Then by good fortune in New York he became one of the first owners of some pots by the extraordinary George Ohr from Biloxi, Missisippi (sharing this distinction with Jasper Johns, who also painted them). These paintings by Wilkins of objects by Rie and Ohr must be a high point in the relation between modern ceramics and the art of painting. The bowls themselves had been a large presence in his life, always visible in his house, and stared at continuously in his own study, educating him by constant repetition of the possibilities of scale and presence. Yet the first effect of this appreciation was his painting of the Romanesque cathedral at Perigueux.

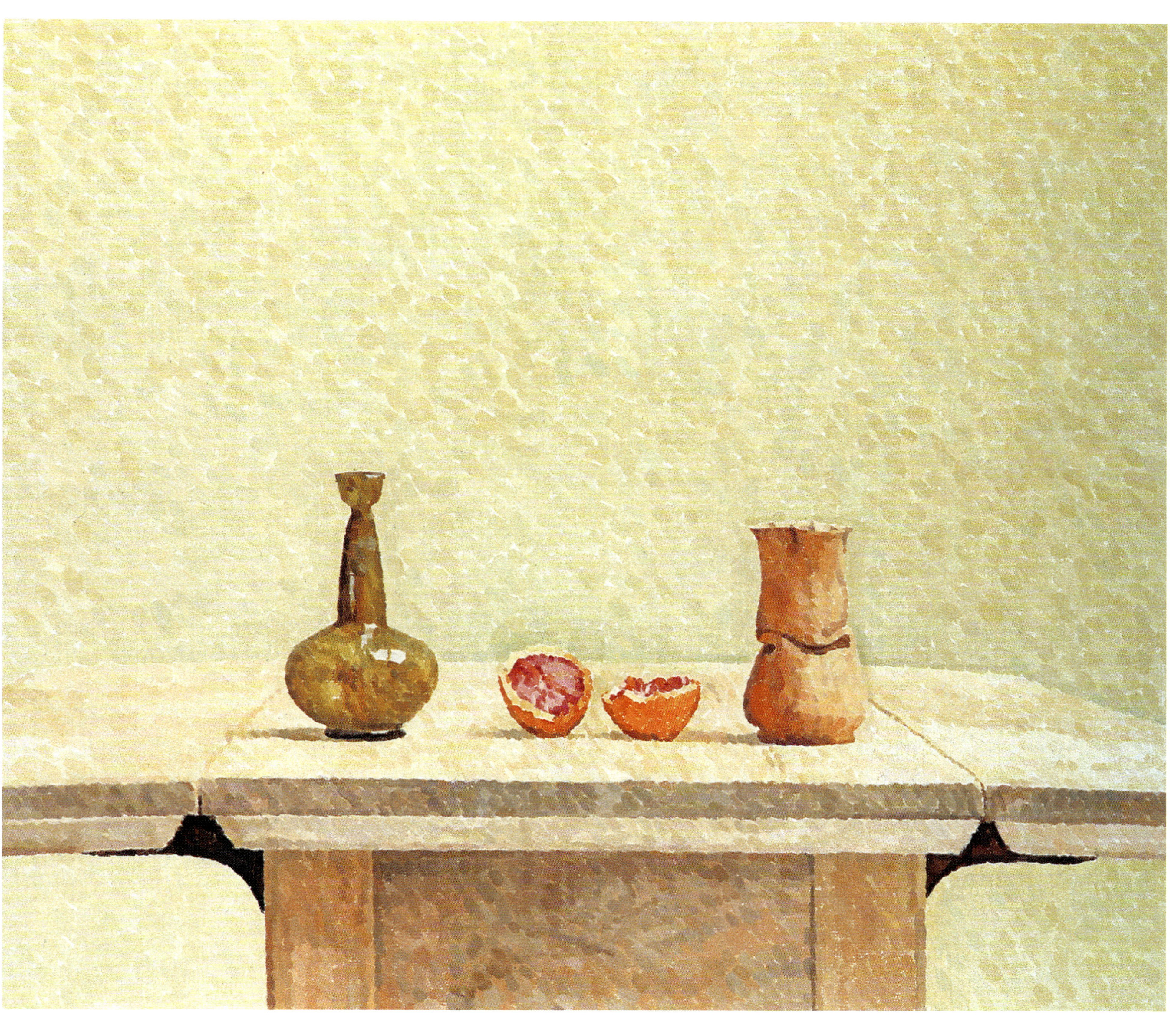

Still Life with Blood Orange, 1986, oil on canvas, 50 x 60cm, Private collection.

He had painted the exterior of the church at Loches, and then in 1979 visited the cathedral of Saint-Front in Perigueux, an amazing building with a cross plan of shallow domes on pendentives, and massive stone unpainted buttresses, restored and bare. He drew inside the church, in his Morandi cross-hatched style, and returned (with an American grant) to set up his easel in the nave, looking up into one of the domes. To the scanning eye noting each minute change of colour as the head turned, the straight edges, made as each point was checked, became slowly curved. His square format painting is a masterpiece of cool looking and visual rhythms. The stippled curves of those huge hand-made surfaces resemble the colour and pitted surface of his own bowl by Lucie Rie, echoing that serene space. An axis is given to the painting by the slightly curved hanging of the huge golden candelabrum. Maybe without seeing the bowl he would never have devoted the time to this upwards view, nor decided on this view that cut off the stability given by a ground level. The painting is reminiscent of the church interiors of Saenredam, both so empty and so full.

In the still lifes of ceramics these bowls are worshipped, set centrally or in relation to polished table tops, and they seem a substitute for the occasion to be able to paint in great church interiors. Ceramics are enjoyed by touching as they take on a feeling of a body, and the memory of the hands that made them. In Wilkins' still lifes they are often on a table that projects a forward and backward perspective, as if of a human body in balance between the present and the future. The space made by the touch of paint parallels the touch of the hands, and shows its mix of overall simplicity and immensely careful and painstaking assembly. In each case the geometry is simple, but the sense of a mysterious space is given by the withheld entry into the interior of the bowl. The greatest architecture, which is so rare, gives also this feeling of an ordered space that has its own odd life, measured and enacted in its own terms.

In 1987 Wilkins began an annual prolonged visit to Venice in the summer and autumn, reserving rooms for the period. There, eventually, over the years, he took on painting the two fourteenth century gothic churches, of the Dominicans and the Franciscans, with their vaulted and tie-beamed ceilings, and again he looked upwards, usually not showing the floor. These interiors were painted, of course, on the spot, negotiating with the church authorities for permissions, trekking in with easel and paints, and numbering how many tiles from a column to place his easel, with another count for where to stand. These are later paintings, and by now the pictures are more abstracted, and yet can take on more complex structures. The detail and accuracy of these interiors are astonishing, given the larger size of the touch of paint. The church interiors are of three materials: stone columns, brick walls and plastered vault, and Wilkins gave to them a grey, a warm pink and an ochre, with the light of the windows, all crossed and lined by the wooden beams like a syncopated Mondrian, with linear structure and limited colours, rich with paint. The verticals are kept straight (unlike at Perigueux) but the tie-beams bend and arch, reach and stretch, marking the turn of the head. Slicing off the floor induces a dizziness. The painting of the ceiling of SS Zanipolo is static and magnificent, but within the view the head has turned vertically to see so directly above. That of the Frari is in a visual tension in the turn from nave to aisle. These are sophisticated images of space, with few colours and an even, granular structure of surface, but beyond that there is a sense of the eye pushing through the network of beams, and opening out into a new space.

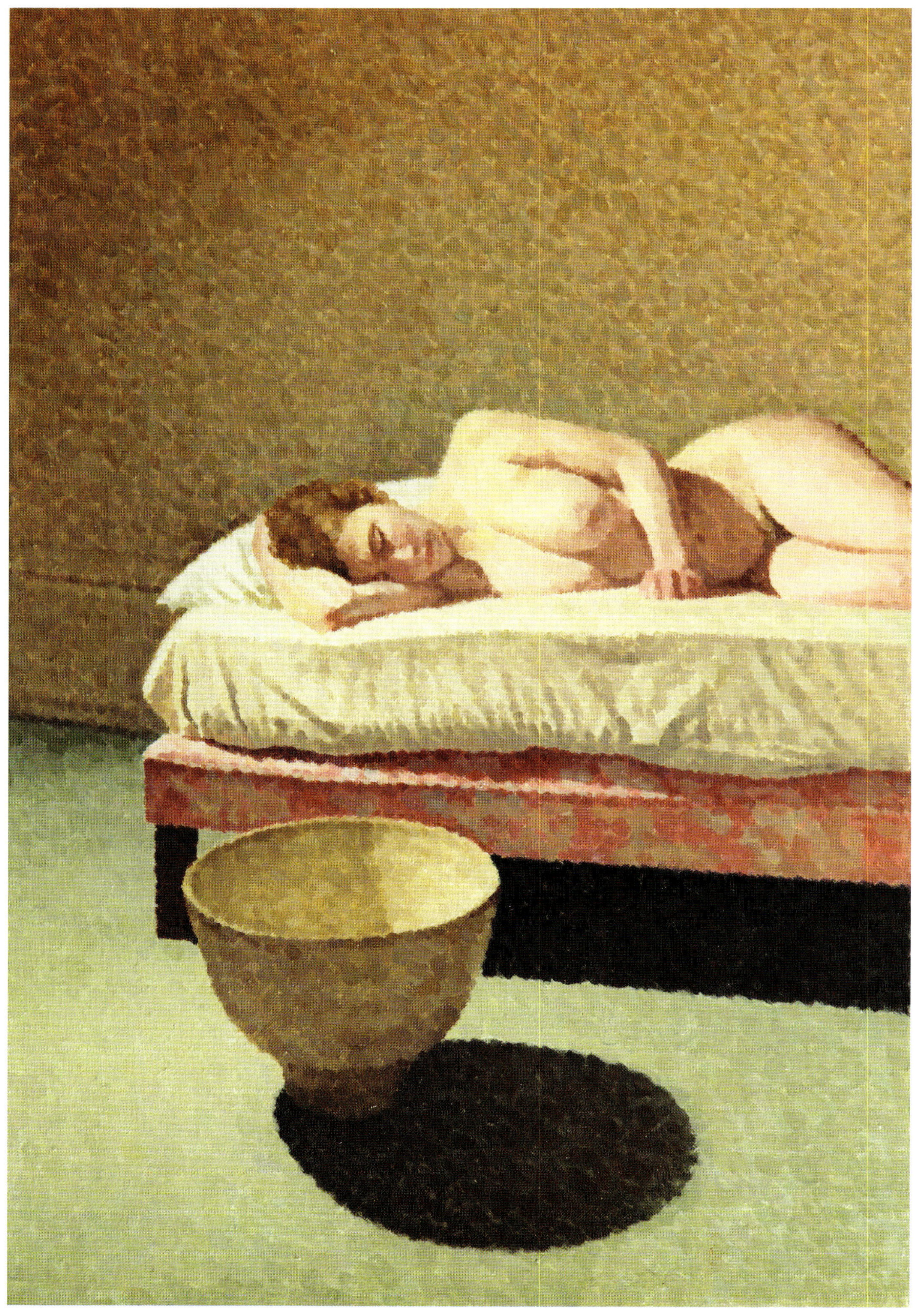

Nude with Bowl, 1978, oil on canvas, 35 x 25cm, Private collection.

Light

A presence of light in a painting has to be earned, and does not come simply from the contrast of light and shade. Pictorial light is something of its own kind, a glow that can unite a painting. This is one reason to paint the nude, as the surface of the human body has itself a glowing radiance, as if light and warmth were bouncing off the skin, so that the light becomes a sign of life. Wilkins' earlier painted nudes are tonal, and make their shapes in space from shadows. In the 'Nude with Bowl' (1979) the model's breasts and the outline of her hips are shadowed boldly by the strong downward light, and compared to the interior shape of the Rie bowl in the foreground. Both model and bowl are linked together by this similarity of concave and convex, like parts of an orrery that show the phases of the moon and the planets in the light of the sun, here offstage at the left. This is exactly a painting of chiaroscuro.

But there had been a transformation by the time that 'Seated Figure' (1982) was painted. This is an image of utter simplicity, like a Gwen John, and the model is shown easily placed in free space around her. The green carpet, like a well-cut lawn, radiates this colour upwards, and her own skin is modelled with a lighter key of colours so that she seems constituted within the space and light. There is a radiance about her body that makes it self-contained and secure in shape, yet there is also a distance, given by the extent of free light around her, and the presence of a mirror. This was calculated presentation, deliberately constructed.

The nature of this device was shown for itself in Wilkins' tall self-portrait with a full length nude 'Two Standing Figures (Self-Portrait)' 1984. The model is posed with her left hand turned oddly in front of her, as if shielding her sex from the gaze in the mirror (she was a dancer who also worked as a model for the Slade School, and was able to hold this difficult pose). And she steps onto the red carpet, so that the touch of her foot just shares with the artist a second space in the mirror. The painting holds two lights, and two worlds, in contrast, but they are shown in an equivalence as a kind of Annunciation, with the difference that here the man demands no coercion. Areas of red and blue and yellow on walls and carpet show what means the artist possesses, just material colours, but they can be used to put together this beautiful and independent figure, leaving the artist in his different compartment, yet both of them in a shared contact.

There is an extreme of full light in the 'Seated Nude' (1984) who sits radiant in front of the junction of yellow and blue backgrounds, her independence almost a hostility, acknowledged in the overt leer of the musician in the framed engraving after C.W. Dietrich, on the wall, now as a kind of Anti-Annunciation. But the light that comes from her body glows like a lamp, with a highlight on her temples, her blonde hair like a Van Gogh sunflower. The ability to endow a painting with light can give sufficient power of independent life to suggest potential movement. In this way Wilkins' Japanese 'Standing Dancer' (1986) pauses in mid movement, again a difficult pose. She is completely self absorbed, the structure of her body and muscles given by the accumulation of coloured paint, and her nakedness (rather than nudity) totally unembarrassed.

Wilkins painted few nudes in the 1990s, until in 1998 for some seven years he took a studio in Llandeilo and hired untrained women to pose. By then his painting had changed, and he used larger touches of paint in a single layer, in much stronger colours. With each fragment only covered once, and as always no drawing, these paintings were especially demanding. He returned to heavy shadows and intense artificial light, and just as the figures have the ordinariness of people from round and about who have taken off their clothes, and sat and lie still, the models are underplayed. They are summary presences, more or less unknown, and seem secondary to the light, as if it were light itself and colour that made the painting, into which these figures happen to be present.

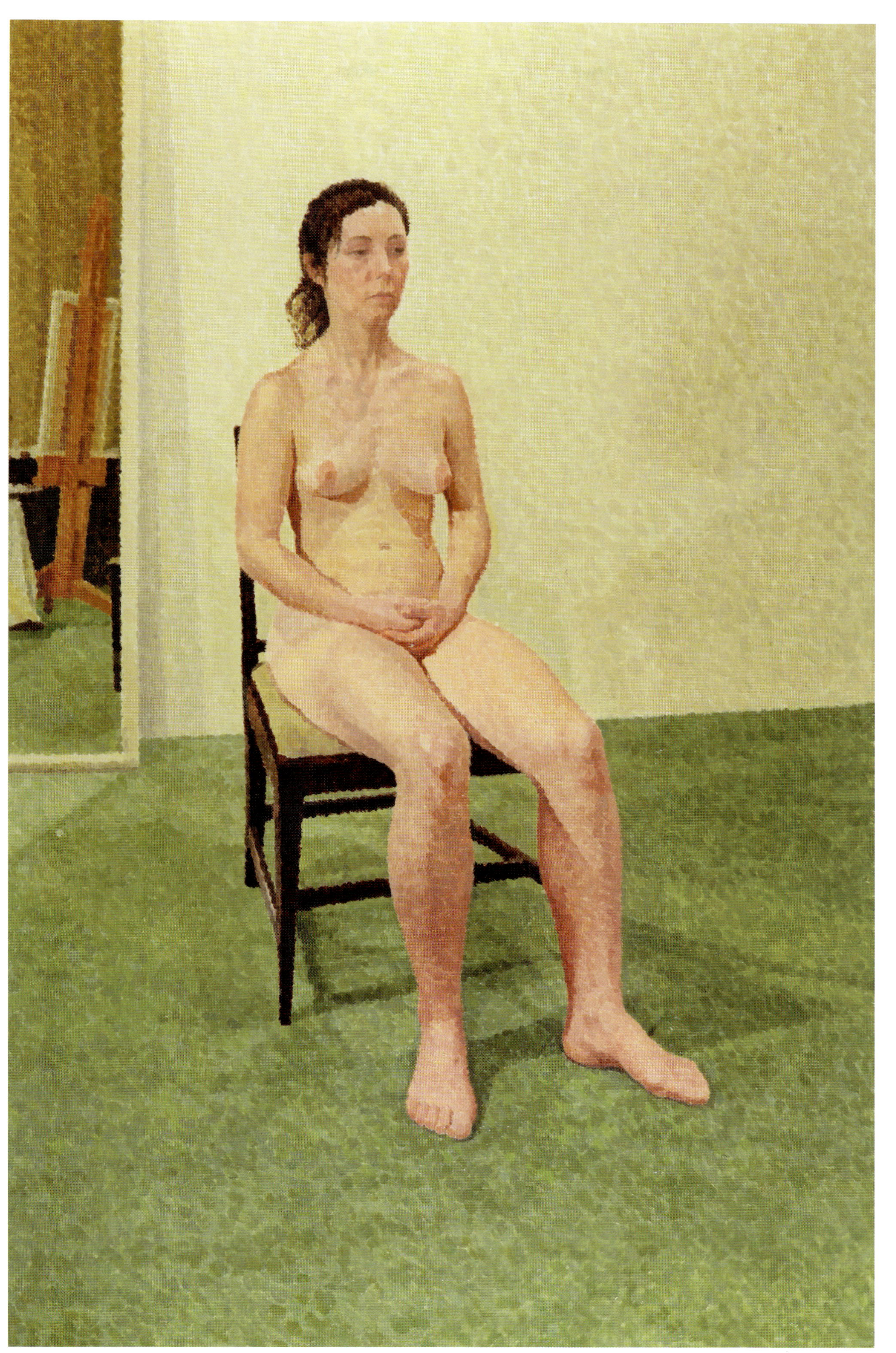

Seated Figure, 1982, oil on canvas, 55 x 35cm, Private collection.

Colour

The higher keyed colours used by Wilkins from about the mid 1990s he found in nature, that is in the garden and woods in Carmarthenshire, and in his summers in Venice. Wilkins first painted his family's garden in Wales in about 1981, as before that he was working on the restoration. It was a few years later that he first went to paint in Venice, though he had drawn the city in 1974, in wide and low cross-hatched pencil drawings. At first the pictures of Venice were not known in Britain, as they were sold in America, and from year to year his unfinished paintings were kept in store in Venice.

In both garden and Venice it was necessary to look away from the obvious, especially in the latter from the example of Monet. Monet's Venetian paintings in the Davies collection at Cardiff show very clearly his search for extraordinary new colours, and his well known structure of corrugated paint on the canvas surface, both of these ratchetting up the emotional metaphors of light seen at a momentary extreme. Wilkins' Venice has none of the astigmatically over-cooked look of Monet, but are calmer, much smaller and more modest, with a speciality of wide and empty foreground planes that drain into the distance towards a thin row of buildings and monuments. They are slightly like some of the Neo-impressionists' paintings of St Tropez, by Henri-Edmond Cross and Paul Signac, with large points of colour.

In Venice the weather was reliable, and finding somewhere relatively free of pedestrians he was able to work, reserving the different quarters of the day for particular views. Often in his pictures the sun is reflected from water, but it does not drench the buildings, which are usually in shade. The crinkled horizon striplet of Palladian churches and terracotta roof tiles look like an unexpected travel poster intruding into an abstract painting, since what matters in these pictures is the colour of the lagoon and sky. These surfaces have the compelling space-making out of colour of Bridget Riley's abstract paintings, which often have a sense of horizon, despite their seemingly exclusive abstraction. Venice gave Wilkins the opportunity to research colour, to find new tints and a way of painting that avoided darks. In comparison to Seurat's coastal views of Honfleur the overall

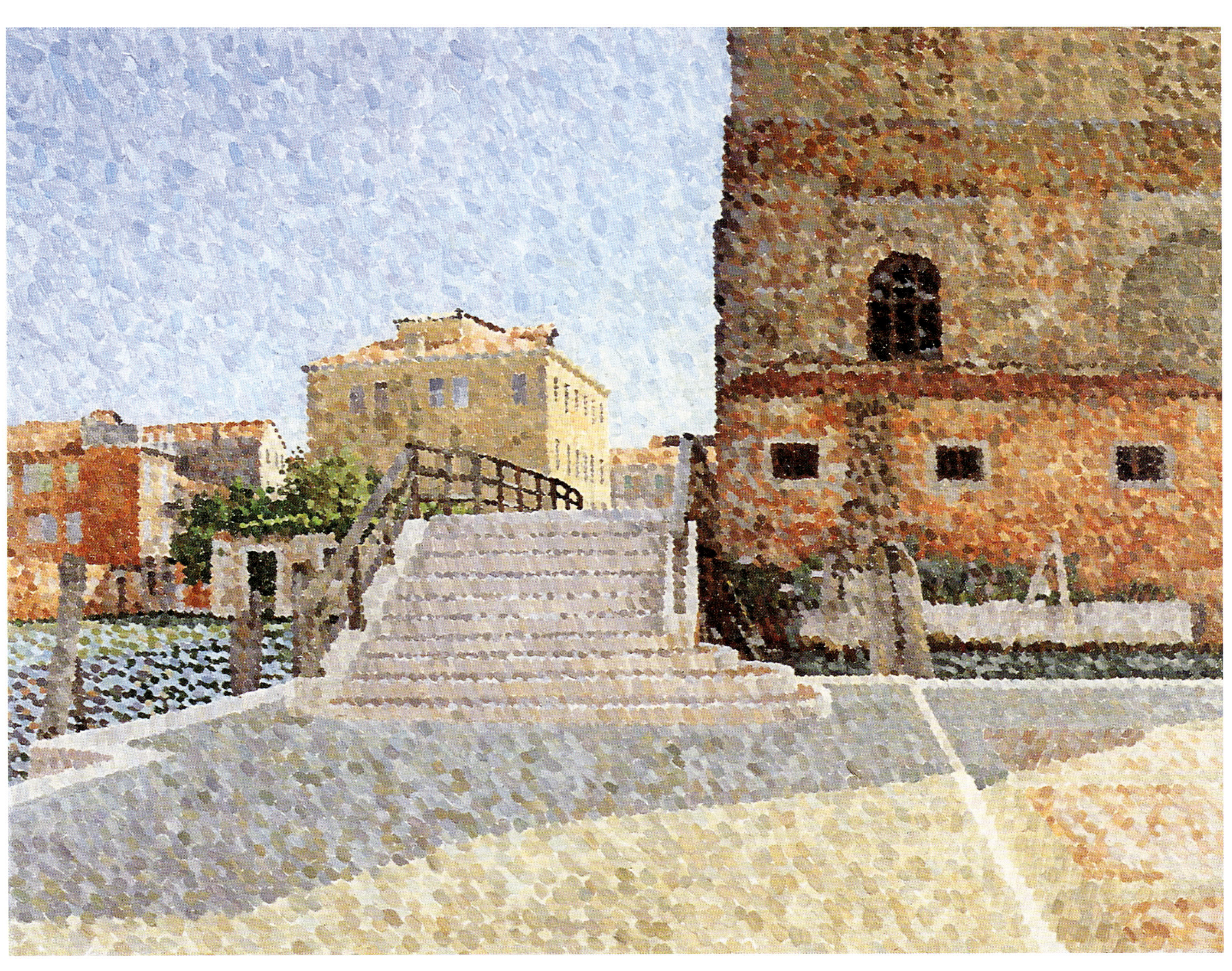

Scuola Grande della Misericordia, Venice, 1999, oil on canvas, 46 x 60cm, Private collection.

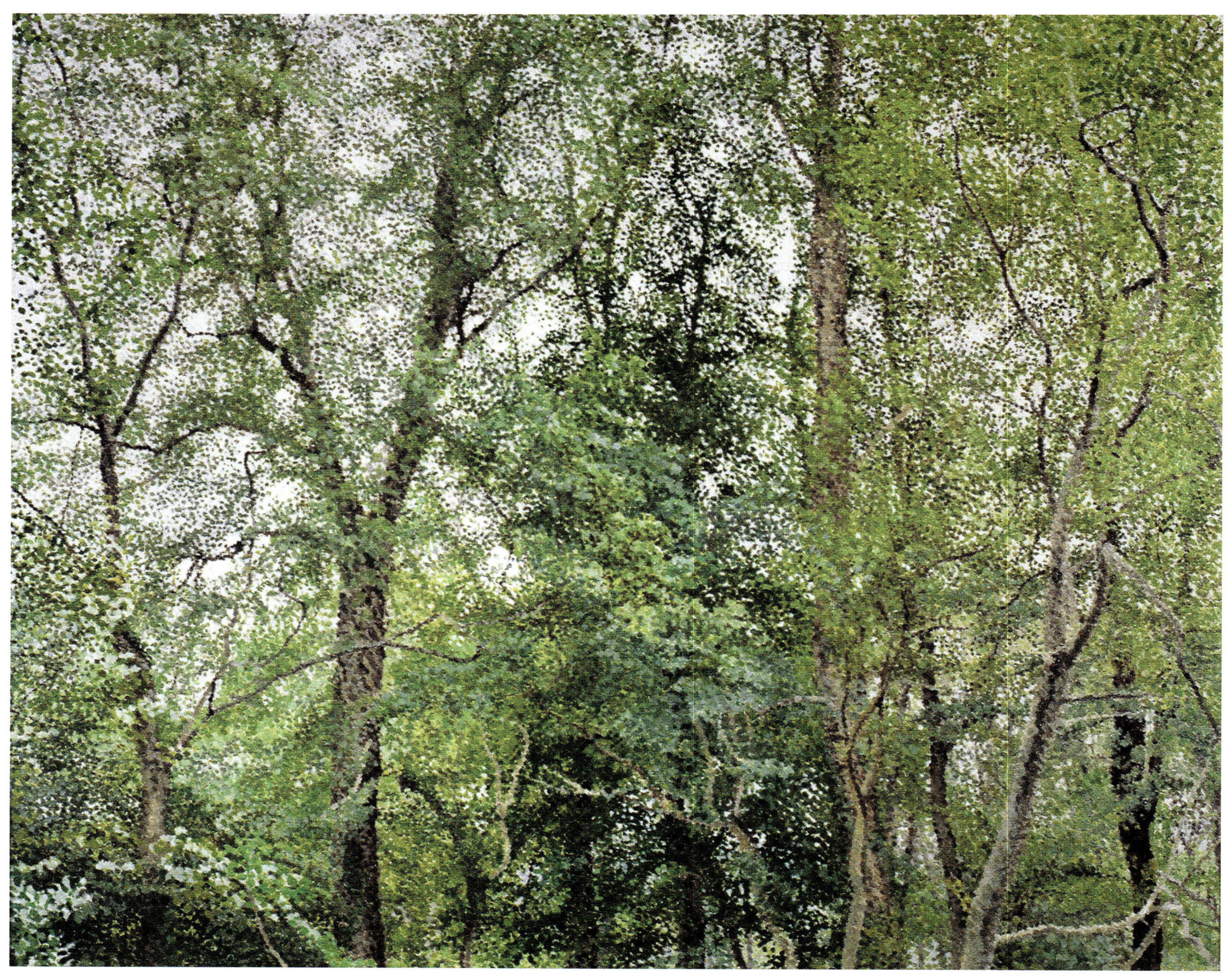

The Jubilee Plantation, 1980, oil on canvas, 35 x 45cm, Private collection.

colour key is higher, and the larger touches of paint emphasise colour alone. Wilkins' Venice is similar to his paintings of nudes, the city looking like a woman reclining on a bed of the lagoon, tracked by the eye from feet to outreached arms.

The garden paintings typically pitch husbandry against competitive nature, in a natural palette of green and gold. It was here that he first allowed colour to break free. To begin with, in for instance the small 'The Jubilee Plantation' (1979-80), a shower of varied green dots, like drops of rain on a window, compete against the wriggling brown tree trunks, one all scatter, one all thrust, yet all of them merely coloured dots, like clothes over a body. This series charts on a huge scale the changes of season in the same place, but also charts his creation of a garden, from an empty but beautiful stage to the progress of known trees and collections. If shown together, it is difficult to imagine that anything apart from Giverny could match this place. Impressionism might have been made for gardens, and these pictures become Pontoise-sur-Towy. They have a homeliness and gentleness, and it is only here that Wilkins

could have taken on the variableness of western weather, painting in sunlight, in grey light, at particular times of day.

Some of these garden pictures appear to be of nothing but colour, that nevertheless by a twist of the eyesight turn into undergrowth, tree trunks, shrubbery. Each touch can be a sunlit leaf, and in the high key of these small sketches he discovered a way to a luminosity that had eluded the earlier attempts of the French and of the Camden Town painters. These paintings sparkled at his 2010 exhibition at Martin Tinney Gallery, Cardiff, especially those of inconsequential corners of the garden, almost unrecognisable, without sky or distance. 'Afternoon Sunlight, Autumn' shows scarcely anything. It follows experiments of the year before, restricting the colours in order to discover the effect of small changes. When these little paintings were begun, they were just touches of colour here and there on a white ground.

Now in Venice Wilkins turned his attention to the covered alleyways and enclosed corners of pedestrian routes, places of human access like rabbit holes, where the touch of his warm colours lay across the surface evenly, but the sudden perspectives of passages and depth emerged clearly and mysteriously. He had begun to add figures to his drawings of Venice, figures that were almost invisible in the dense network of darks concealing these 'sottoporteghi'. Drawing had become for Wilkins a matter of seeing the gaps between things and marking intervals, most beautifully in Venice in close views of the narrow streets and sudden openings to canal or bridge. People in Venice depart and arrive from view by surprise, darting into doorways that turn out to be sidestreets, and these figures feel themselves into the space in the way that Wilkins had all along been training his eye to find. And so, in these small paintings of these alleyways, there are sometimes feet and bodies that scuttle into some unsuspected access.

Artists are makers of images – of course, what else could they be. A painter of traditional subjects might have an advantage in that the way the pictures should be judged seems apparent, but also a problem in that there might be few images left to find. But John Currin can still find a new Madonna and Child. And, despite the comparisons above to Dutch and to Impressionist painting, there is hardly any picture by Wilkins that looks, as an image, in the slightest like anyone else's. They are all strange – models standing on a bed; Venice appearing over a table-top of water; ceramics paired across two mahogany tables. Even in the garden there appears a riot of branches, and within Venice the eye reaches along a passageway probably never before painted.

If his pictures were displayed in one of the old master galleries, would they seem to hold their place with the masters like Saenredam and Seurat, or would it be with the Berkheydes, or some secondary artist? This is the one test of art, of any kind, whether it would seem to deliver a power of originality as an image, with the unity of all the means that make that image. A contemporary painting can become a picture-in-residence with the famous, even if not showing in the same room, though that was what Freud (at Dulwich), Auerbach (at Ordovas) and Hirst (at the Wallace) have approved. Amongst recent British painters, Wilkins particularly admires Andrews, Caulfield and Scully, all good enough in my opinion to be displayed anywhere, for the sheer tearing impact of what they have made.

To my eyes his own pictures seem of the best. A seated nude in full light; the interior of a great church; an avenue of trees: this is a full world of my own visual experience – whether personal and sexual, or in consideration of the current basis of old beliefs and their buildings and decoration, or in the process of walking alone in the ordered nature of Britain. It is not that these are comfortable places. These images throw open edgy situations, examining on a prolonged basis and in personal isolation what is valid and what can be salvaged.

Wilkins has made paintings inside museums, putting his own work implicitly in comparison to old art. There is an early painting of his showing the interior of the V&A looking towards their display of stained glass, his own former metier. In the foreground is a man looking into the museum with his back to us, wearing a denim jacket of dense blue, like the famous lost colour of thirteenth century glass. Beside him is the 'Effigy of a Knight' of the title, in ochres with touches of pink, mostly, and in a glass case. This was how the museum looked, and this painting is as if to say 'Look! Here is the old stained glass, and here a living, lovely blue, and here a dead warrior – so maybe these colours could be revived to bring back to life the art of the past, and to link our own lives with that time'. It is a painting of a potential Resurrection.

The great Venetian churches are themselves museums of sculpture and painting, of monuments to the Doges and altarpieces, and are better than museums, since the art all has its proper architectural frame, and is still a part of the original liturgical purpose. One of Wilkins' views of the interior of SS. Zanipolo shows also the polished tile floor, looking toward the inside of the entrance façade. It is an unusual viewpoint, avoiding the most famous sights, but showing a group of wall monuments in the far corner. Beside the wooden panelling and seating in the distance is the warm colouring of a huge painting, in fact an old copy of Titian's 'Death of St Peter Martyr' (the original was commissioned for this church, but was destroyed). In about 200 touches of colour, all in a single layer from a stiff hog-hair brush, the remarkable colouring is re-created, of rich blues and reds, out of a sombre background. That classic Venetian colouring of the Renaissance, that cannot usually be found in contemporary life, is here turned inside-out, as Titian's glorious colouring re-inhabits this vision of the whole church interior. A full palette of colours is used, of a kind best known in modern art in some architectural painting by early Mondrian and by Paul Klee.

This is a contemporary painting amongst the old masters. It has a mastery of colour and image as much as Caulfield and Scully, and who knows, as much as Saenredam or Seurat.

David Fraser Jenkins, April 2014

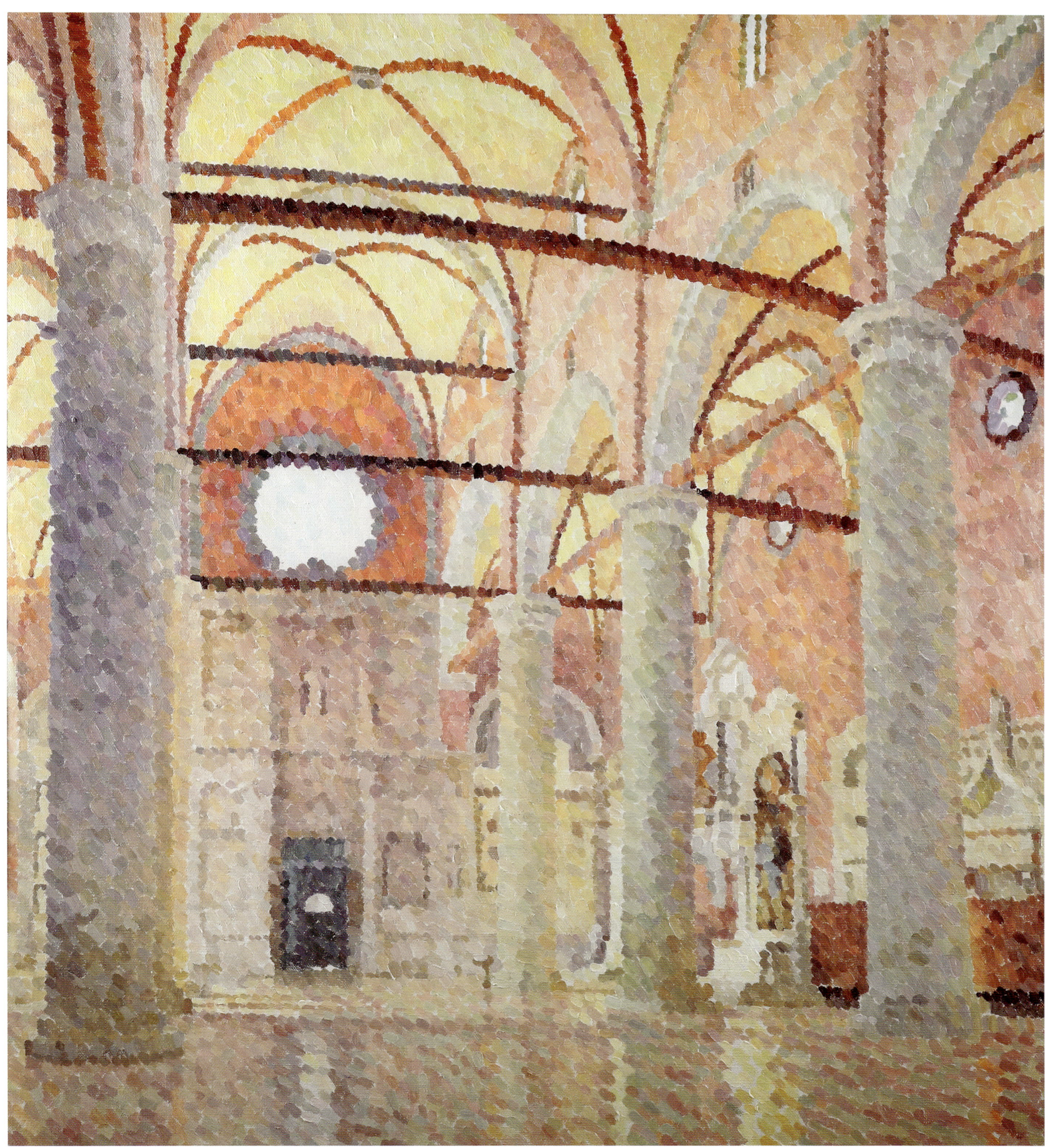

Santi Giovanni e Paolo, Venice, 2006, oil on canvas, 70 x 65cm, Private collection.

WILLIAM WILKINS: PROFESSIONAL ARTIST AND CREATOR OF GARDENS

DAVID MOORE

At Carreg Cennen house and garden, William Wilkins' elegant classical home near Llandeilo overlooking the romantic ruins of a medieval castle, a life driven by a finely-tuned visual sensibility is evident. In his domestic environment, architecture, garden and carefully-arranged artworks and ceramics form harmonious visual relationships. The four-acre garden with its bee-bole wall, extensive lawns, orchard and trees is well maintained through the seasons. It is a structured world which reflects Wilkins' deepest interests as well as his art.

The house, built in 1807-8 and attributed to Samuel Pepys Cockerell, had been his mother's family house since the early 1850s. She was descended from the last of the Physicians of Myddfai. Wilkins, born in Suffolk in 1938, moved there with his parents when he was two years old. His earliest memories are of his grandfather running it and the estate 'in a state of Edwardian perfection.' Sadly, this was not to last. His parents moved to Tenby in 1944 and they separated shortly afterwards. Much to Wilkins' shock, the family estate was sold in 1954. He determined that, one day, he would buy back the house.

Wilkins' great-great-grandfather, who shared his Christian name, had designed both the National Gallery and University College in London. Wilkins' father, William Vaughan Wilkins, felt that his son, too, should become an architect. Yet he had himself worked from 1934 as an historical novelist, following a career in journalism. William Wilkins had, however, only ever wanted to be an artist. He had drawn compulsively from an early age, receiving serious encouragement from artist Arthur Giardelli since the age of eleven. Intriguingly, at the age of fifteen, he had also been a great admirer of Rubens as both an artist and a successful public servant.

It was natural that Wilkins would become an art student. At first, he specialised in stained glass, attending Swansea College of Art from 1955 until 1957, where he studied under Howard Martin. One of his 1958 windows may be seen in the chancel of St John the Baptist Church, Templeton, Pembrokeshire. At the Royal College of Art, between 1957 and 1960, he continued to study stained glass. Lawrence Lee and Keith New, who had made their reputations working on the glass in Coventry Cathedral, ran the

department. Wilkins realised, however, that he had made a bad mistake in specialising as he felt that, for him, it was too limiting a medium. Seeking a fresh start, he started evening life drawing classes at Hammersmith School of Art.

Although Wilkins plays down its significance, perhaps his most notable achievement while at the Royal College was as a founder with Ken Baynes, in 1958, and chair, in 1960, of Anti-Ugly Action, a campaign which aimed to combat a perceived lack of imagination in contemporary architecture. This archetypal duffle-coated sixties student movement, often to the accompaniment of a jazz band, encouraged the appreciation of livelier modern buildings, attacked bad schemes, held demonstrations, disseminated posters and leaflets and petitioned councils. At the laying of the foundation stone for the Barclays Bank new headquarters in Lombard Street in 1959, Anti-Ugly Action turned up with a coffin containing, symbolically, the ashes of British architecture. Pauline Boty, another student in the stained-glass department, scattered rose petals. The campaign benefited from Wilkins' evident flair for publicity and attracted considerable press coverage. He and his colleagues were even interviewed by Alan Whicker on BBC television's modish current affairs programme *Tonight*.

Wilkins entered the teaching profession, firstly part-time in west London. For much of the rest of his time he painted and drew and made abstract works, some of them shallow cardboard constructions. Little work of this period survives. The modernising headmaster of Malvern College, Donald Lindsay, invited Wilkins to reform the school's art department. Between 1964 and 1968 this expanded greatly in both students and space. Sculpture and ceramics were introduced. An opportunity arose with the progressive Leicestershire County Council but Wilkins, with a clear vision of his own future, made the firm decision that he needed to spend more time on his own creative work. Teaching, he felt, was drawing on the same part of himself as his art practice.

Wilkins secured a strictly nine-to-five job as information officer in the Greater London Council's Architecture Department from 1968 until 1977. He determined, like the poet T.S. Eliot, to keep his life as an artist separate from the business of earning a living. The job, nevertheless, evolved. Initially, he had been employed in the Town Development Division concerned with promoting better public understanding, through publication and exhibitions, of new town developments and the communal spaces and gardens on estates for London overspill. Later, he became responsible for these matters for the Architecture Department as a whole.

In another decisive and symbolic move, in 1970, Wilkins was able to buy back Carreg Cennen house and the garden. For sixteen years it had been a guest house. It was, by then, in a poor state of repair with water descending the cantilevered staircase. The garden had been, effectively, destroyed. His mother and aunt looked after the house and, when staying, Wilkins worked on the garden, for which he had a long-term vision.

Wilkins' development as a professional artist evolved in parallel with his time working for the Greater London Council. Feeling inadequately trained, he disciplined himself to learn how to draw again. Over a six-year period, he devoted

three hours a night to drawing for five days
a week as well as eight hours a day for three
weekends out of four. Committed to figure
drawing, with some architectural and still-life
work, he abandoned abstraction. For ten years
he lived and worked in his flat off Holland
Park Avenue.

Exhibiting opportunities came along. During the
late 1960s, Wilkins had developed a fascination
with Brittany, for its ecclesiastical architecture,
stone crosses and carvings, calvaries and
pietàs. Raymond Eyquem, a lecturer at
University College Cardiff and an enthusiastic
promoter of modern art from Wales, offered
Wilkins his first exhibition in 1971. *Drawings
of Brittany and Some Others* was also shown
at University College Aberystywth. Wilkins was
able to develop his interest in Brittany with
a Welsh Arts Council bursary to draw and to
study the way church plans were the key to
understanding space and light in buildings. An
exhibition followed in 1972 at the Welsh Arts
Council's headquarters in Cardiff.

London galleries began to represent his work
and other exhibiting opportunities occurred.

By 1973 Wilkins was being exhibited by the
American Howard Abramowitz, art critic of *The
Spectator*, at his short-lived Covent Garden
Gallery. Wilkins was able, too, with British
Council advice, to take advantage of a 1973
GLC lecture tour in Warsaw to exhibit his work.
Wilkins' drawings, in particular, were popular
and works were bought by his GLC colleagues.
His work was included in shows at Agnews and
at Roland, Browse and Delbanco. He had solo
shows at the Langton Gallery off King's Road,
London, and at University College Swansea.

By 1975 Wilkins' pointillist oil painting technique
had become the main focus of his artistic
output. At the same time, Wilkins was invited to
join the 56 Group Wales, a member of which he
would remain until 1999. His promotional skills,
from 1978 until 1986, were employed to good
effect as its publicity officer. Regular exhibiting
with the Group, particularly visits to France,
Italy and Czechoslovakia, added to his sense of
purposefulness as an artist.

Following a chance meeting with American
figurative painter Lisa Zwerling, while drawing
in London's Hyde Park, Wilkins felt encouraged
to approach New York dealers directly.

Two of his works were included in an eclectic exhibition at the Allan Stone Gallery in 1976. There followed, between 1977 and 1981, a series of three successful solo shows with Robert Schoelkopf Gallery in Madison Avenue. Wilkins showed landscapes, still lifes, nudes and architectural works. After enthusiastic reviews from Hilton Kramer in *The New York Times*, these sold out. 'The most auspicious debut of the season so far - and indeed of many a season this writer can recall - is that of William Wilkins,' Kramer wrote in 1977. 'Seurat's is a powerful and demanding vision,' he continued, 'and any painter who falls within its orbit risks being swamped by an invidious comparison. Mr Wilkins survives this peril unscathed. He commands not only the requisite touch - which in his case is actually somewhat freer and more painterly than Seurat's - but also the feeling for structure that is its necessary corollary.'

Much encouraged by such enthusiasm for his art, Wilkins, not surprisingly, gave up his job in 1977 to become a full-time painter. He received a Welsh Arts Council grant to develop his work the following year. In 1980 the Ingram Merill Foundation supported him to paint in Périgueux Cathedral, Dordogne. That year, too, he became artist-in-residence with the Artists for the Environment Foundation at Delaware Water Gap National Park, New Jersey. Part of the park was being returned to wilderness and he lived, newly married and with a young family, in an abandoned village working with art school post-graduates.

Despite his success as an artist, however, Wilkins realised that he would be limited by his time-consuming technique and an inability to produce more than twelve to fourteen paintings a year. It took him two years to paint enough work for an exhibition. Advised that Schoelkopf was not developing his reputation enough, Wilkins approached other dealers. In 1983 a solo show at the Duke Street Gallery in London was reviewed in *The Times* by John Russell Taylor. 'I can think of few modern painters,' he wrote, 'who can paint a group of bowls or pots on a polished wood surface to such ravishing effect.'

In New York in the mid-1980s Wilkins held two exhibitions at Barbara Mathes Gallery. His prices were increased and the shows sold well. She recommended him to galleries in Palm Beach, Florida, and in San Francisco. Through Lisa Zwerling he showed, in 1986, at the Payne Gallery in Moravian College, Bethlehem, Pennsylvania. Gruenebaum Gallery, New York, acquired work on a regular basis prior to a projected show until, sadly, it went out of business. Since 1987 he has also spent a month or more each year in Venice.

In Britain, Cardiff's Andrew Knight Gallery included Wilkins in a 1985 group show, *Painting in Wales, 1850-1980*. Bath's Artsite also featured him in its touring *The Self-Portrait: A Modern View*. Marina Vaizey in *The Sunday Times* reviewed a 1988 Albemarle Gallery show, writing: 'Wilkins takes traditional subjects, but updates them using his own version of pointillism, with specks of colour like the kind found in glistening sand, often subdued but sometimes brilliant, which give his compositions a luminous sheen.' The following year, Swansea's Glynn Vivian Art Gallery showed a retrospective, *Themes and Variations, William Wilkins, 1979-1989*. Edward Lucie-Smith's essay questioned the positioning, by some critics, of his work as post-modernist because, 'despite a strong emphasis on design and proportional relationships, there was little that is overtly classical about Wilkins' art'. A 1991 Piccadilly Gallery show in London was also well received.

A New York show in 1994 at Maxwell Davidson Gallery was of a high quality although, with a slump in the art market, sales were not as good as they had been. Subsequently, Wilkins gave up on New York as he felt that he was unlikely to be able to continue making a living as a full-time painter. Also, he was frustrated by being insufficiently known in London and Wales. With his extremely slow technique he would not, if he continued to show in New York, have been able to produce enough work to improve the situation.

Living at Carreg Cennen full-time from 1990, Wilkins took on extra-mural history of art teaching for the University College of Wales, Aberystwyth. Through Kyffin Williams,

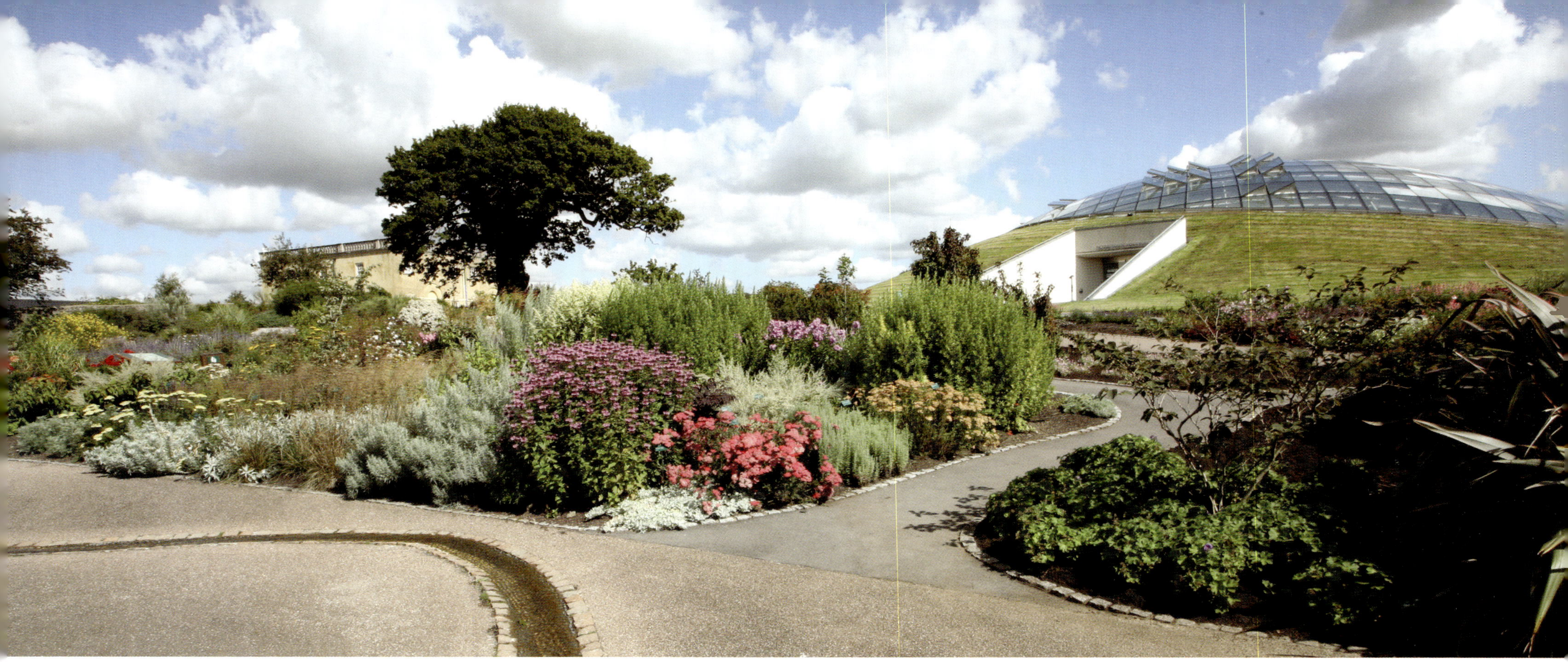

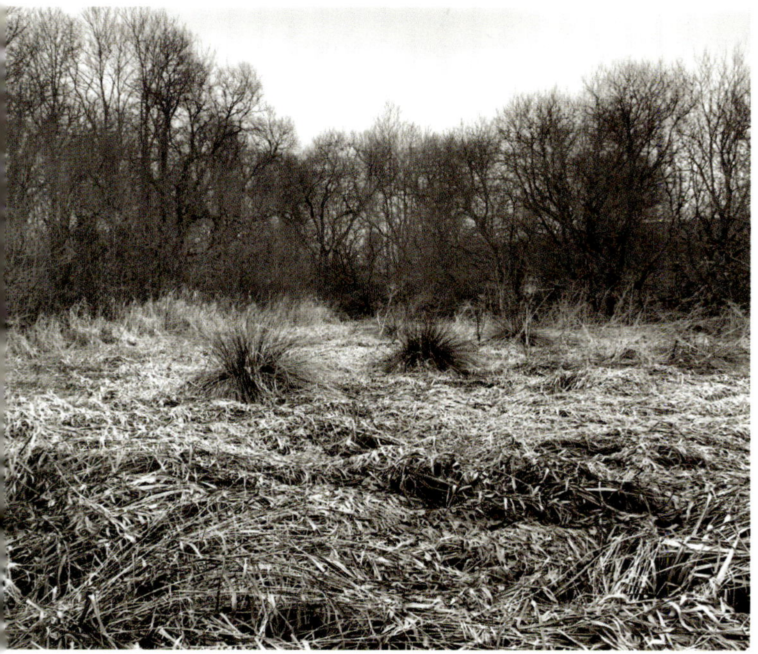

Photo by Colin Baglow.

Bed of one of the abandoned lakes around 1990.
Photo by Miranda Walker.

he became, in 1993, a Royal Cambrian Academician. From 1996, and while involved heavily in major garden projects, he felt that Martin Tinney Gallery, Cardiff, would be a good place to concentrate upon. He has, indeed, built up a strong base of collectors in Wales. In addition, Wilkins has shown in recent years at the National Botanic Garden of Wales and, in London, at the Piccadilly Gallery and at 50 Albemarle Street, where he exhibited mainly drawings.

In Wales, Wilkins became more absorbed in the local community and in major historic garden projects. In the Tywi Valley he became fascinated by three relatively-unrecognised historic designed landscapes at Middleton Hall, Aberglasney and Dynefwr. The latter absorbed the least of his time, its woods and medieval Welsh castle owned by a wildlife trust and, eventually, being managed by Cadw with much of the estate in the care of the National Trust.

The two other historic landscapes, however, have particularly preoccupied Wilkins. Middleton Hall was a former 1793-95 house designed by Samuel Pepys Cockerell for Sir William Paxton with a park originally laid out by Samuel Lapidge. Wilkins' aunt seems to have been the first to have brought to his attention the remains of ambitious water engineering structures in woodland, now identified as the work Cockerell and carried out by James Grier. Owned by Dyfed County Council, these were silted-up and overgrown. Wilkins became interested, contacted the Council, took friends to see them and persuaded the Council to become more seriously concerned about them.

Wilkins became the founding chair, in 1989, of the Welsh Historic Gardens Trust to raise awareness of the huge number of neglected and largely unrecognised designed landscapes. Launched at a conference in Lampeter, publicity was achieved through Wilkins' contacts on *The New York Times*. John Dixon Hunt, editor of *The Journal of Garden History*, visited local sites. Other experts, such as Dr Andrew Sclater, were attracted to the cause, and interest grew in the wider historic garden world. This encouraged the Welsh Office and its agencies to take these landscapes more seriously. Concern for the landscape gardens at Hafod in Ceredigion led to the formation of a separate Hafod Trust.

A Middleton Joint Steering Group was established by the Welsh Historic Gardens Trust and Dyfed County Council. For two years, in the early 1990s, Wilkins became its part-time project director. He provided the scheme with a clear concept, a design, business plan and key funding and support. Surviving eighteenth-century landscape features would be combined with first-class modern design. The idea to create a National Botanic Garden of Wales was, partly, stimulated by the unique surviving double-walled garden. It was Wilkins who persuaded the architect Norman Foster to design the 1997-99 Great Glasshouse which has become an iconic symbol for the project. An application to the Millennium Commission was successful, raising £21 million, half the projected cost.

Two years into the project, Wilkins became ill with cancer. He retired, partly due to ill health and partly because he felt that he did not have the skills to take it to the next stage. The project opened for the Millennium. Although it has been frustrating for Wilkins not to have been involved throughout, he appreciates the new resolve of the trustees to use the potential of the rediscovered Thomas Hornor paintings of the eighteenth-century landscape to stimulate the restoration of the original parkland and its water features.

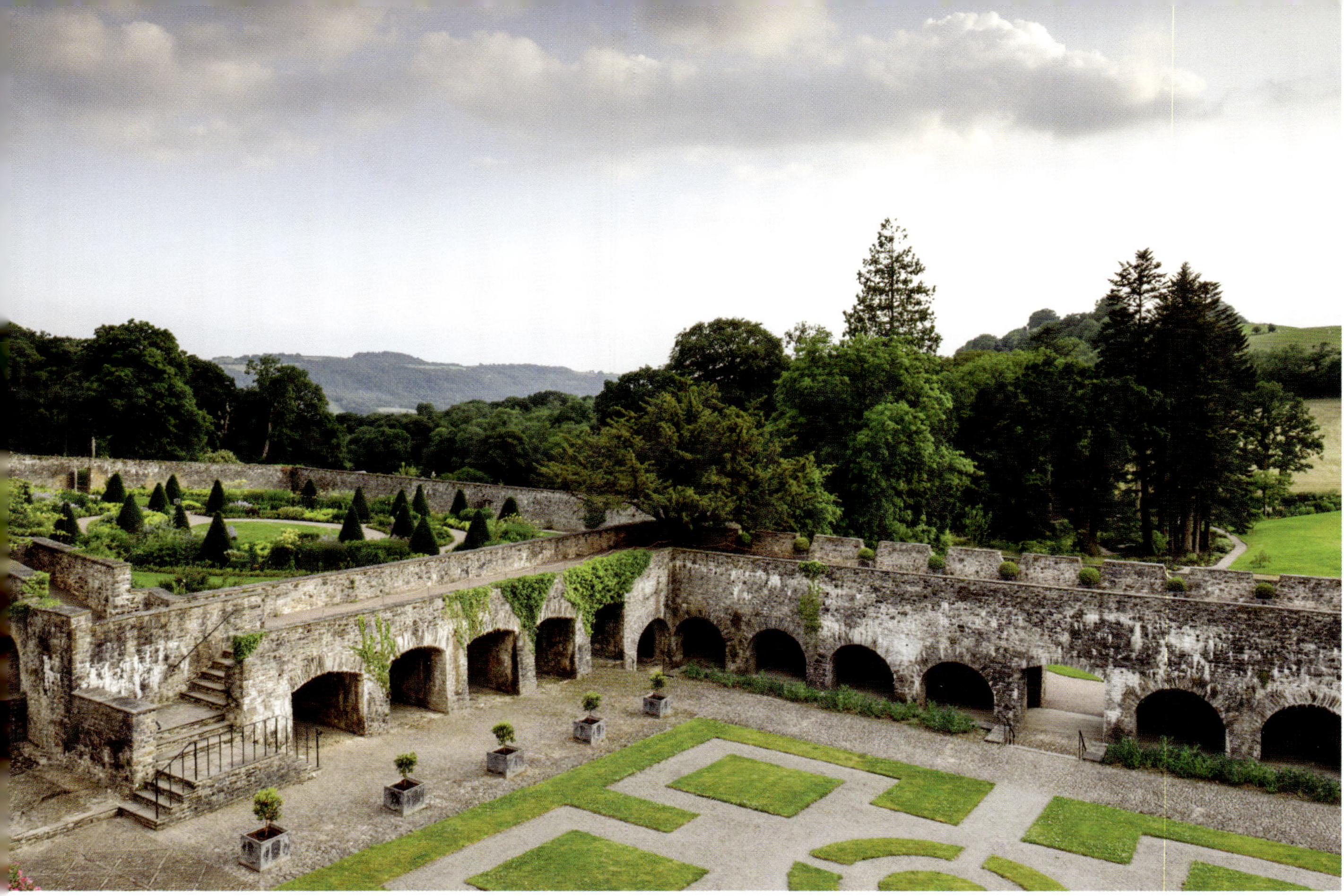

Photo by Jason Ingram

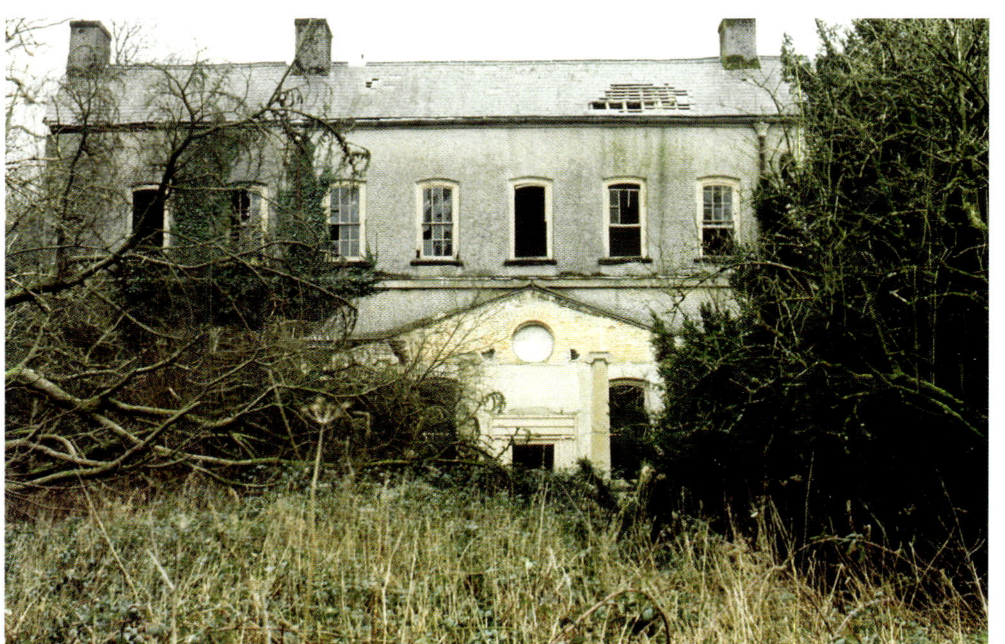

Aberglasney Restoration Trust

The other major historic landscape preoccupation for Wilkins has been Aberglasney. The house and garden were in ruins, overgrown and divided up into multiple private ownership. Rebuilt after 1600 for Anthony Rudd, a bishop of St Davids, the house was again rebuilt c.1710-20 for Robert Dyer and then altered c.1840.

The garden, which dates from the early seventeeth-century, includes a cloister garden which was recognised early on by John Dixon Hunt. Wilkins founded the Aberglasney Restoration Trust in 1994-5 and became its part-time director. This was a project which he very much wanted to see through to completion. With support from Frank Cabot, an American philanthropist, the house was purchased and the various plots into which the garden had been broken up were acquired. Wilkins had attracted Cabot's interest while lecturing in the United States about Welsh historic gardens. The gardens, which were subjected to intense scrutiny, were investigated archaeologically by a team led by Kevin Blockley and opened in 1999 to much public acclaim.

During these major projects, Wilkins managed to continue with his painting, keeping the tasks separate, just as he had achieved in London.

For a while, he had a studio in Llandeilo although he now uses the former servants' quarters at Carreg Cennen. Here, on a dresser, he displays pottery and a photograph of his great-grandfather who developed the house and estate in the nineteenth-century.

The public garden projects have involved different skills to painting. Verbal communication, group psychology, team-building, creating a vision and fund-raising could be exhausting emotionally. Although they have not drained the spirit needed to paint, they have affected the time available for it. Once seated at an easel, however, Wilkins has been able to draw upon different sources of energy, setting aside the stresses of projects. He has also found practical gardening to be therapeutic. It has been important for him to balance these strands in his life.

Wilkins has continued to be involved in heritage projects. Up until 2012 he was part-time project director for the restoration of the seventeenth-century Vaughan family Llanelly House in Bridge Street, Llanelli, which was remodelled in 1714 for Sir Thomas Stepney. Bought by Llanelli Town Council to rescue the property from falling into ruin, it became one of Wilkins' most time-consuming projects. He was the founder of Carmarthenshire Heritage Regeneration Trust which bought the house from the Council and provided specialised oversight of the project. Llanelly House is now open to the public.

In a departure from historic garden and architectural schemes, Wilkins founded and chaired *Artes Mundi*, Britain's largest art prize, in 2002. The idea evolved after Tony Lewis, chair of the Wales Tourist Board, had commented at *Wales Singer of the Year* that it was a pity that something similar did not exist for the visual arts. A feasibility study was commissioned from Wilkins with the support of the Wales Tourist Board, BBC Wales and the Welsh Development Agency. The intention had been, in part, to raise awareness in Wales about contemporary visual art among a broad public. It was, however, to be an international event, building links between Wales and other countries and, hopefully, enriching its cultural and educational life. A greater interest in contemporary art, it was felt, could be fostered through focusing upon the human condition, social reality and lived experience. The selectors were under no obligation to visit Welsh artists although they were expected to be sensitive to the cultural context of the prize. Wilkins has, in addition, become a trustee of the Derek Williams Trust which helps Amgueddfa Cymru / National Museum Wales to acquire artworks. In his local town of Llandeilo, reflecting a keen interest in ceramics, he also promoted a festival, *Ceramica Cymru*, in the early 2000s.

Wilkins, through a disciplined approach to life, has sought to balance a professional career as an artist with the project direction of some of the largest heritage-based tourism projects in Wales in recent decades. Like his early exemplar Rubens, he has always drawn or painted, even when absorbed in other projects. The need to balance these throughout his life has sometimes led to tension and, yet, he has usually been able to redress the balance. His projects have been recognised by the award of a CBE in 2000 as well as honorary fellowships. His meticulously-crafted paintings and drawings, represented in collections around the world, are, by comparison, still known only to a relatively small discerning audience. It is hoped that this book will help to bring them to much wider attention.

David Moore, February 2014

Sources: Interviews with William Wilkins at Carreg Cennen on 8th and 22nd January 2014; William Wilkins' archive; Lloyd. T., Orbach, J. & Scourfield, R. (2006) *The Buildings of Wales: Carmarthenshsire & Ceredigion*, Yale.

EARLY DRAWINGS
1968–1974

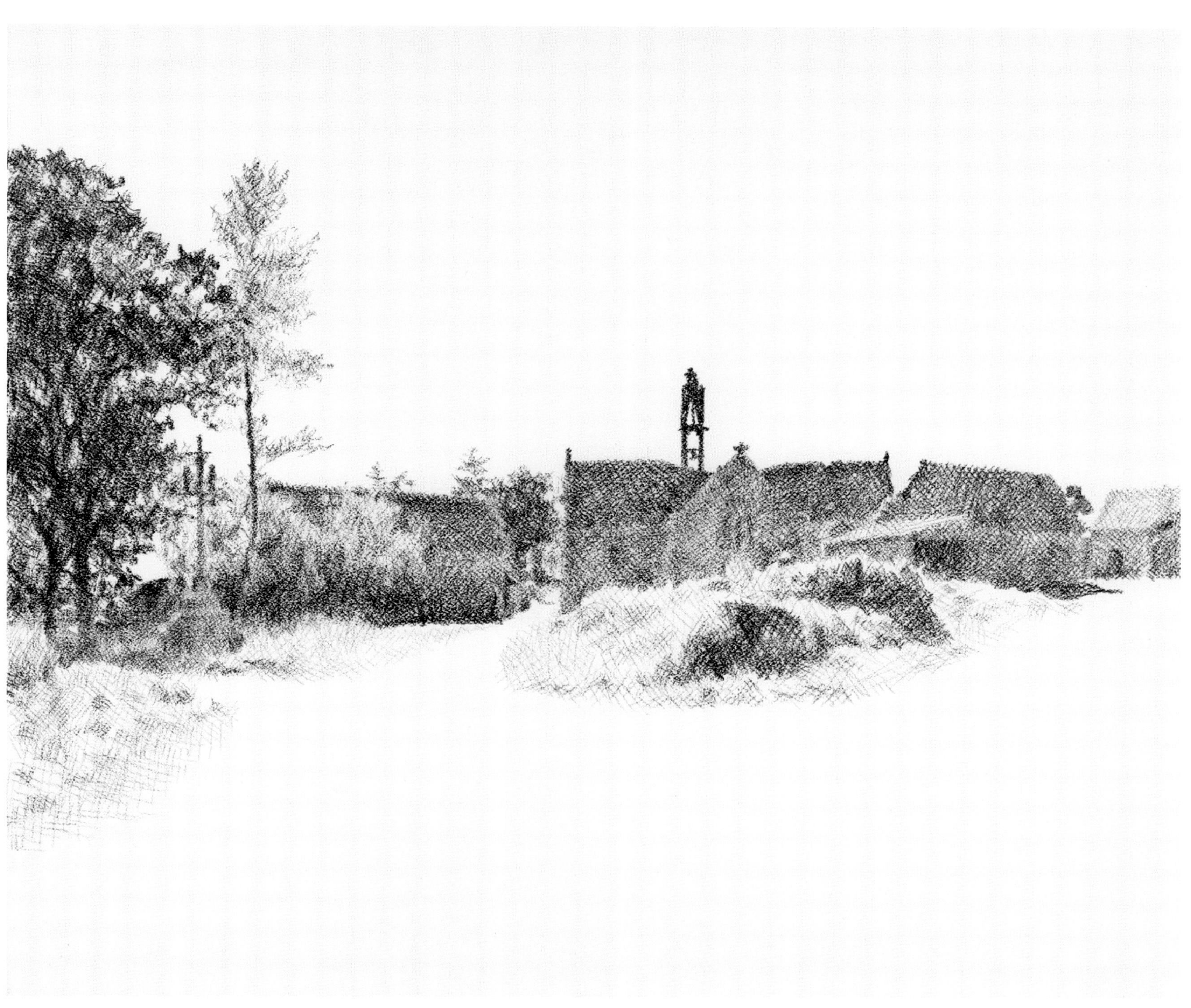

Chapelle de la Madeleine, Briec, 1971, conté crayon on paper, 57 x 68cm, National Museum Wales.

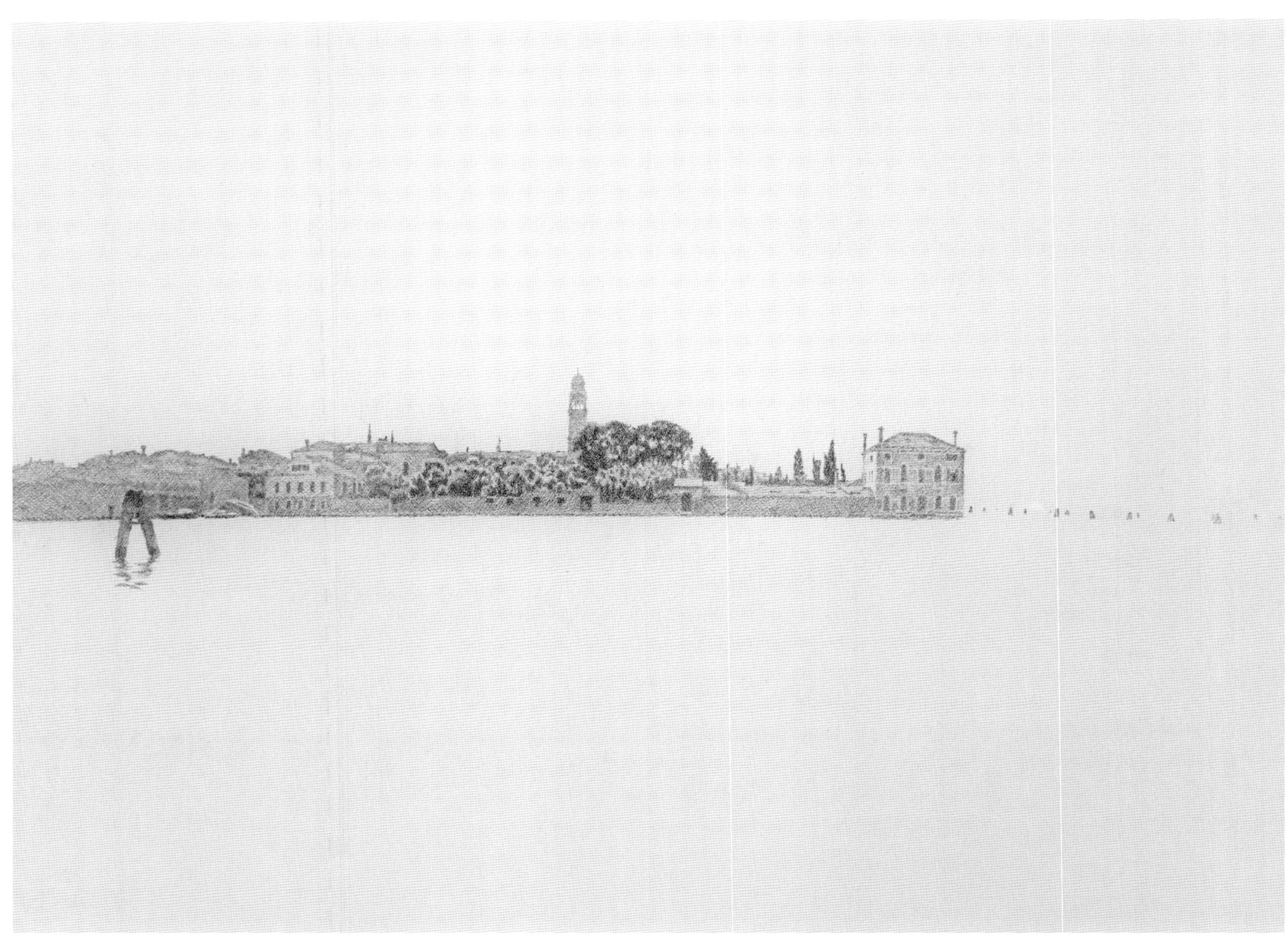

Sacca della Misericordia, Venice, 1974, pencil on paper, 54 x 74cm, Courtesy of the artist.

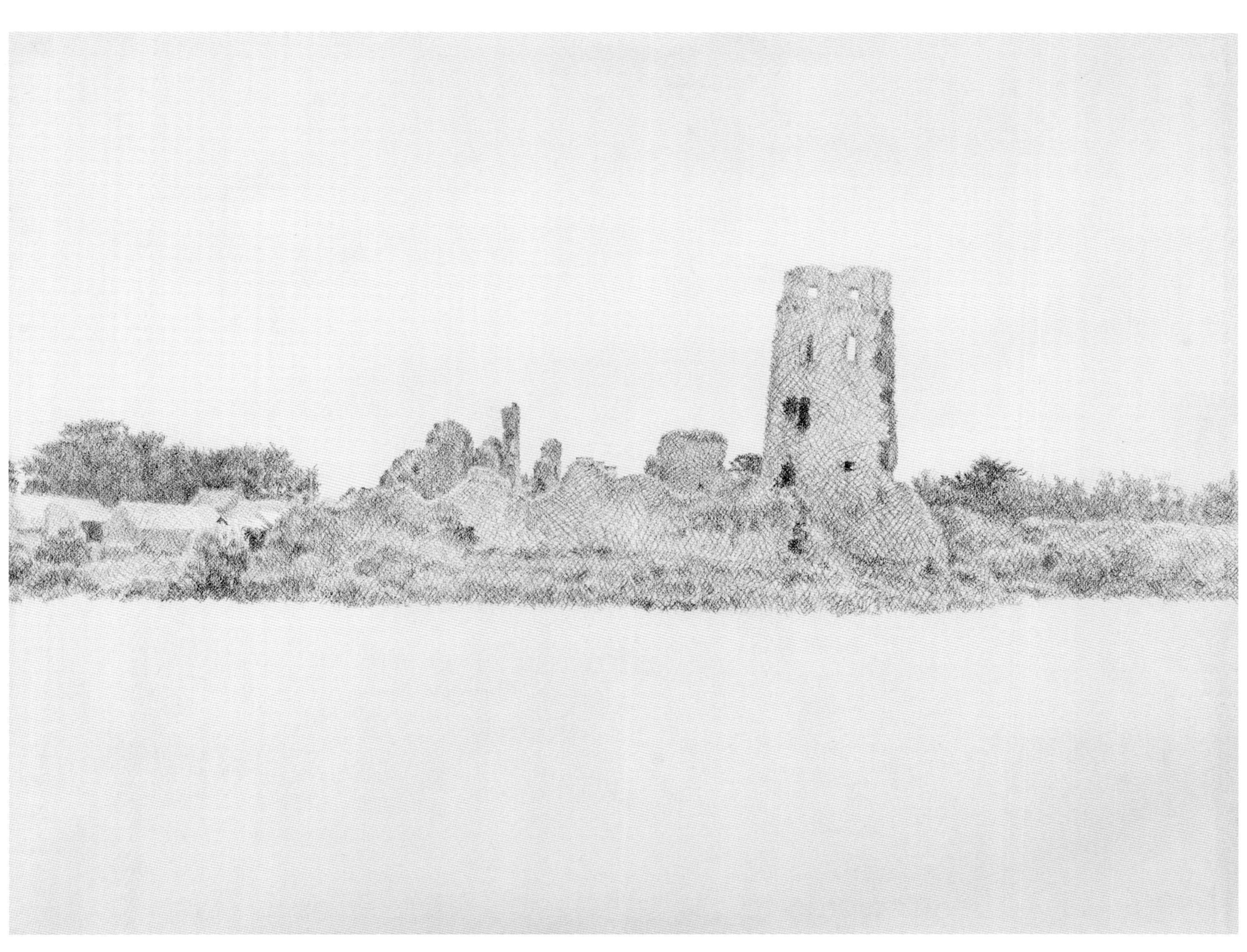

Château de Trèmazan, 1971, pencil on paper, 59 x 80cm, National Museum Wales.

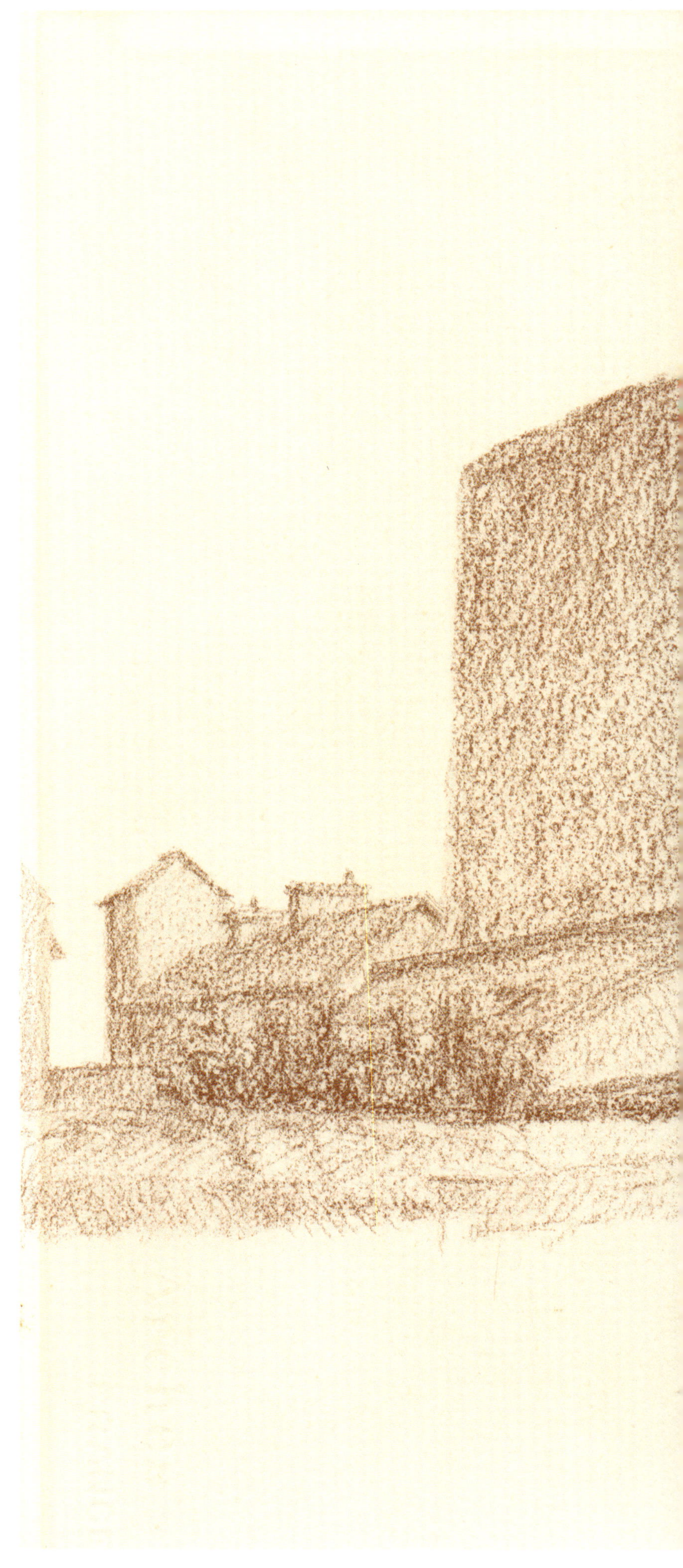

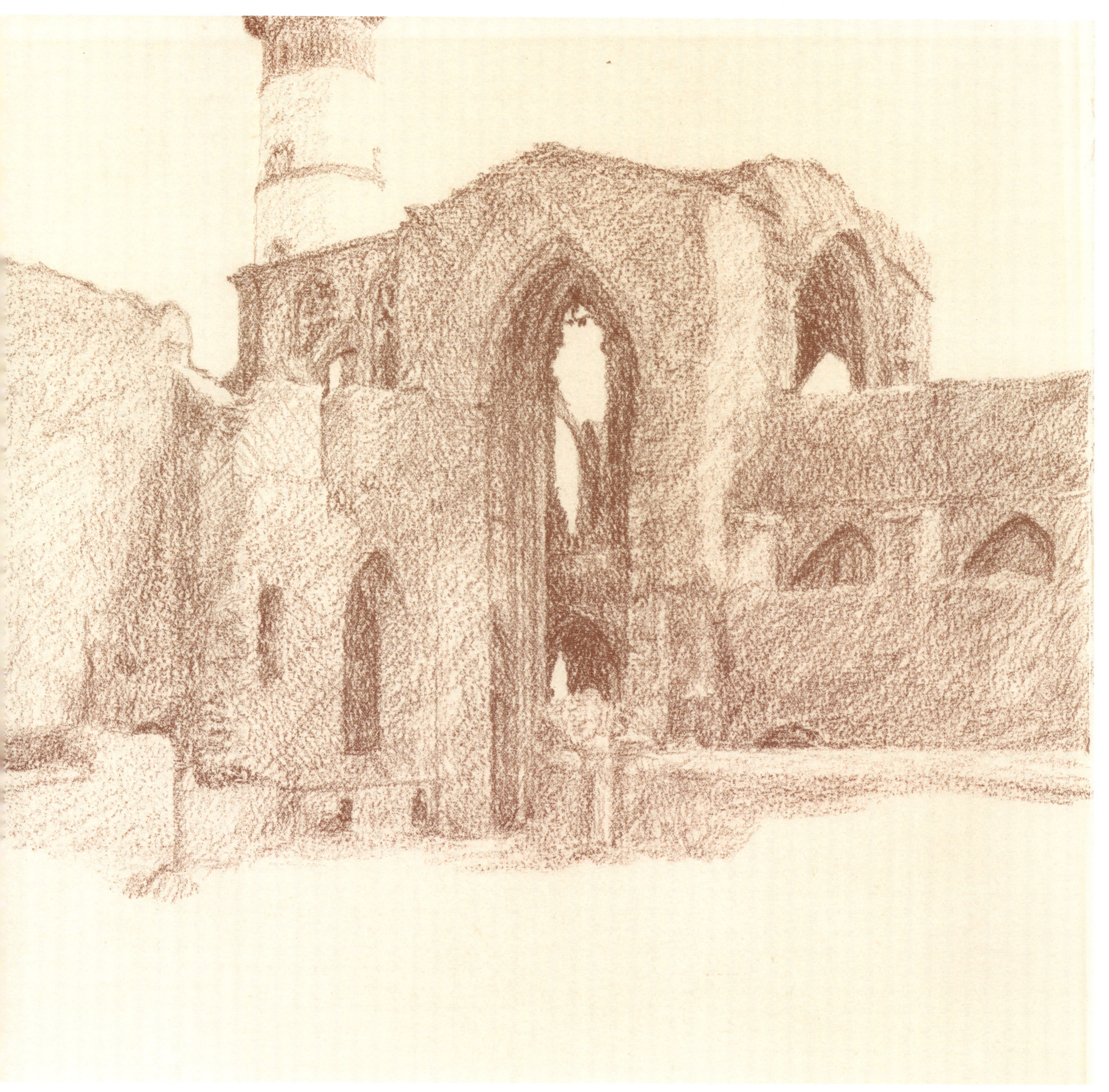

St Mathieu, Abbey and Lighthouse, 1971, red chalk on paper, 38.3 x 57cm, Aberystwyth University.

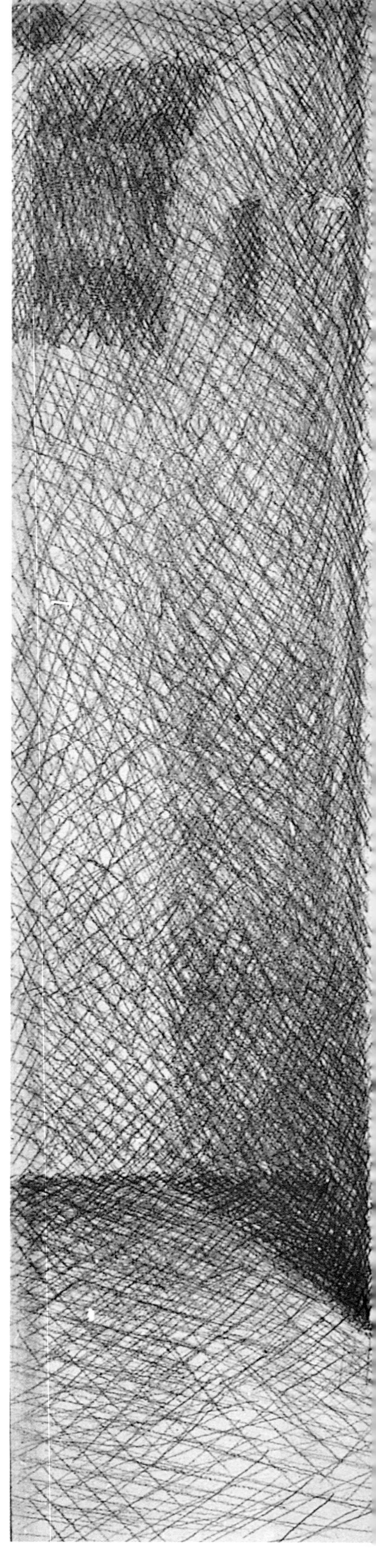

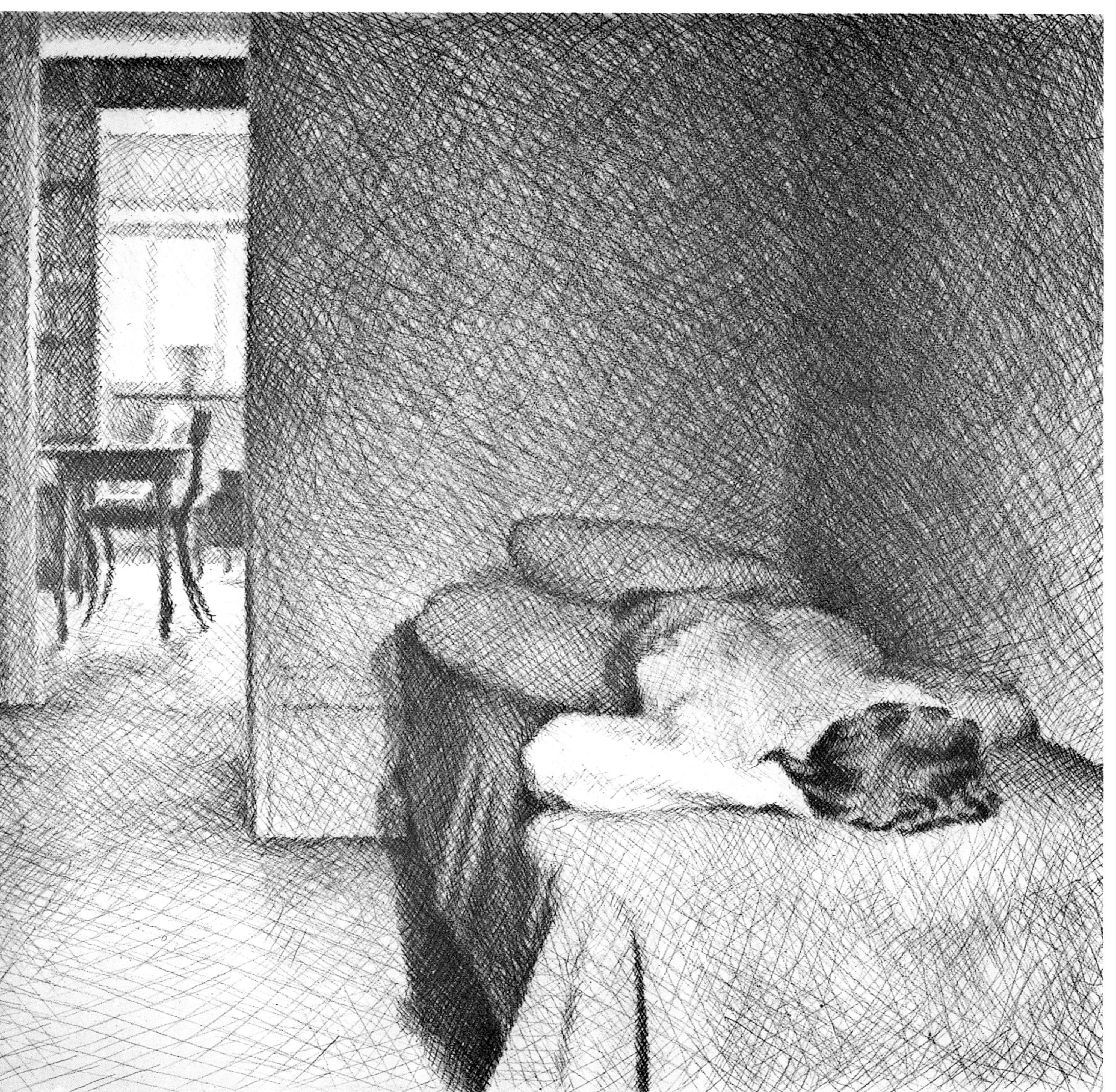

Interior with Nude, 1973, pencil on paper, 25 x 33cm, Private collection.

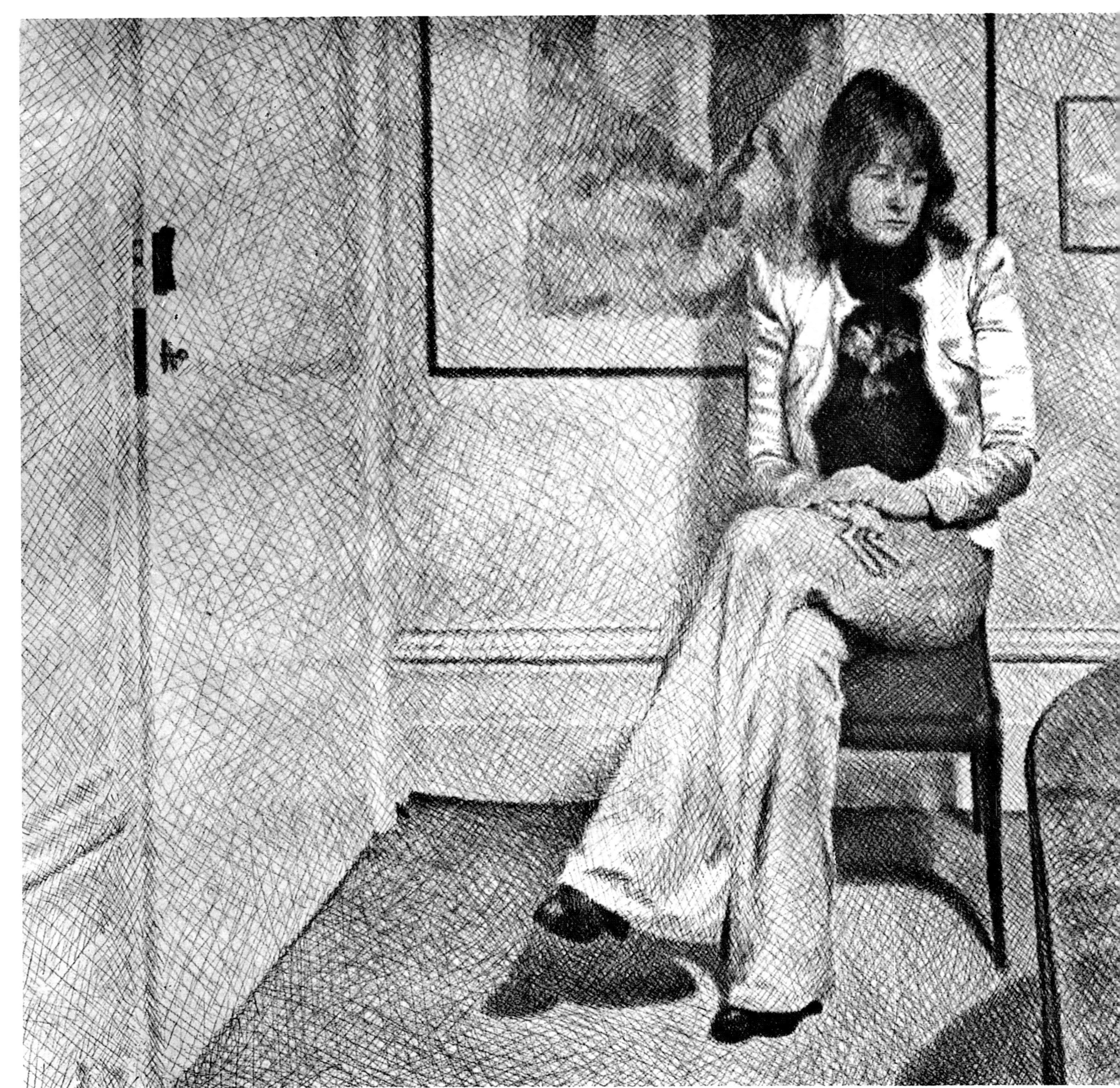

Mair Griffiths, 1974, pencil on paper, 30 x 43cm, Private collection.

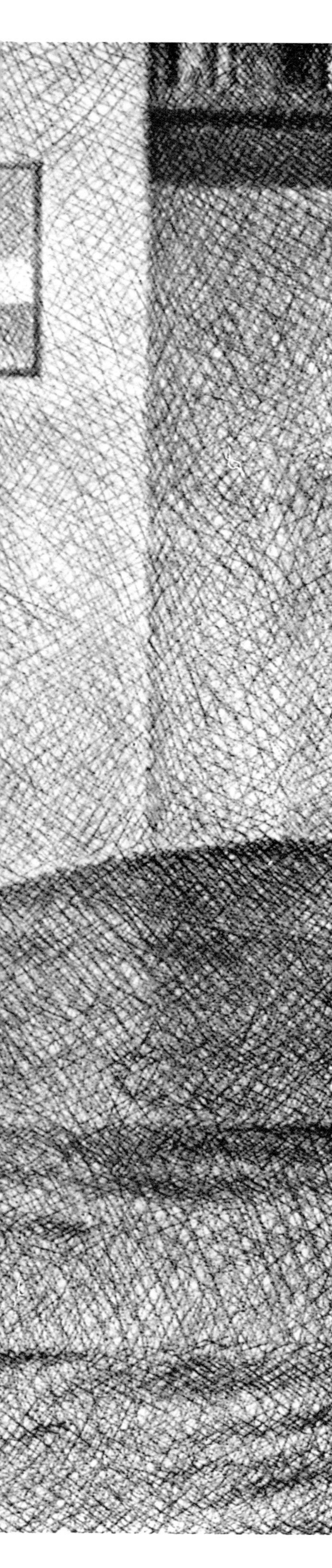

PAINTINGS 1974–1980

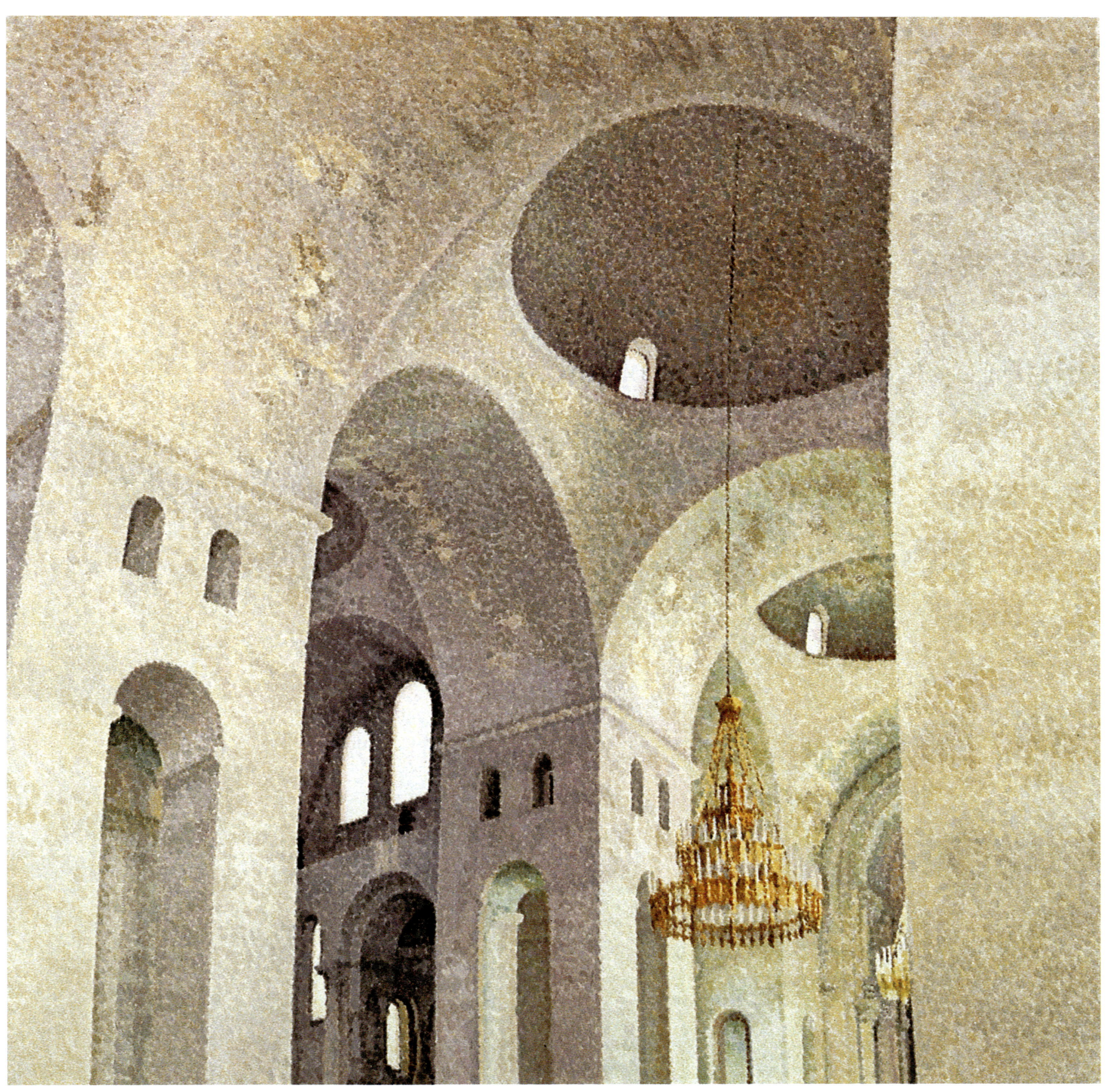

St Front, Périgueux, 1980, oil on canvas, 50 x 50cm, Private collection.

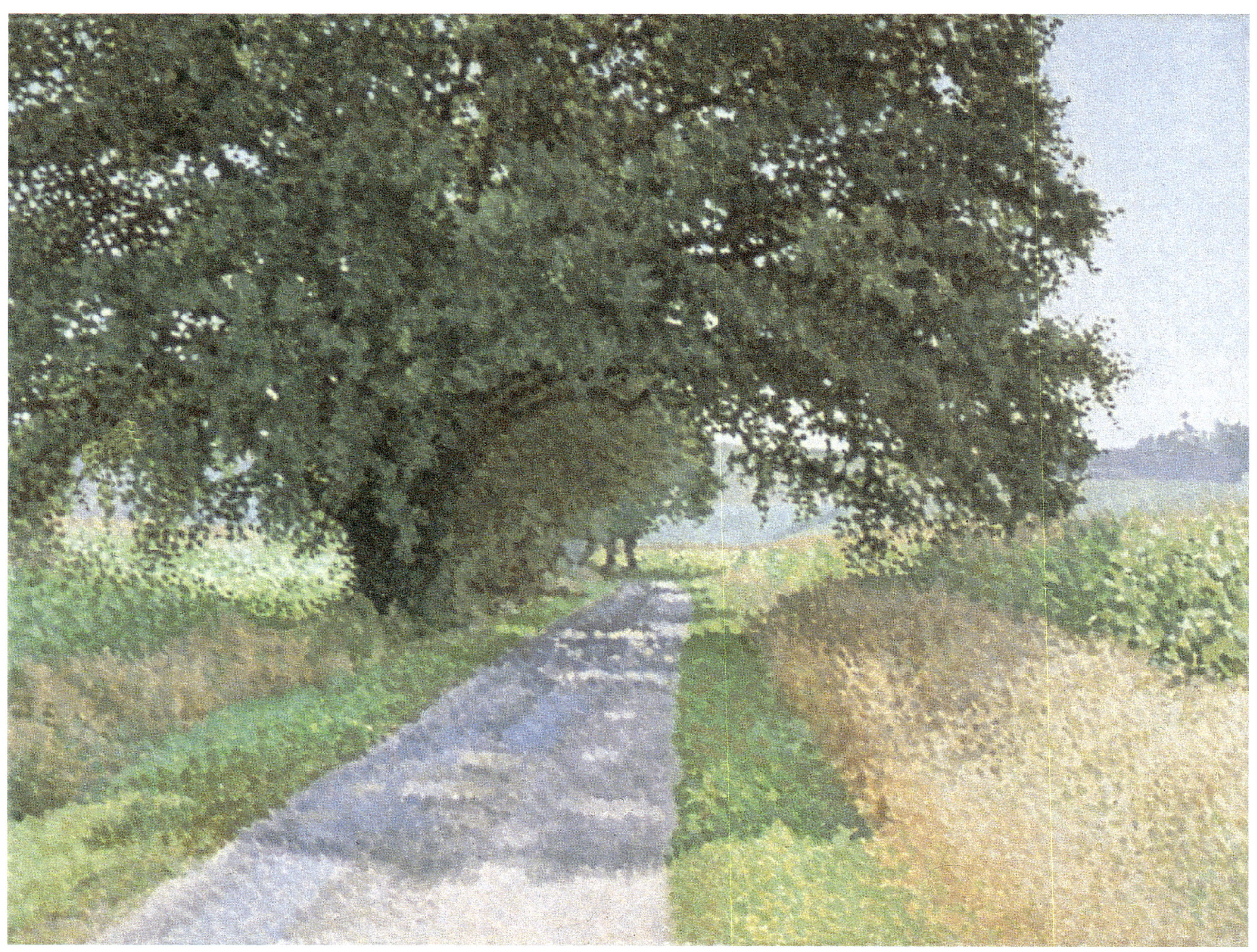

Morning Light, Touraine, 1977, oil on canvas, 27 x 40cm, Private collection.

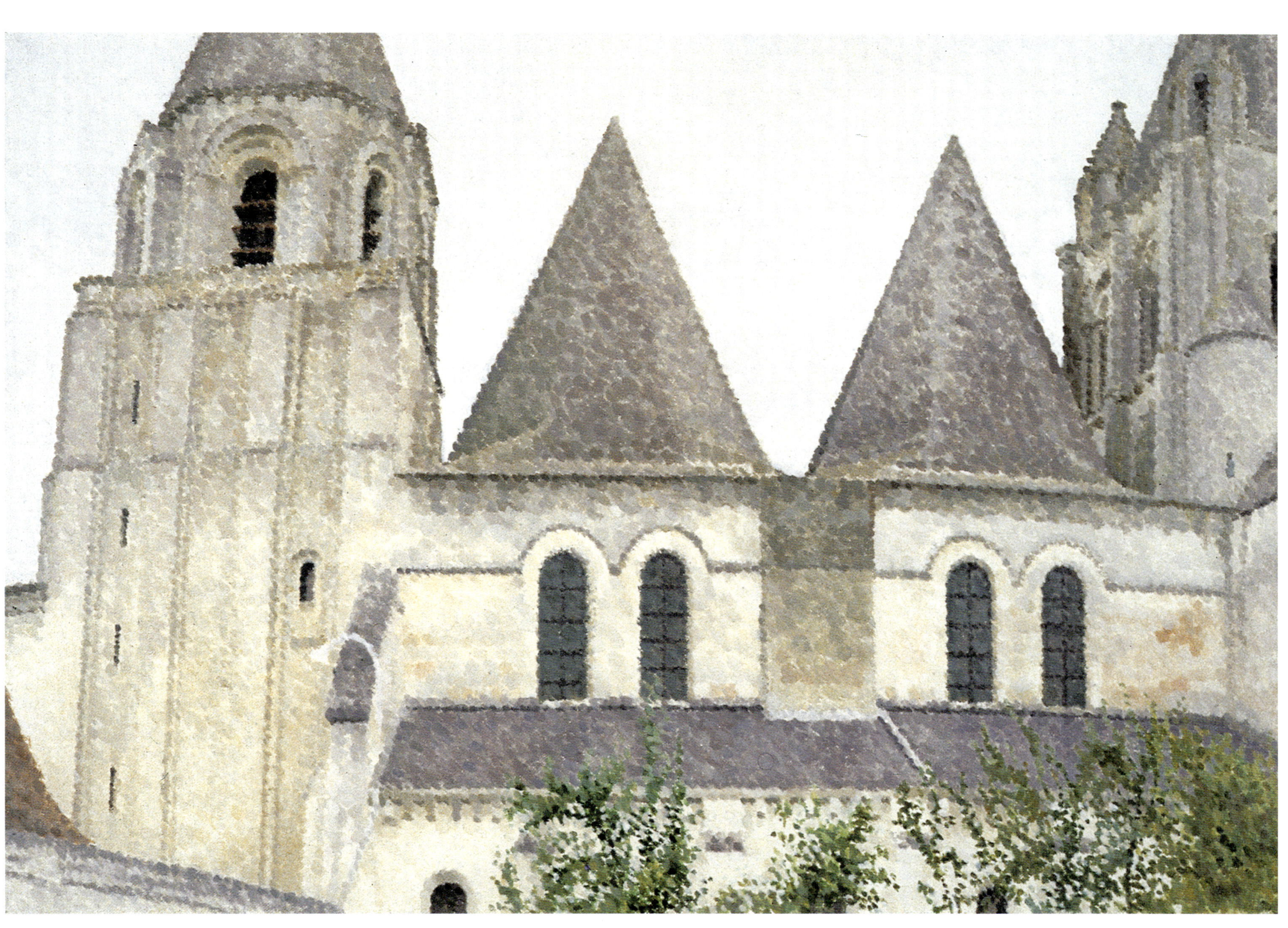

St Ours, Loches, 1977, oil on canvas, 30 x 40cm, Private collection.

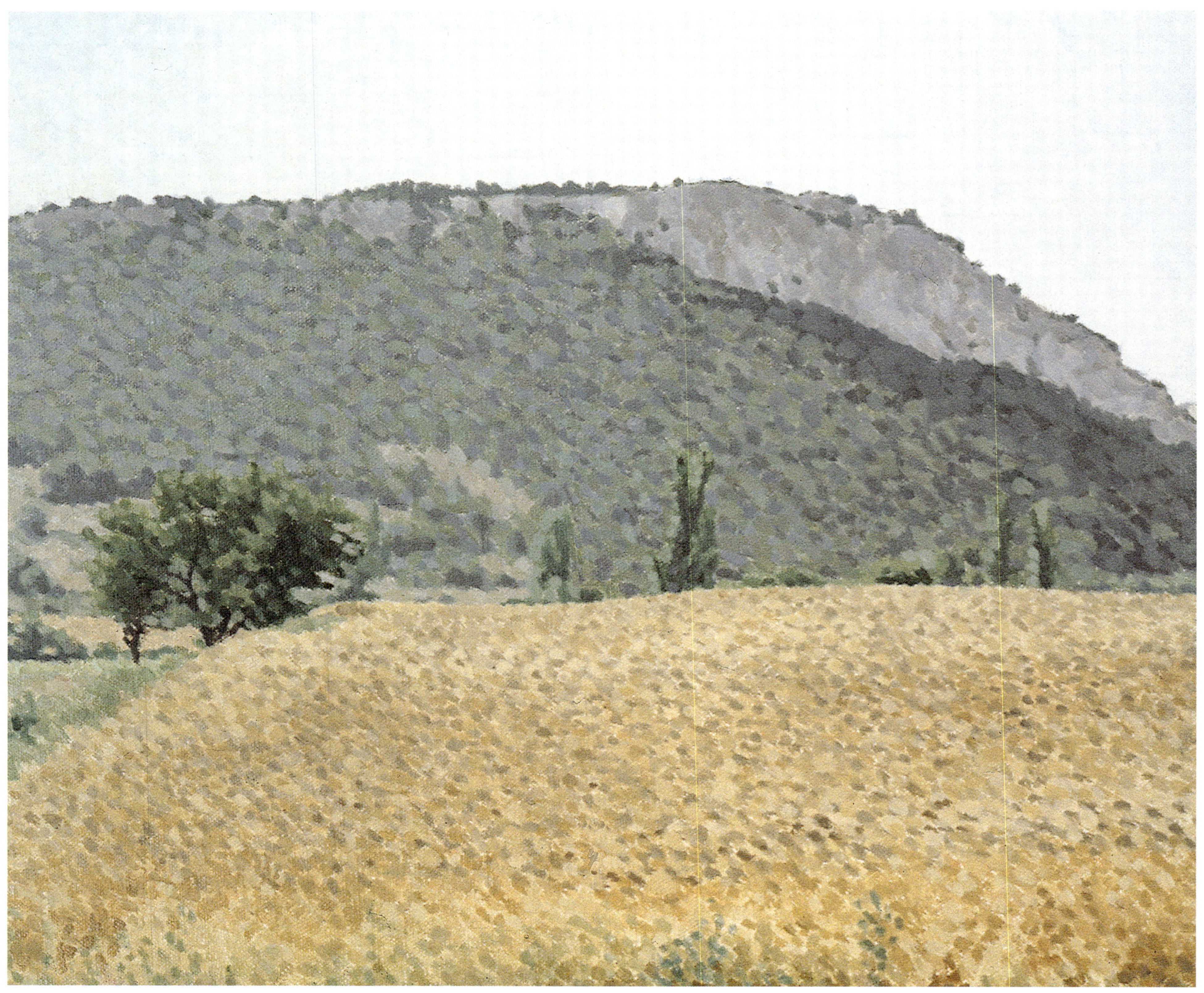

70   William Wilkins

Landscape near Belvezet, 1977, oil on canvas, 25 x 35cm, Private collection.

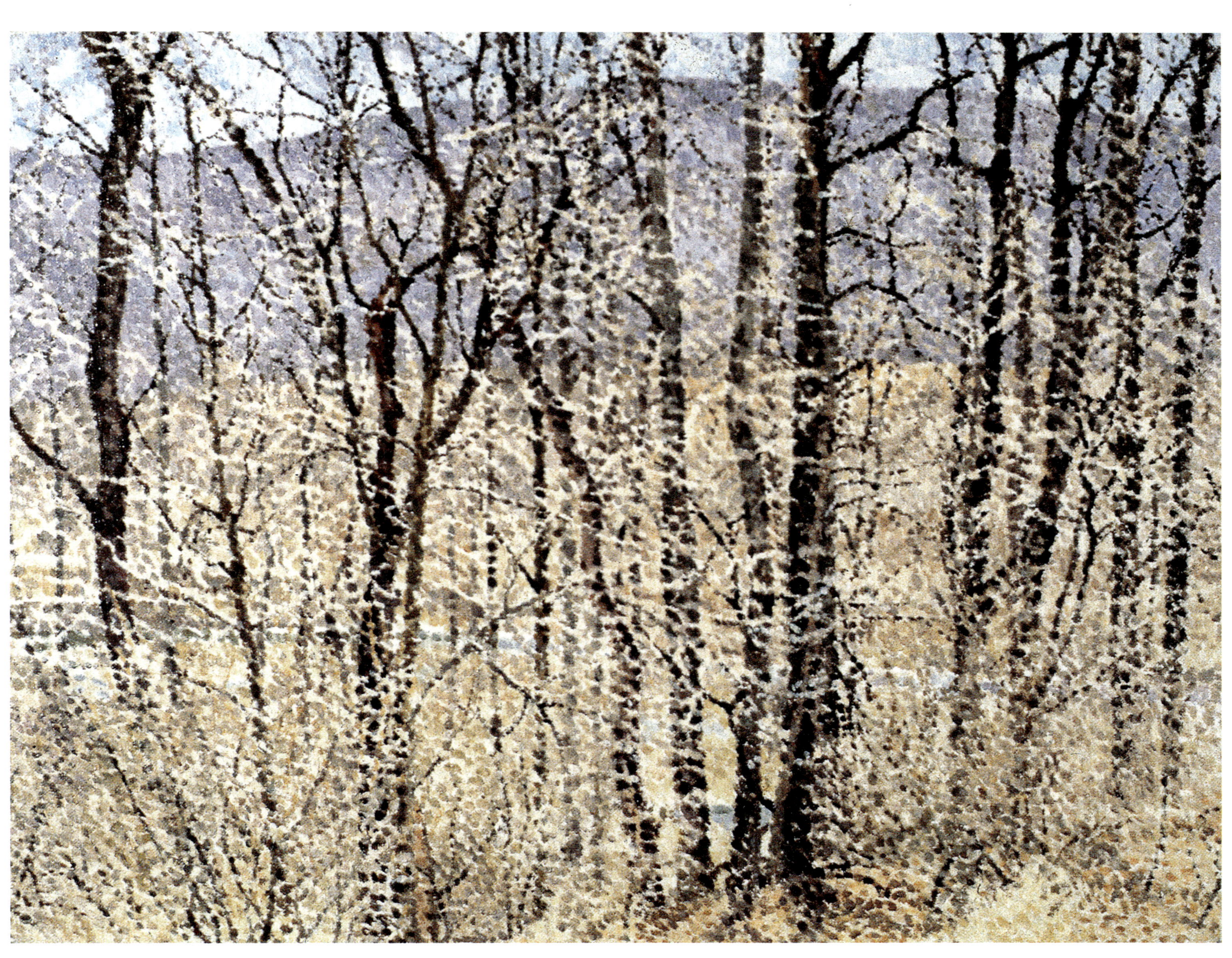

Kittatiny Mountains, Morning, 1980, oil on canvas, 22 x 30cm, Private collection.

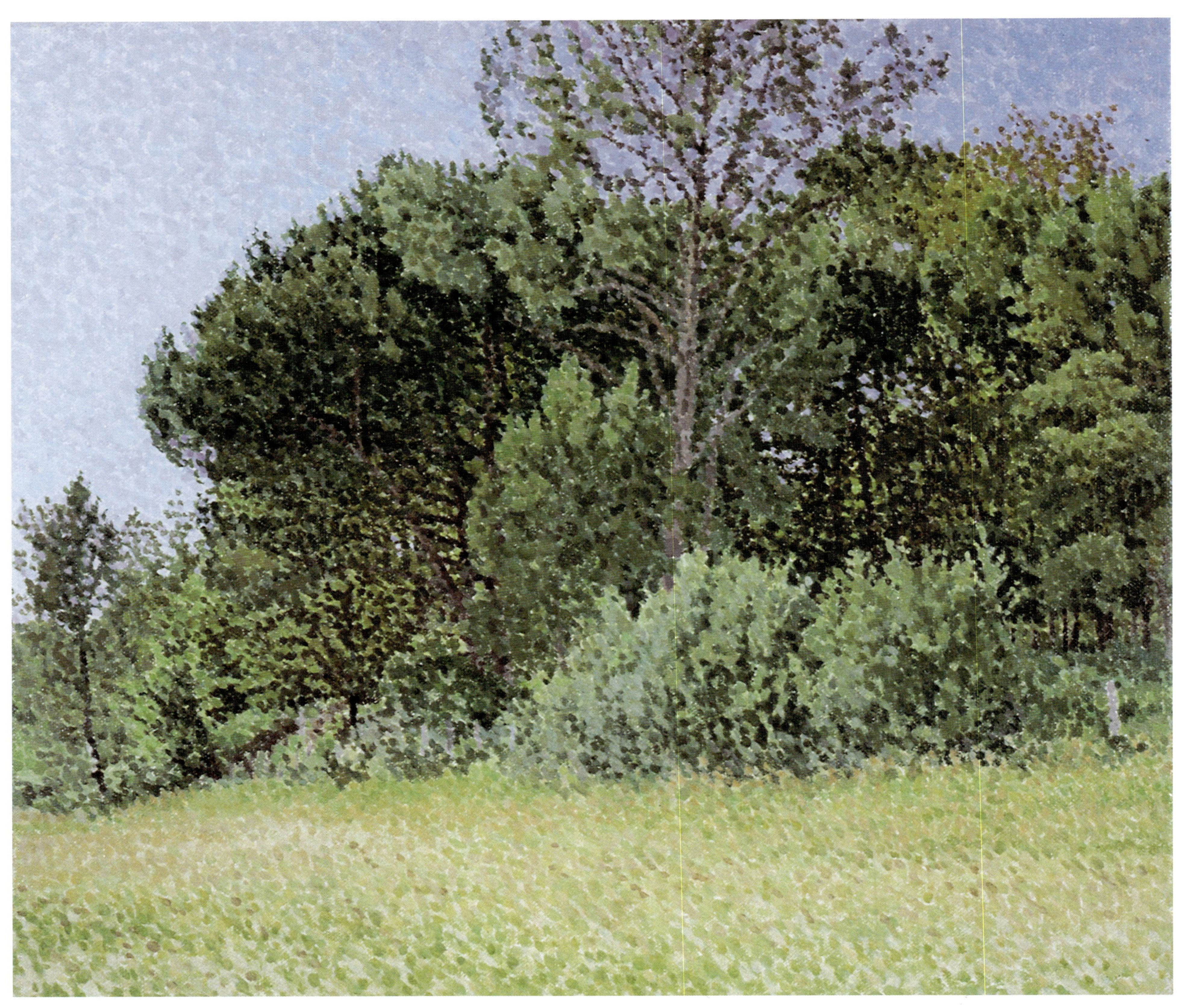

Evening Dordogne, 1979, oil on canvas, 25 x 30cm, Private collection.

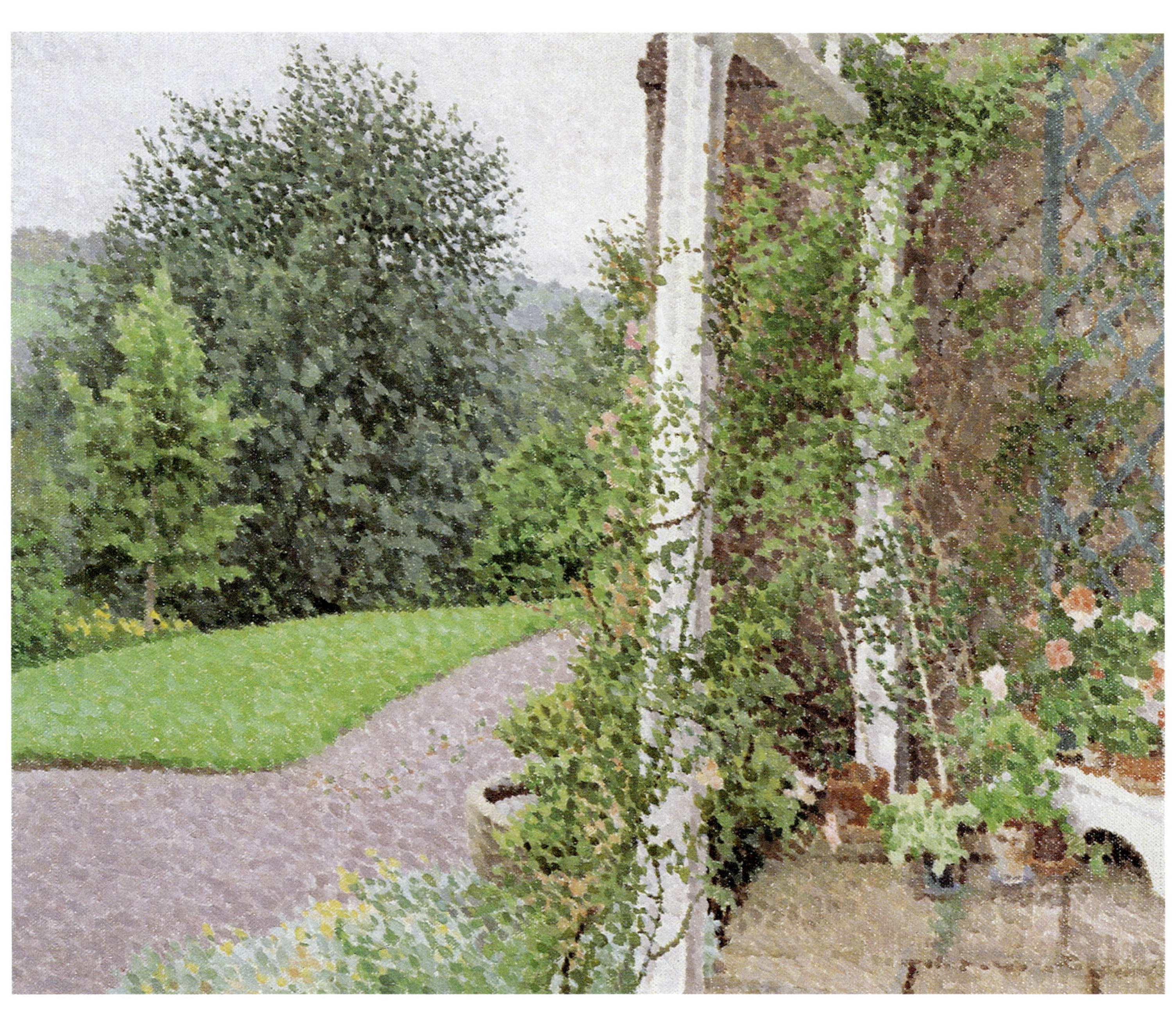

Rain, Carmarthenshire, 1979, oil on canvas, 25 x 30cm, Private collection.

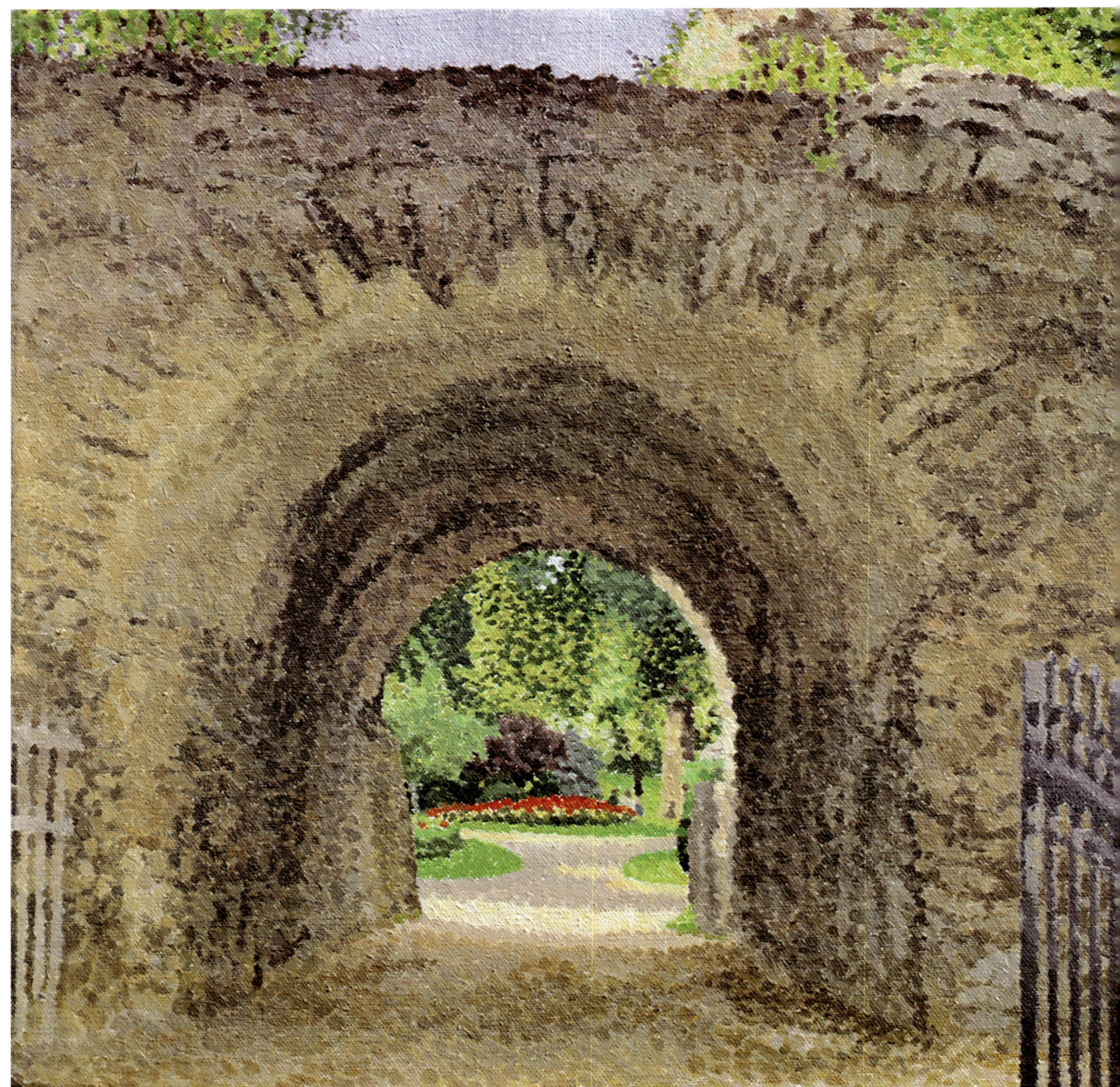

   Jardin des Arènes, Périgueux, 1980, oil on canvas, 25 x 35cm, Private collection.

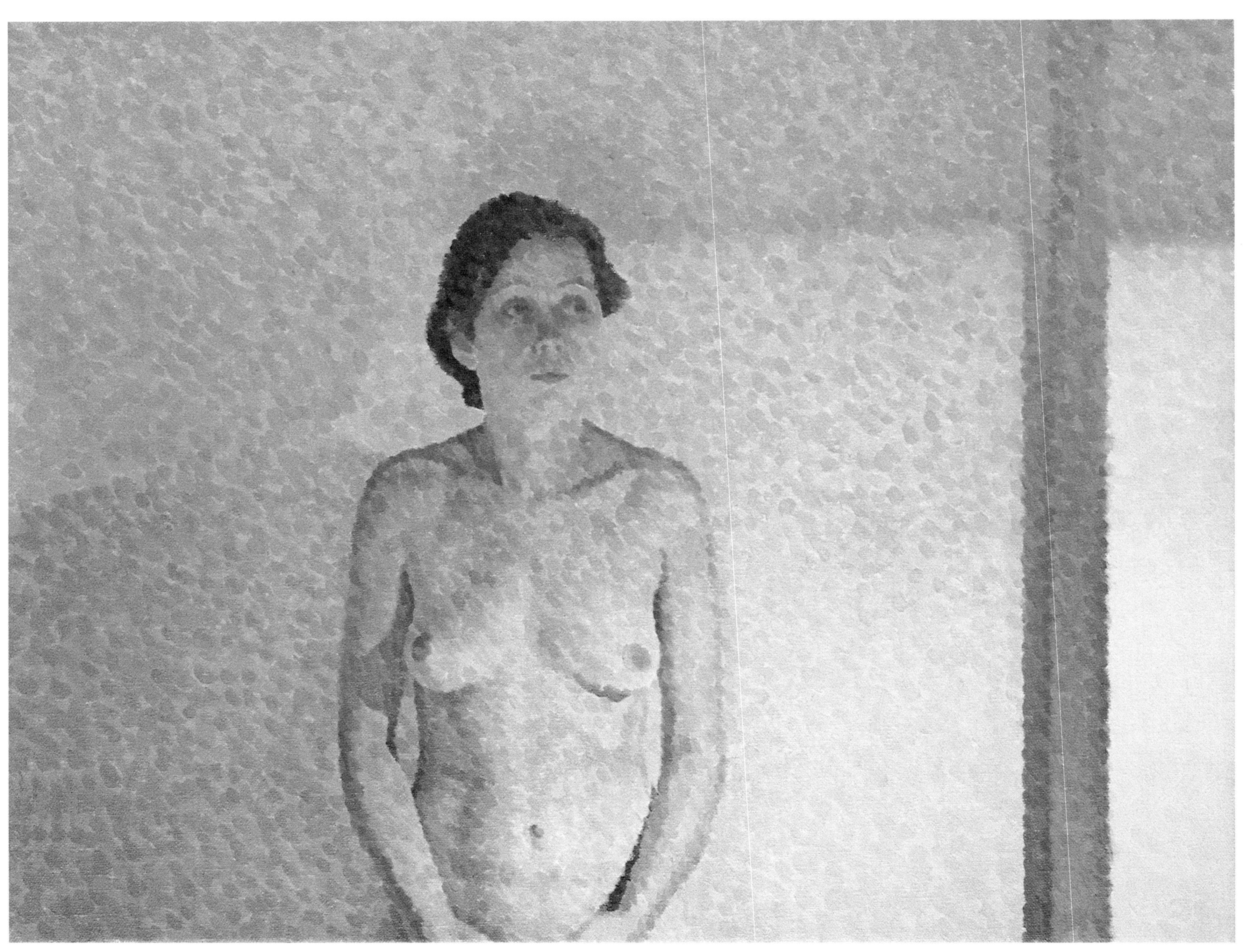

Seated Nude (Mayanne), 1977, oil on canvas, 30 x 40cm, Private collection.

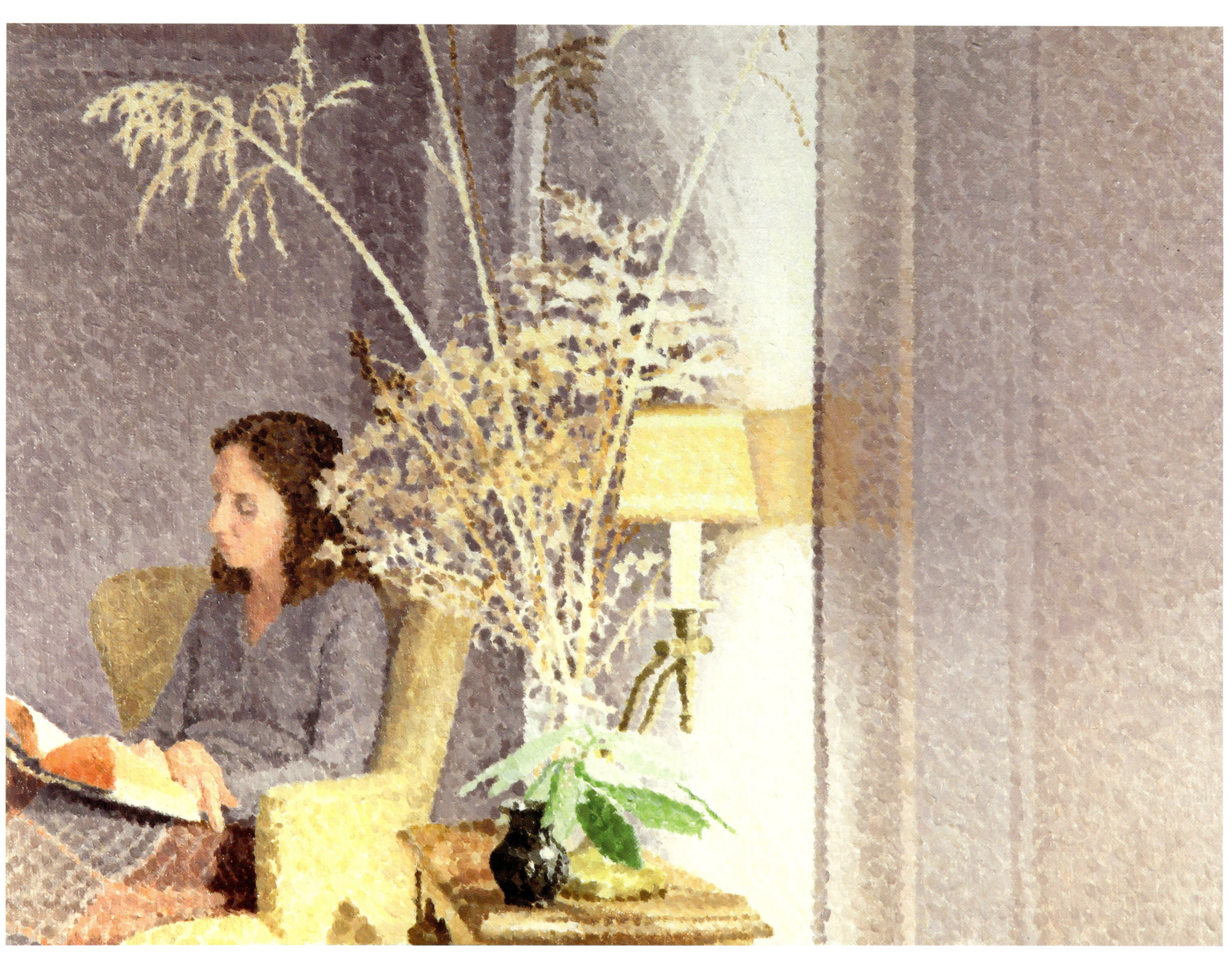

Lynne Reading, 1980, oil on canvas, 23 x 31cm, Private collection.

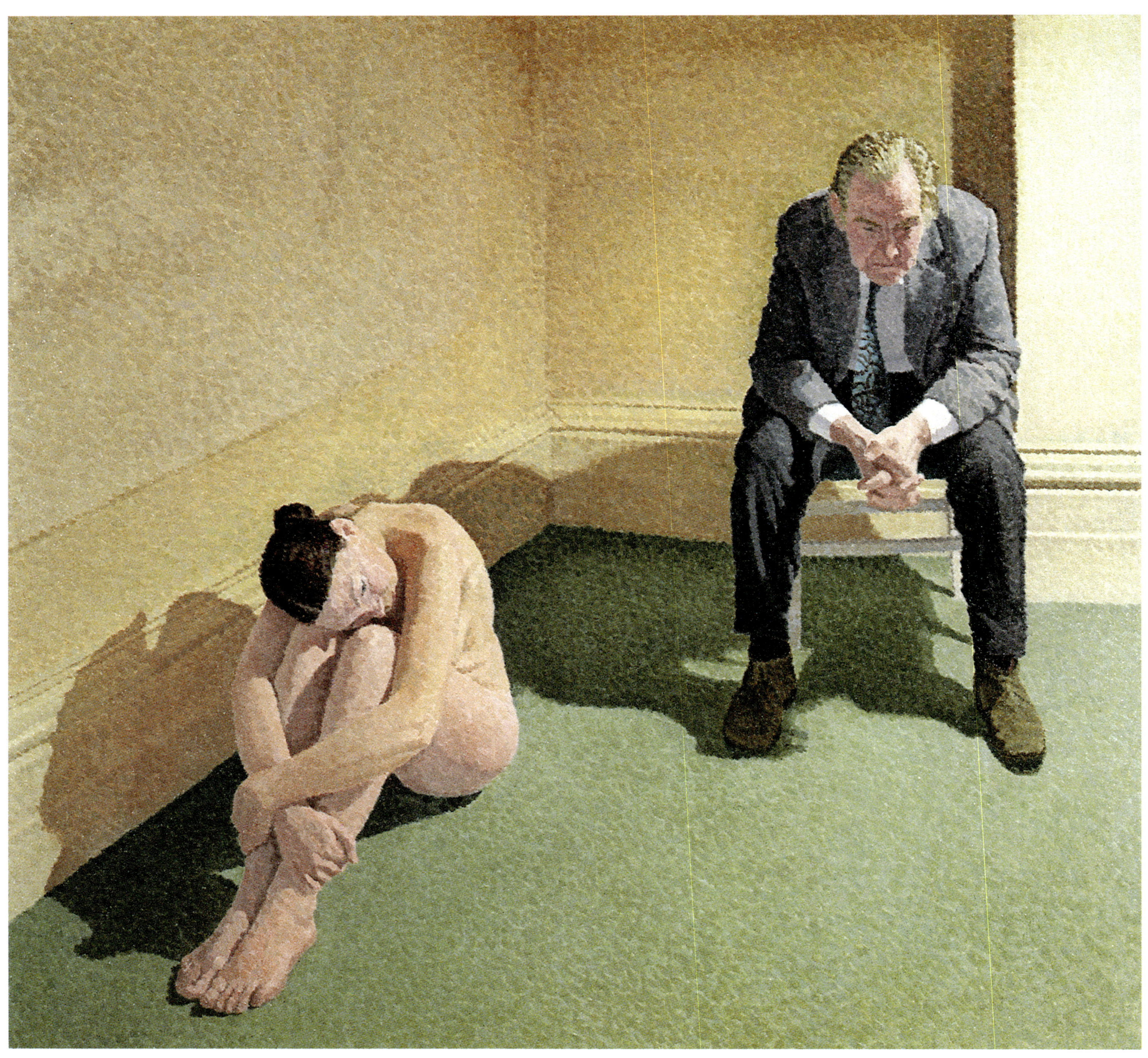

78   William Wilkins   Two Figures in the Corner of a Room, 1979, oil on canvas, 50 x 56cm, Hirshhorn Museum and Sculpture Garden Collection.

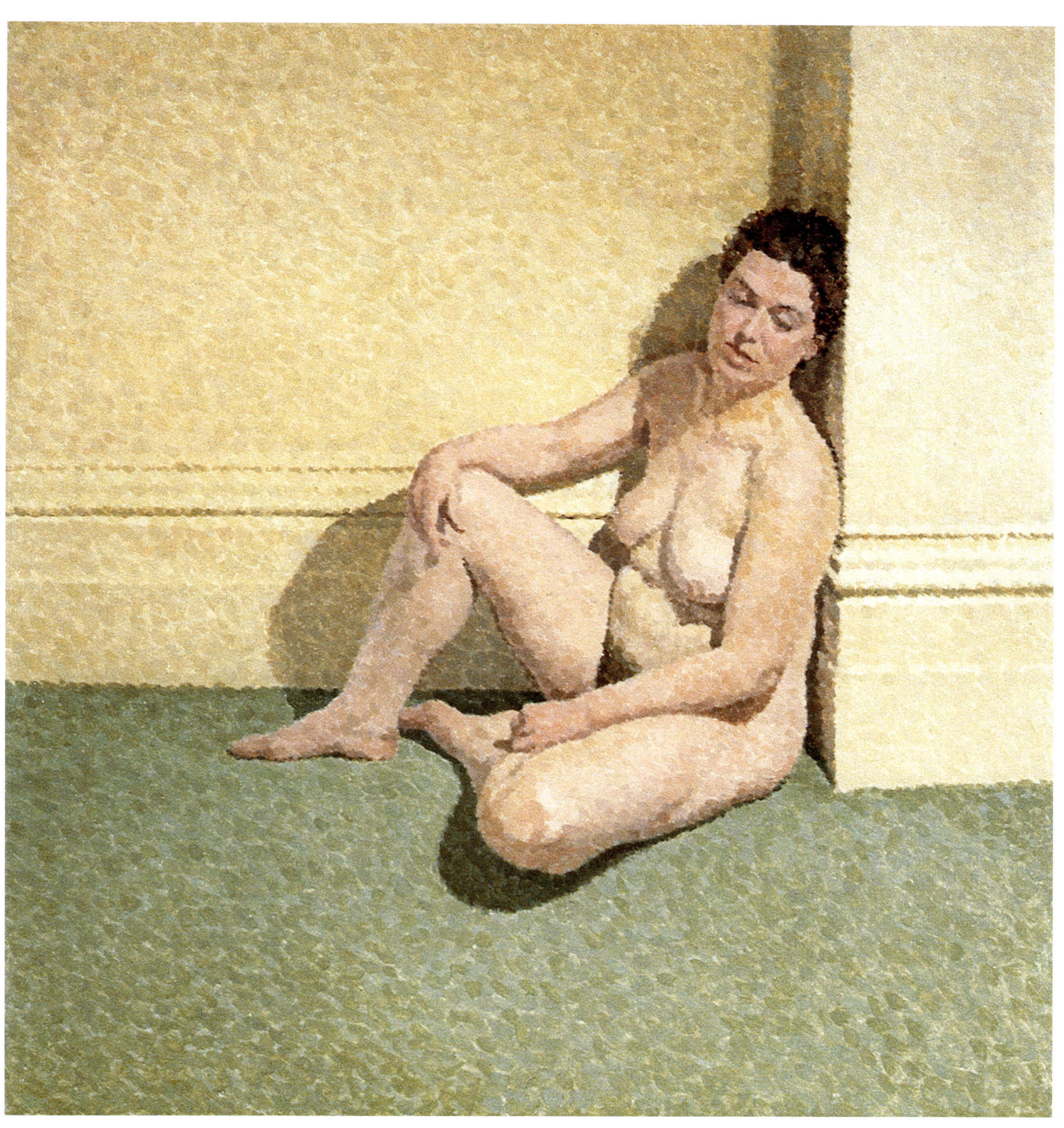

Nude, 1978, oil on canvas, 35 x 35cm, Private collection.

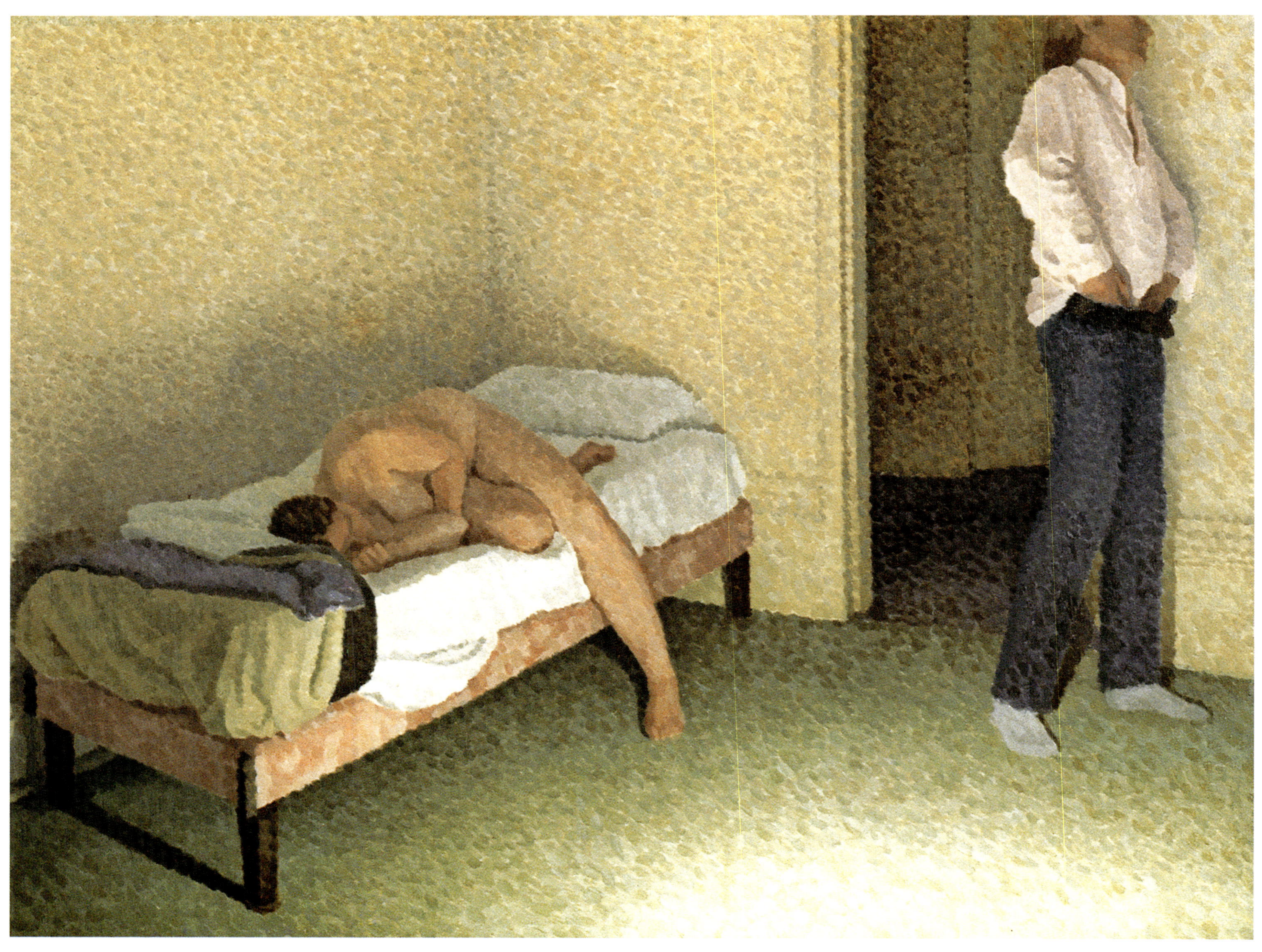

Interior with a Figure Dressing, 1976, oil on canvas, 40 x 55cm, Private collection.

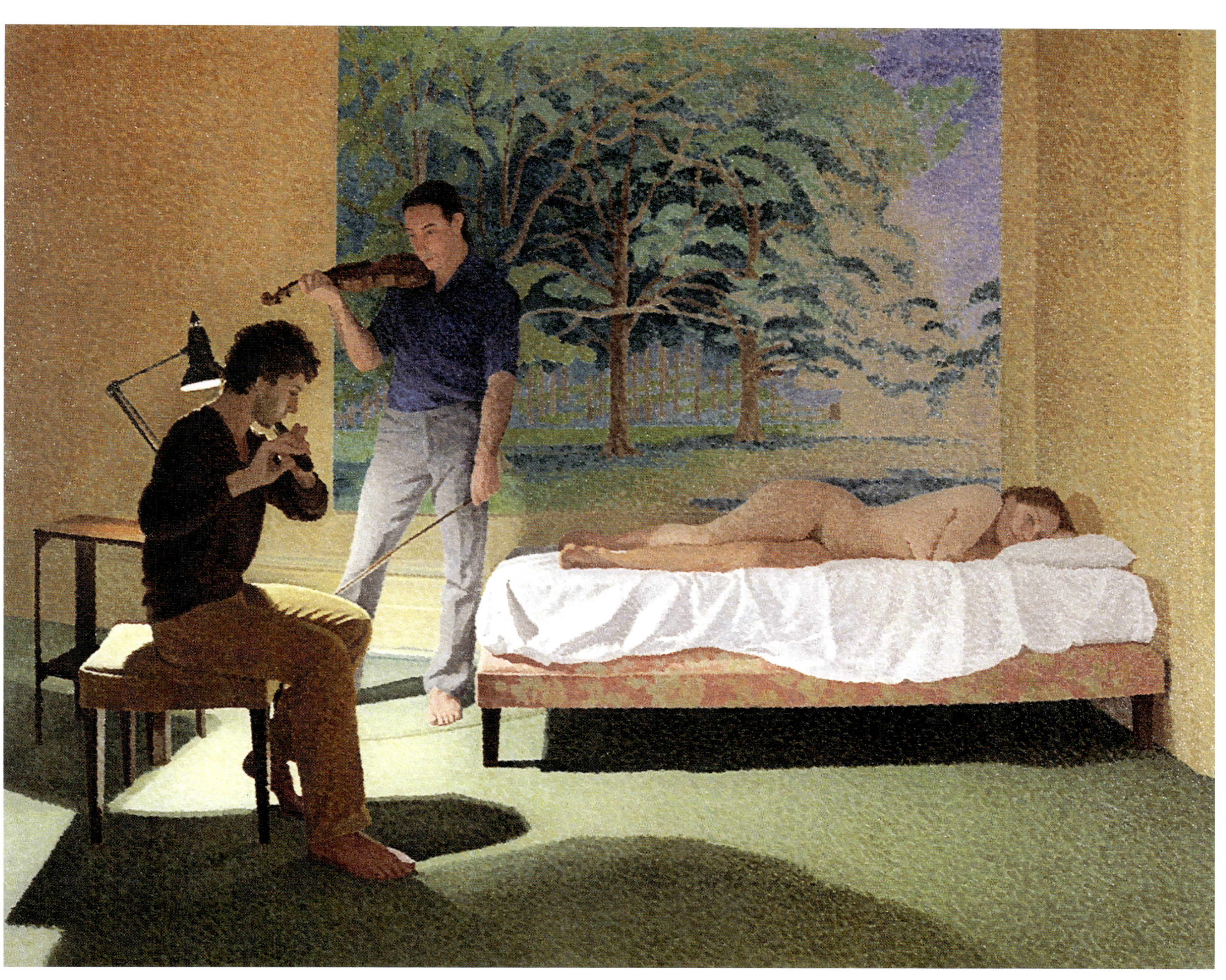

Figures with a Landscape, 1979, oil on canvas, 60 x 78cm, Private collection.

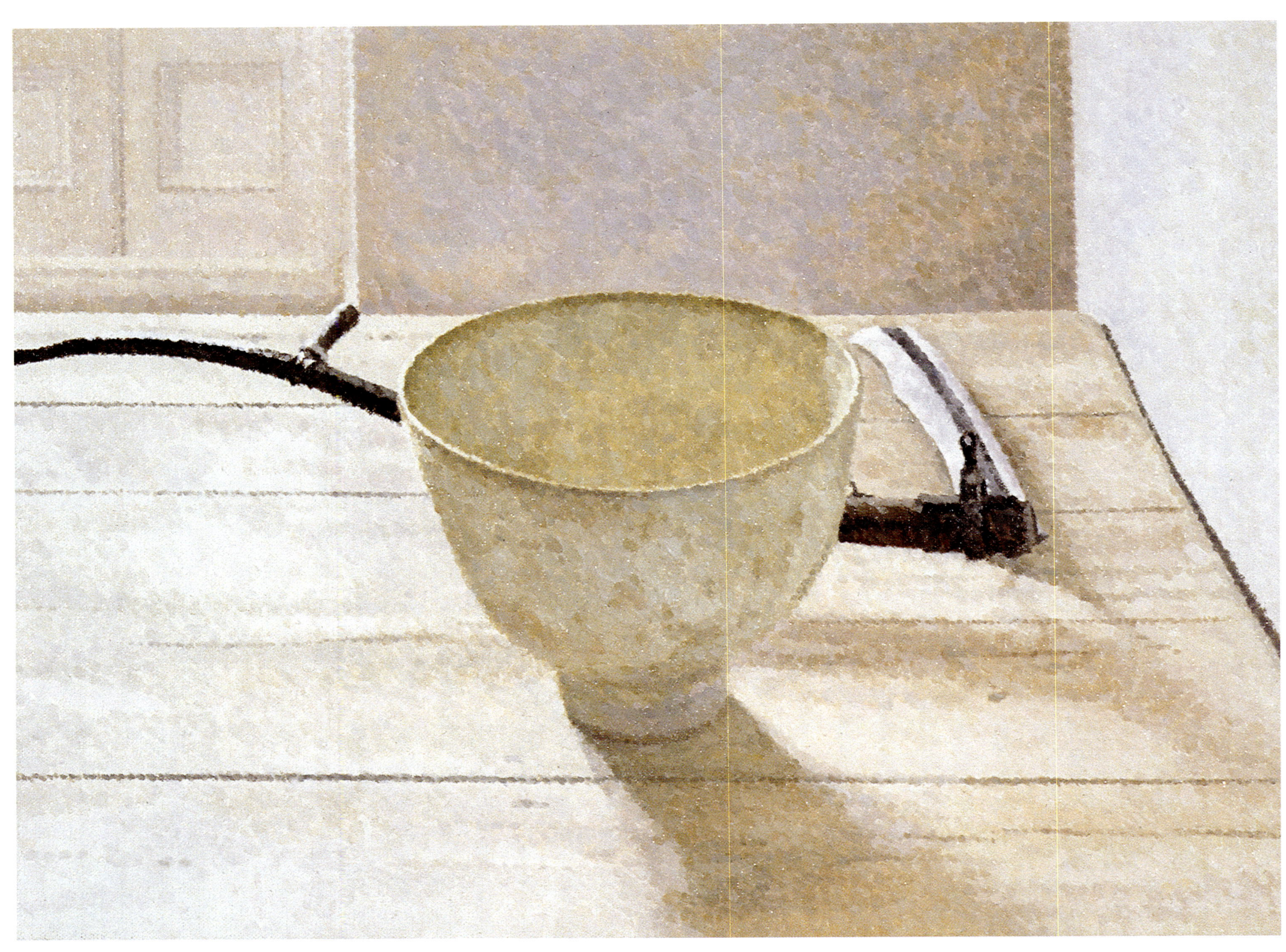

Still Life: Scythe and Bowl 1980, oil on canvas, 25 x 35cm, Private collection.

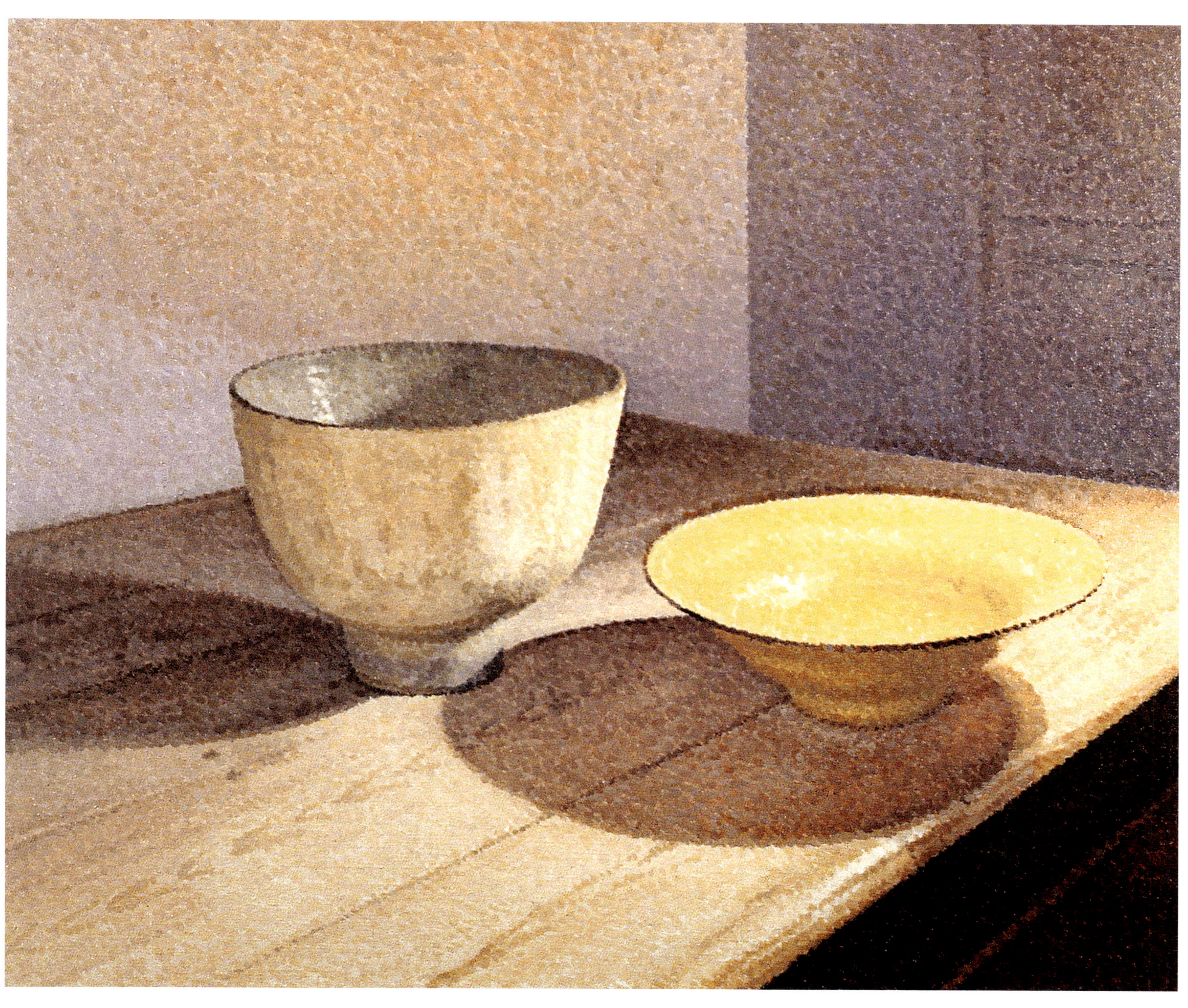

Two Lucie Rie Bowls, 1980, oil on canvas, 50 x 60cm, Private collection.

PAINTINGS 1981–1990

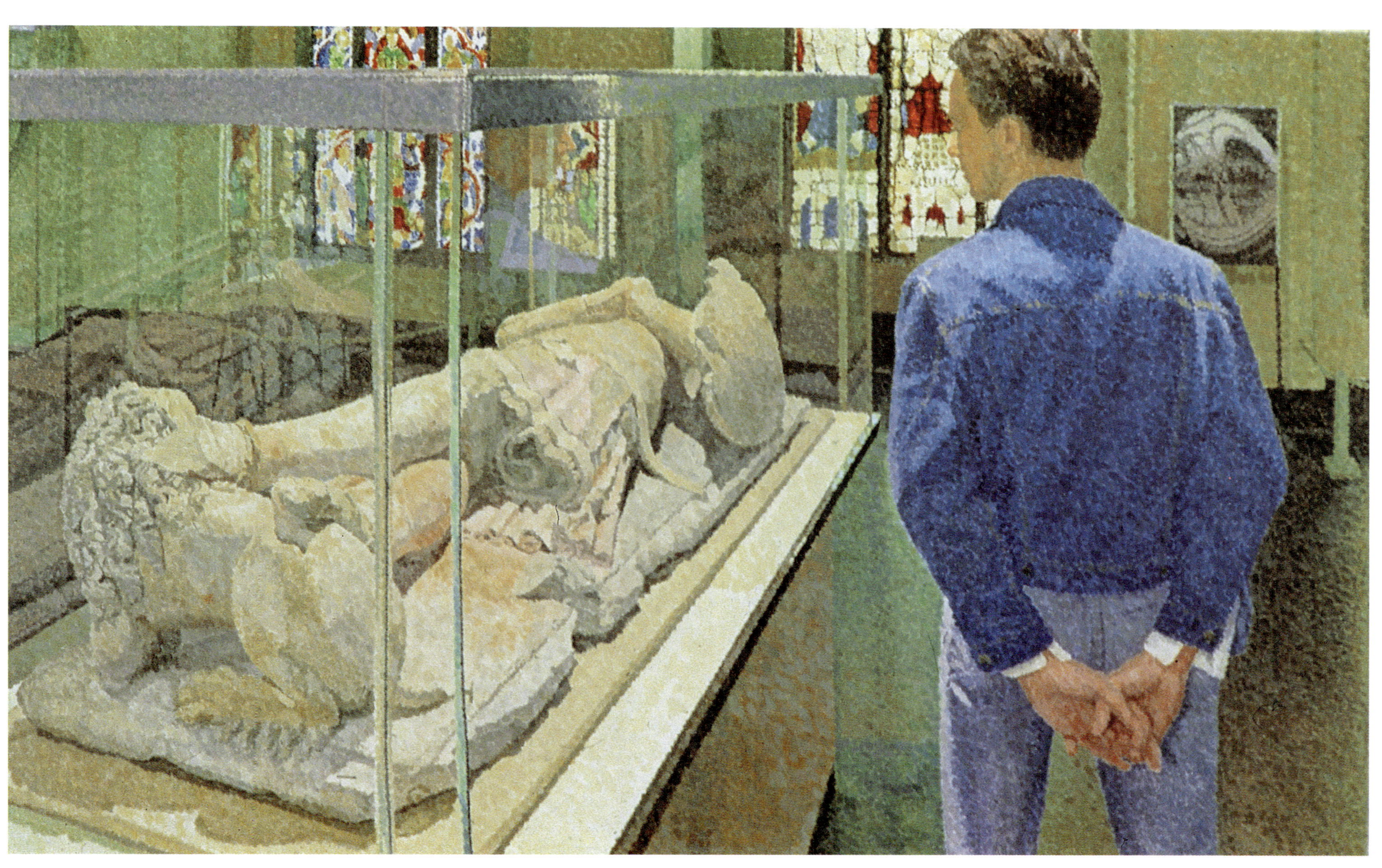

Effigy of a Knight, 1982, oil on canvas, 68 x 41cm, Private collection.

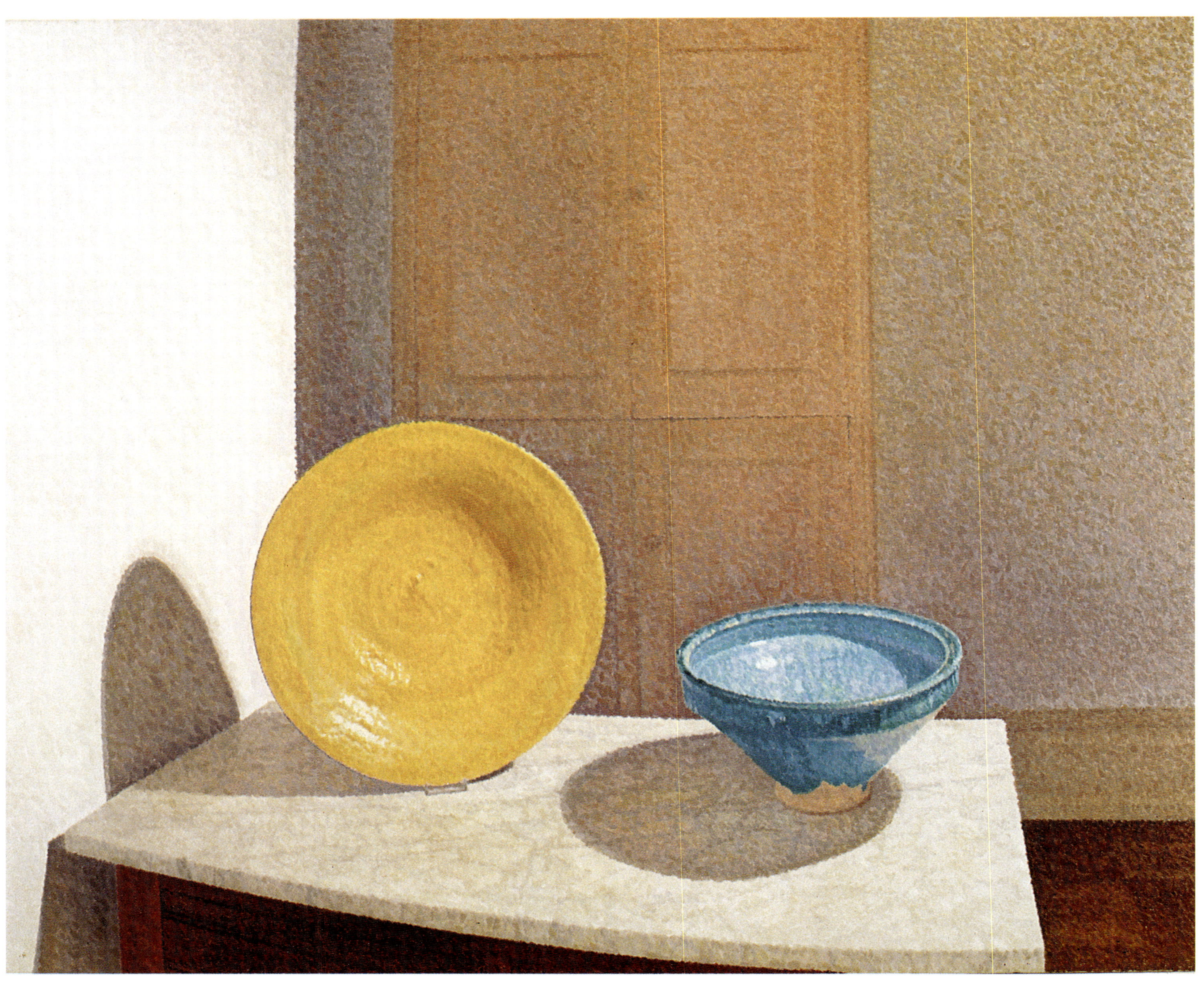

Still Life: Marbled Topped Table, 1984, oil on canvas, 71 x 88cm, Private collection.

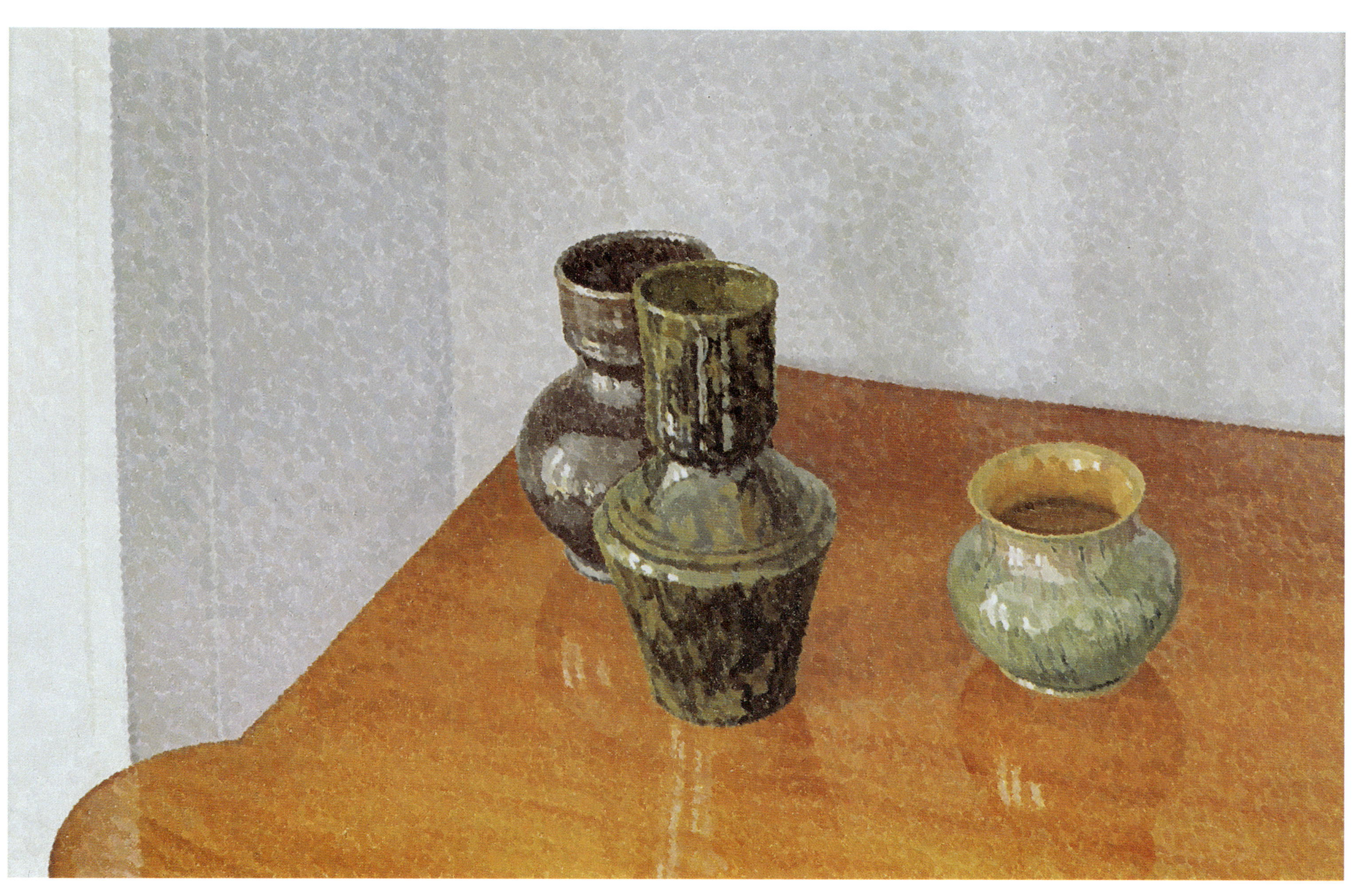

Still Life: George Ohr Pots, 1982, oil on canvas, 30 x 45cm, National Museum Wales.

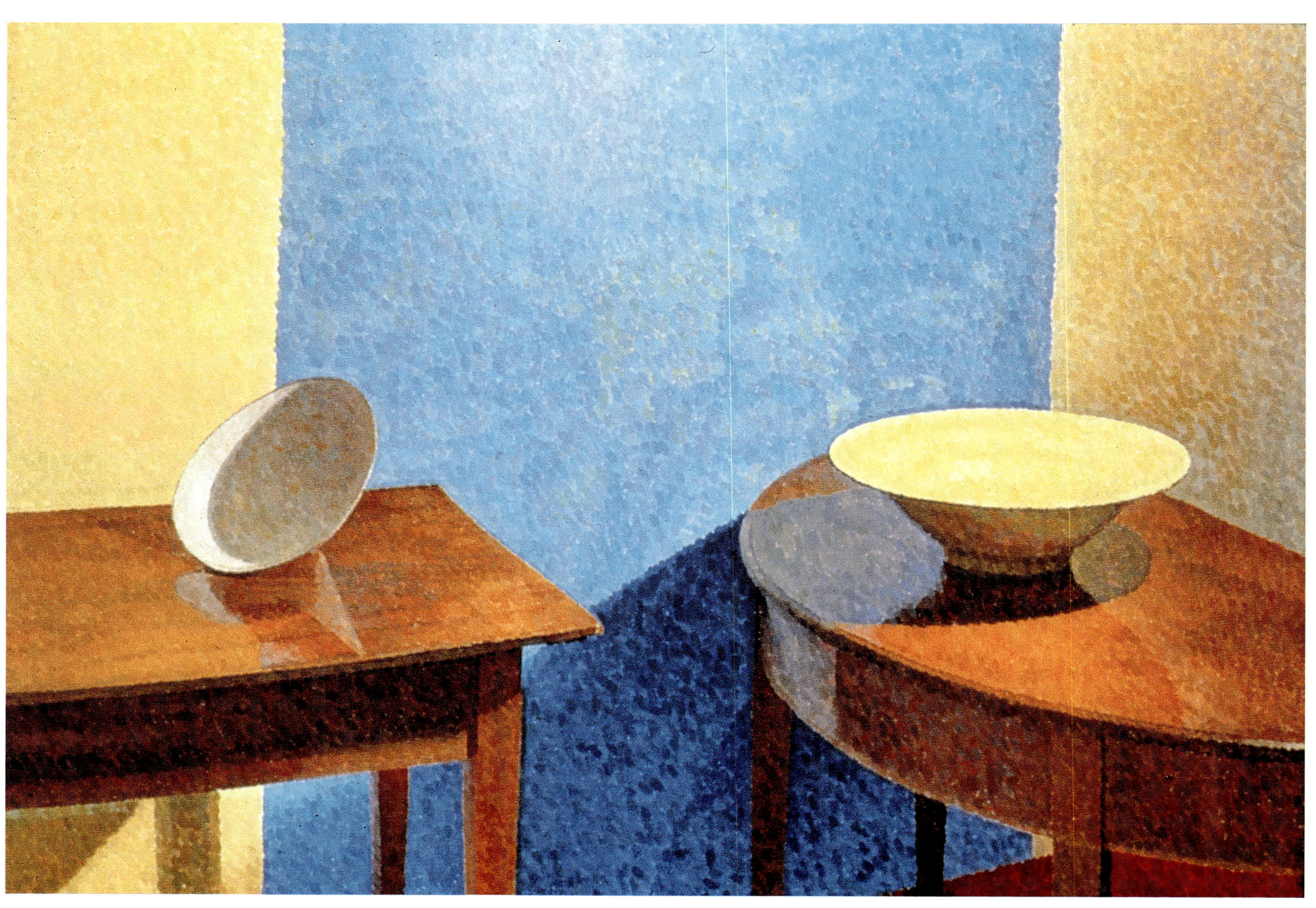

Still Life Two Tables, 1986, oil on canvas, 71 x 101cm, Courtesy of the artist.

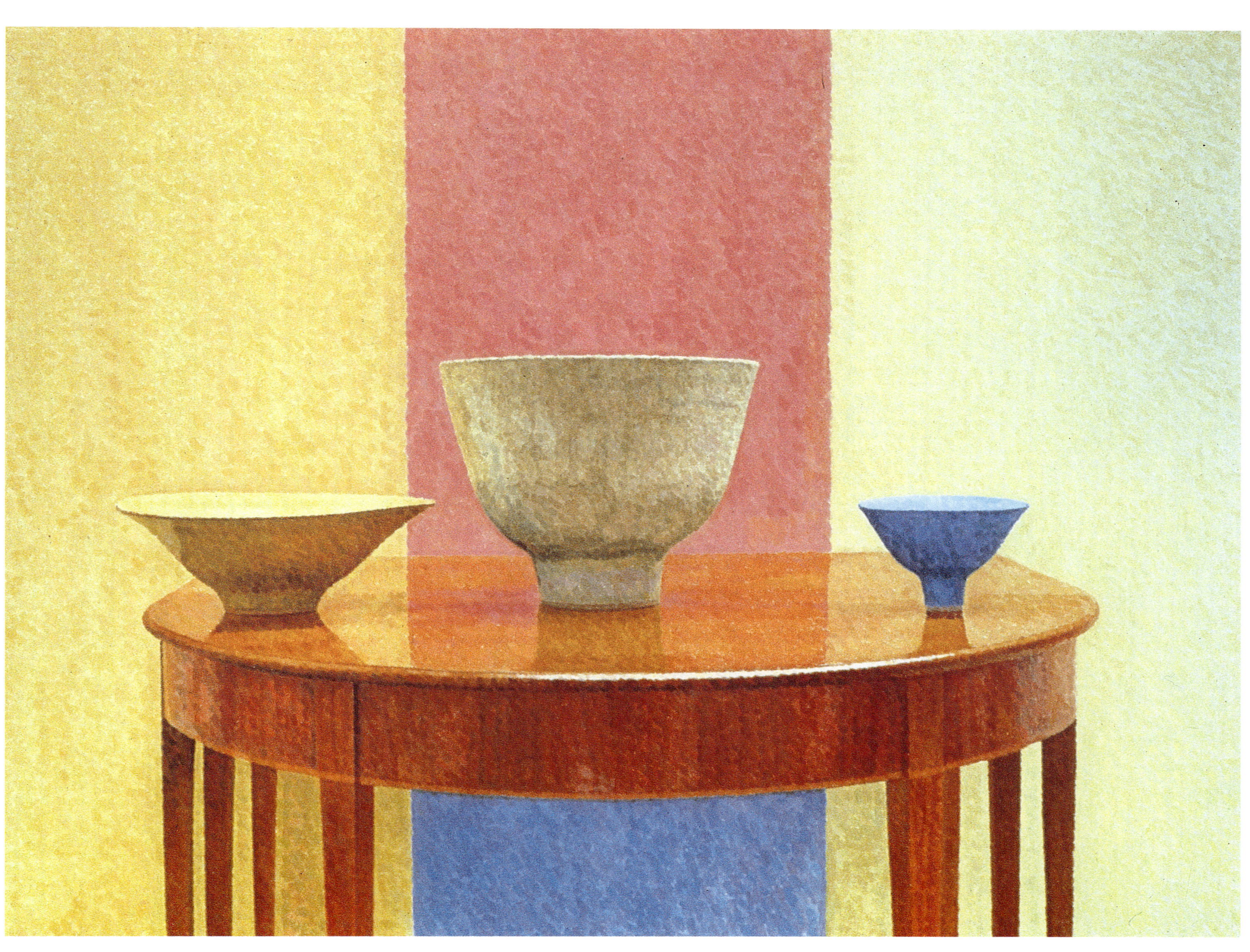

Still Life: Three Lucie Rie Bowls, 1985, oil on canvas, 94 x 126cm, Private collection.

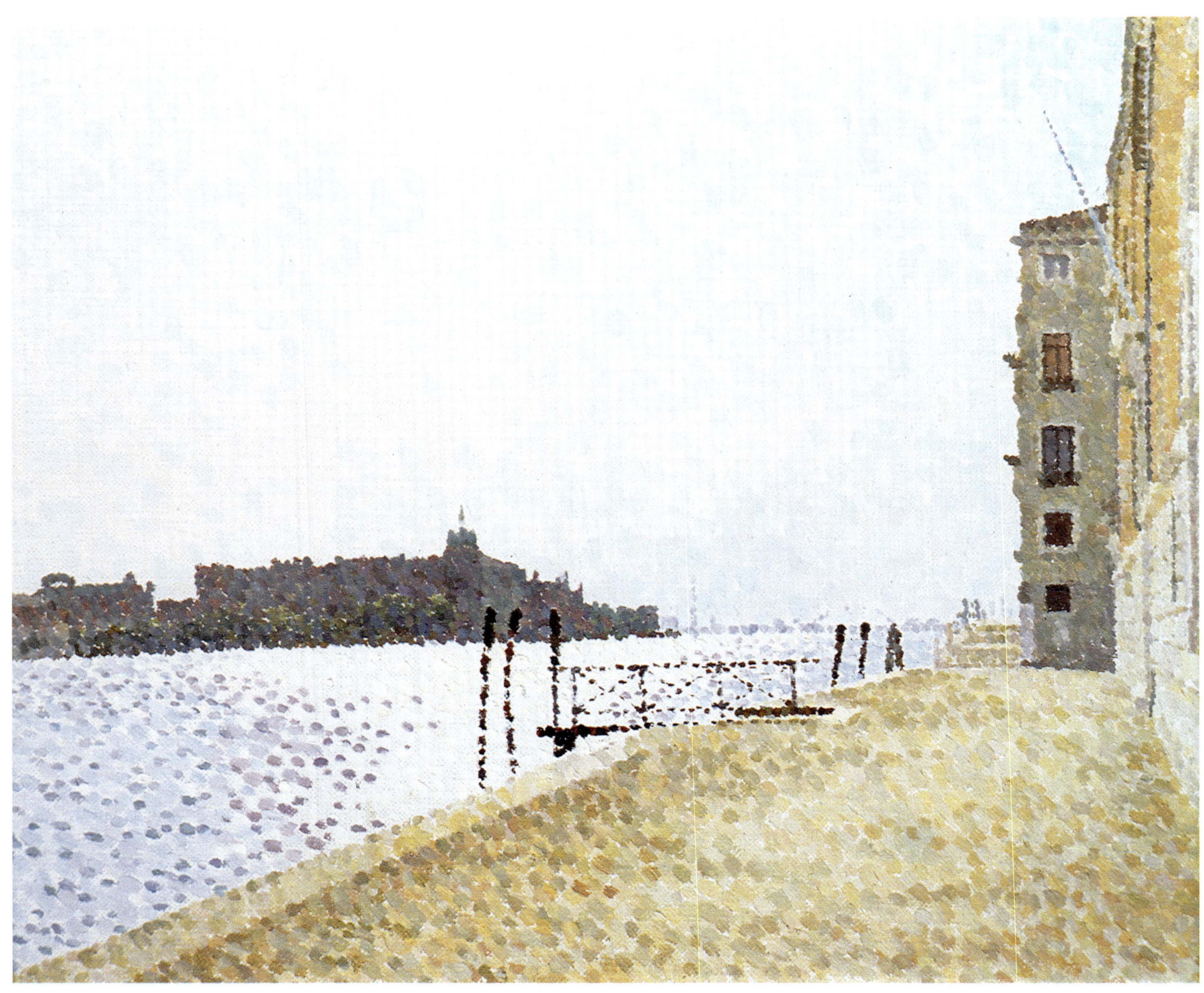

The Stucky, Venice, 1988, oil on canvas, 20 x 25cm, Private collection.

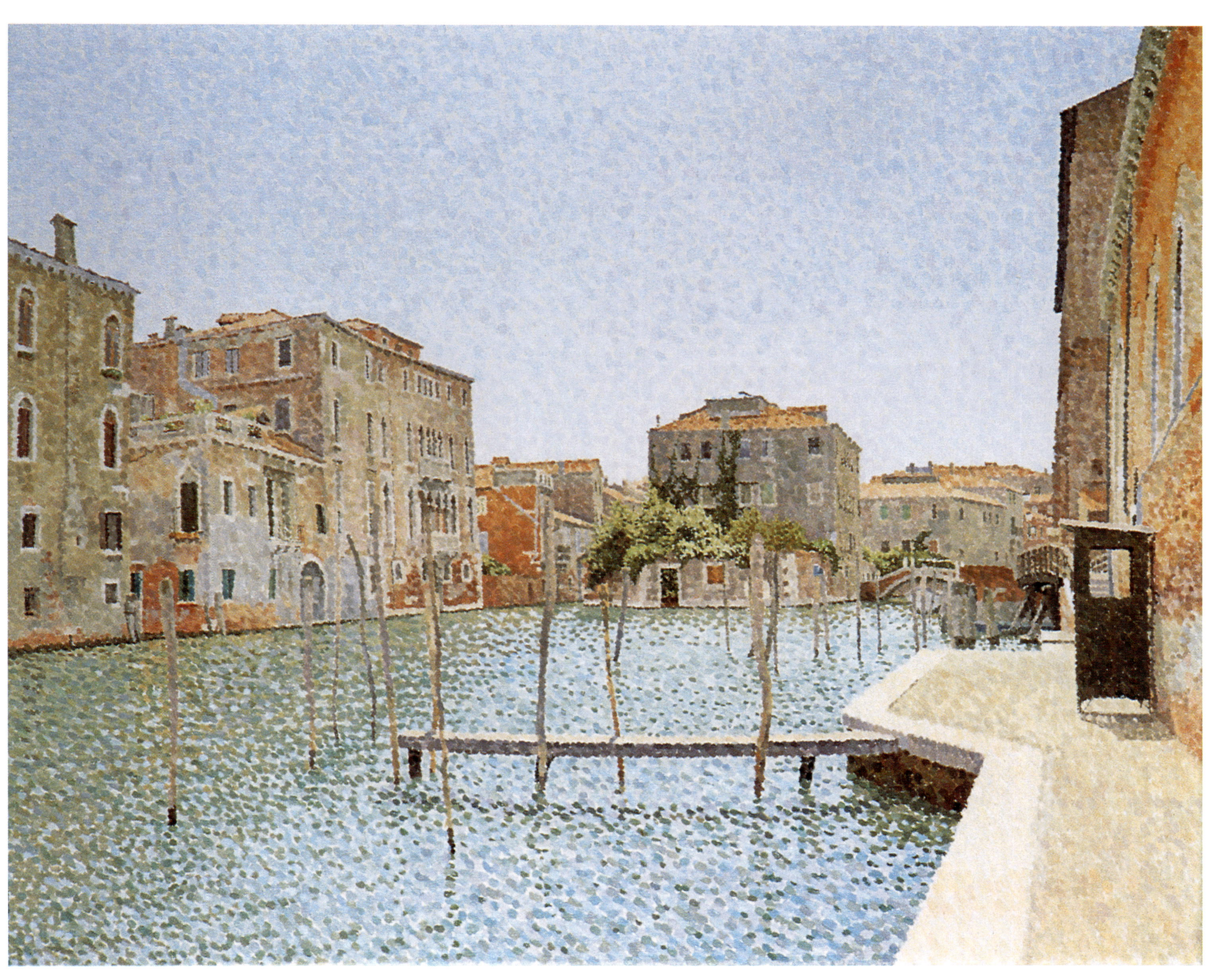

Rio de Noale, Venice, 1988, oil on canvas, 48 x 60cm, Private collection.

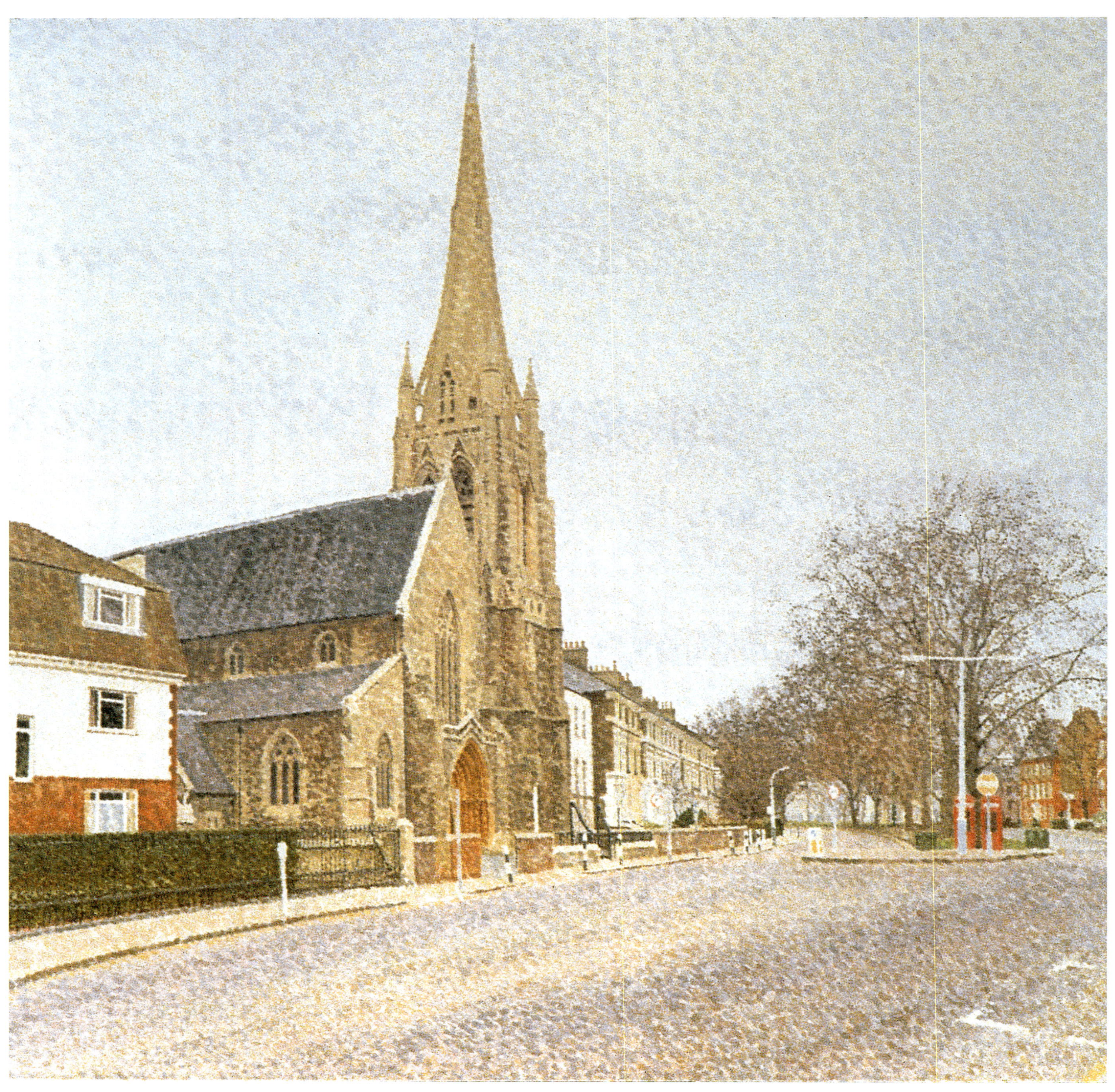

Brook Green, 1985, oil on canvas, 76 x 76cm, Private collection.

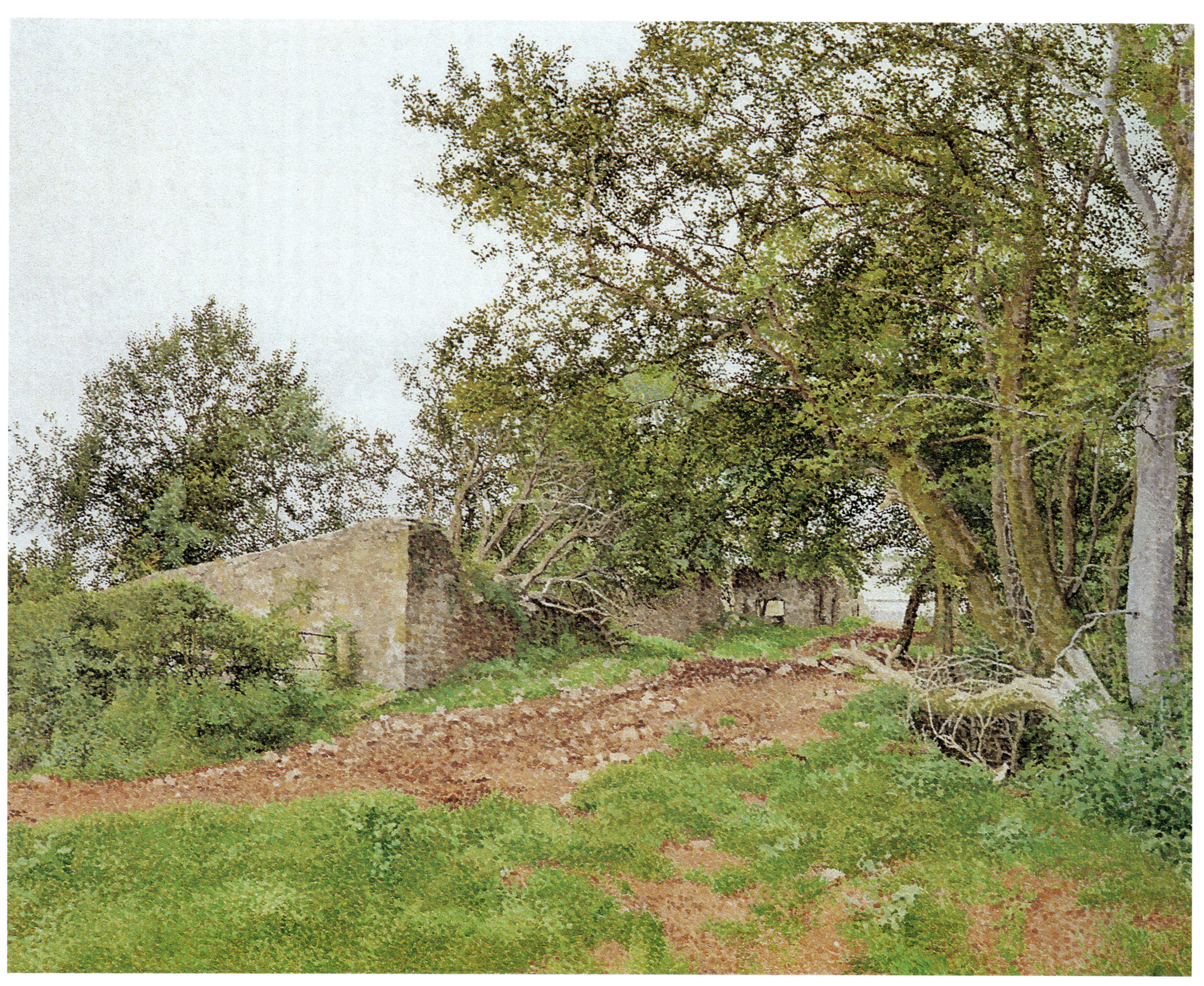

Caedenardd, 1982, oil on canvas, 76 x 58cm, Private collection.

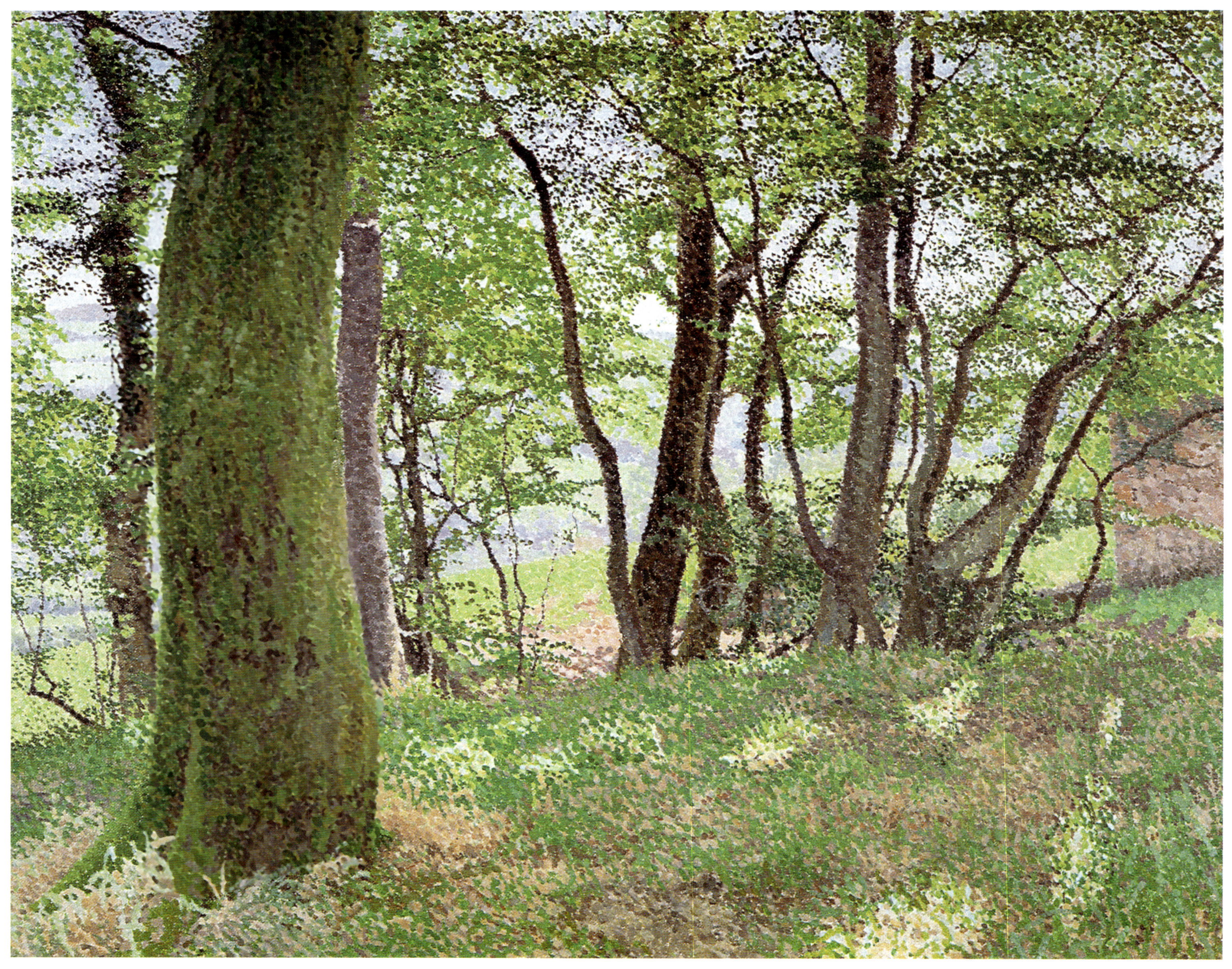

Carmarthenshire Afternoon, 1981, oil on canvas, 35 x 45cm, National Museum Wales.

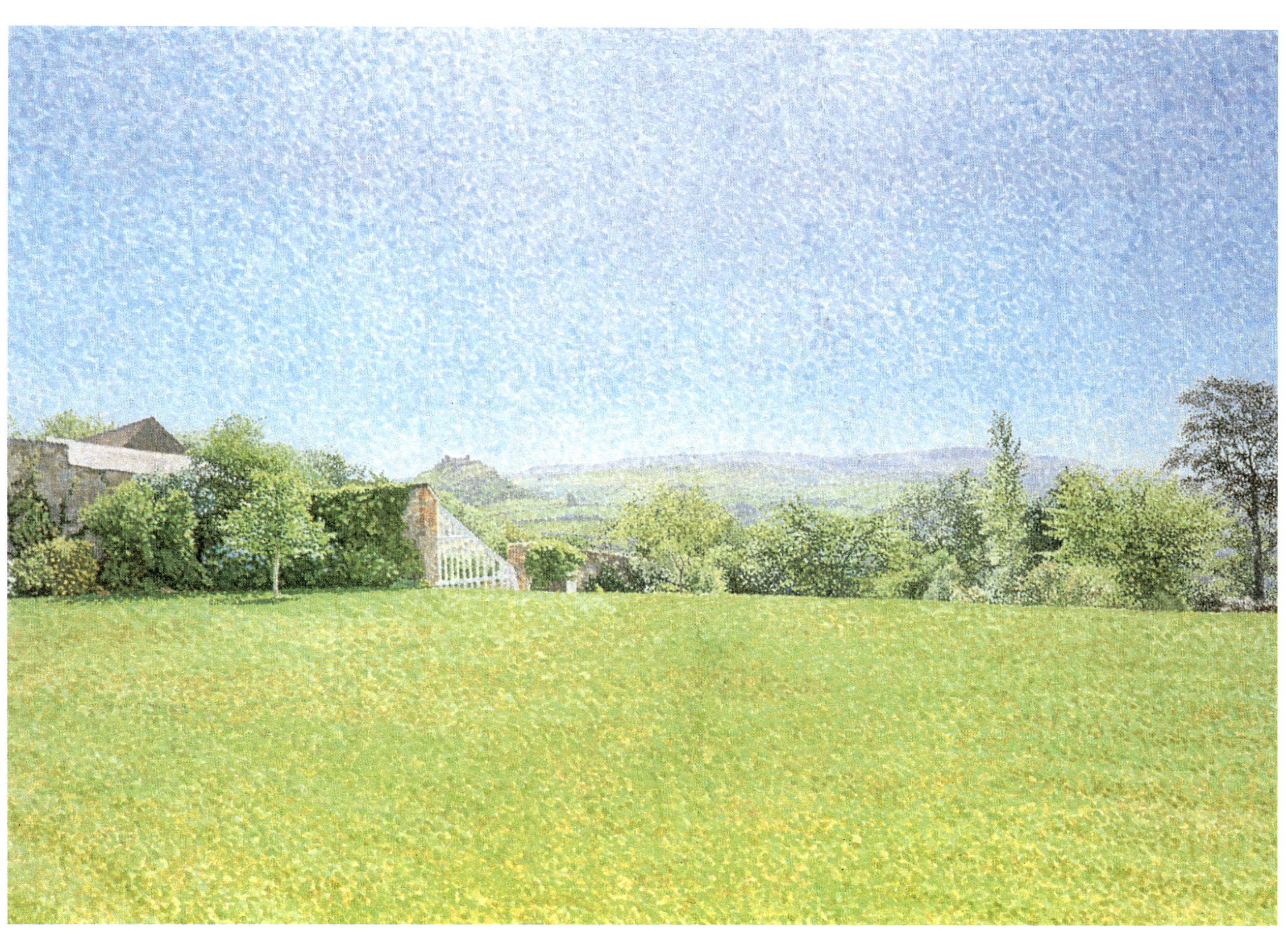

Morning Landscape, Carmarthenshire, 1986, oil on canvas, 78 x 109cm, Private collection.

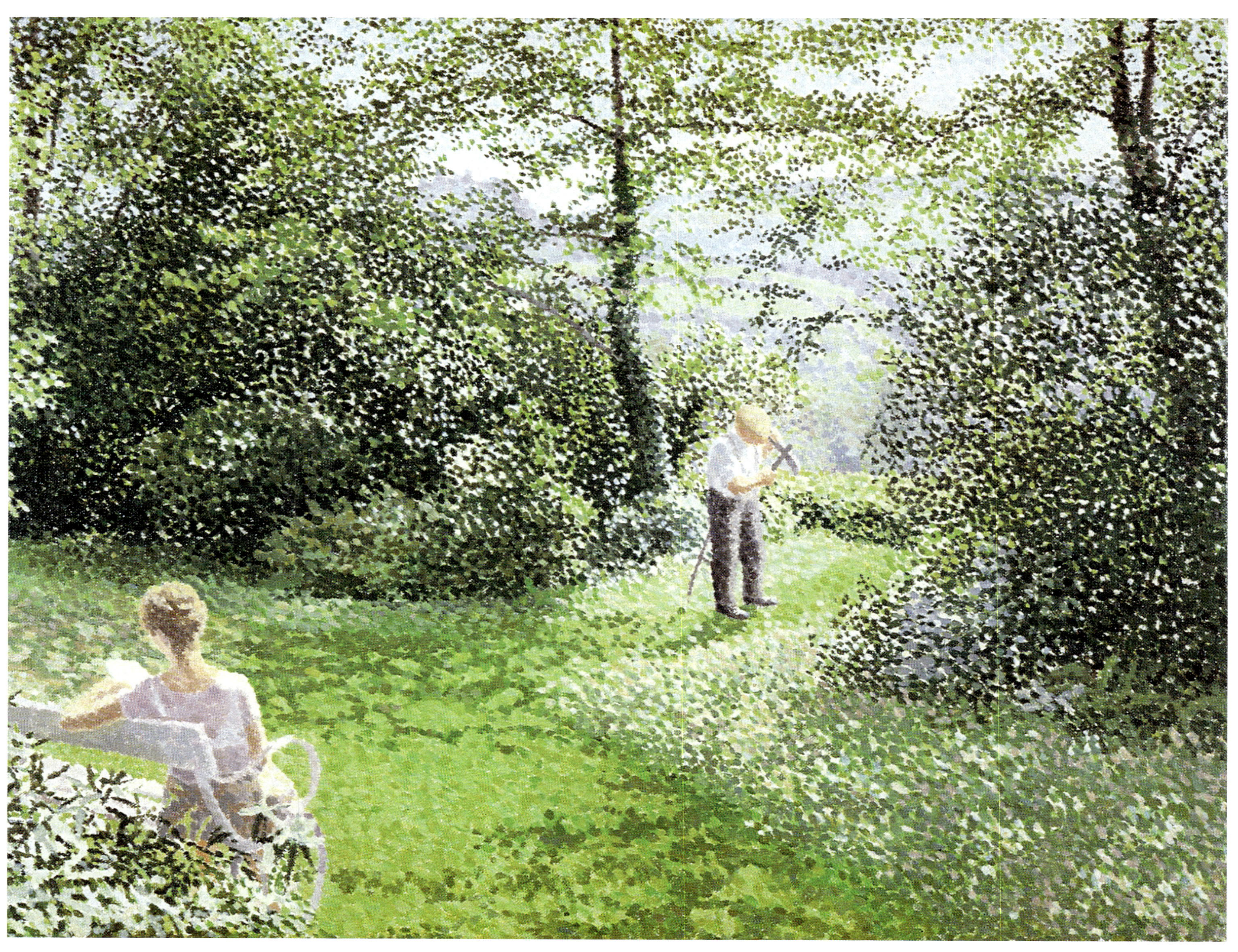

Summer, 1981, oil on canvas, 30 x 40cm, Private collection.

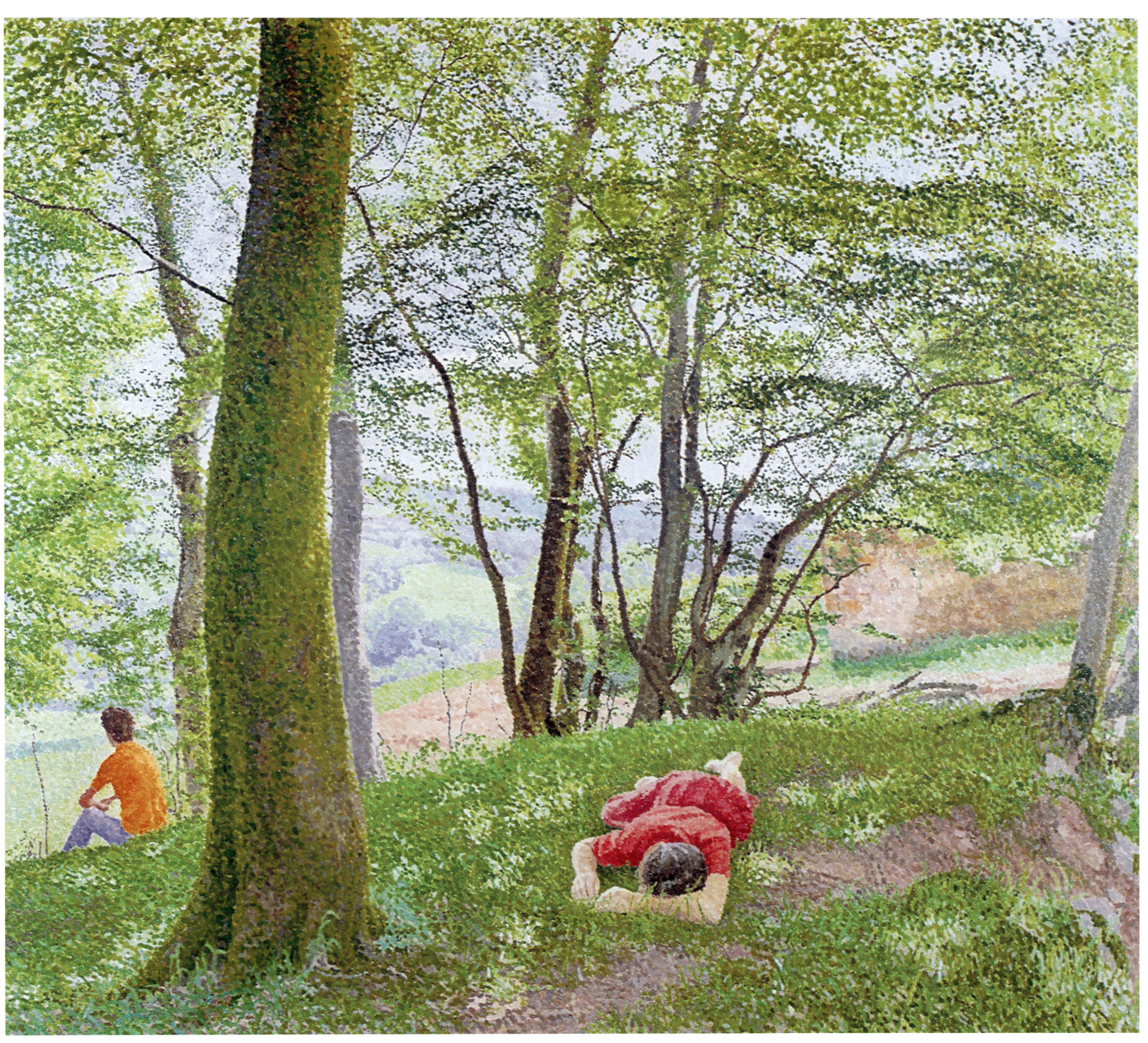

Et in Arcadia ego, 1983, oil on canvas, 60 x 68cm, Private collection.

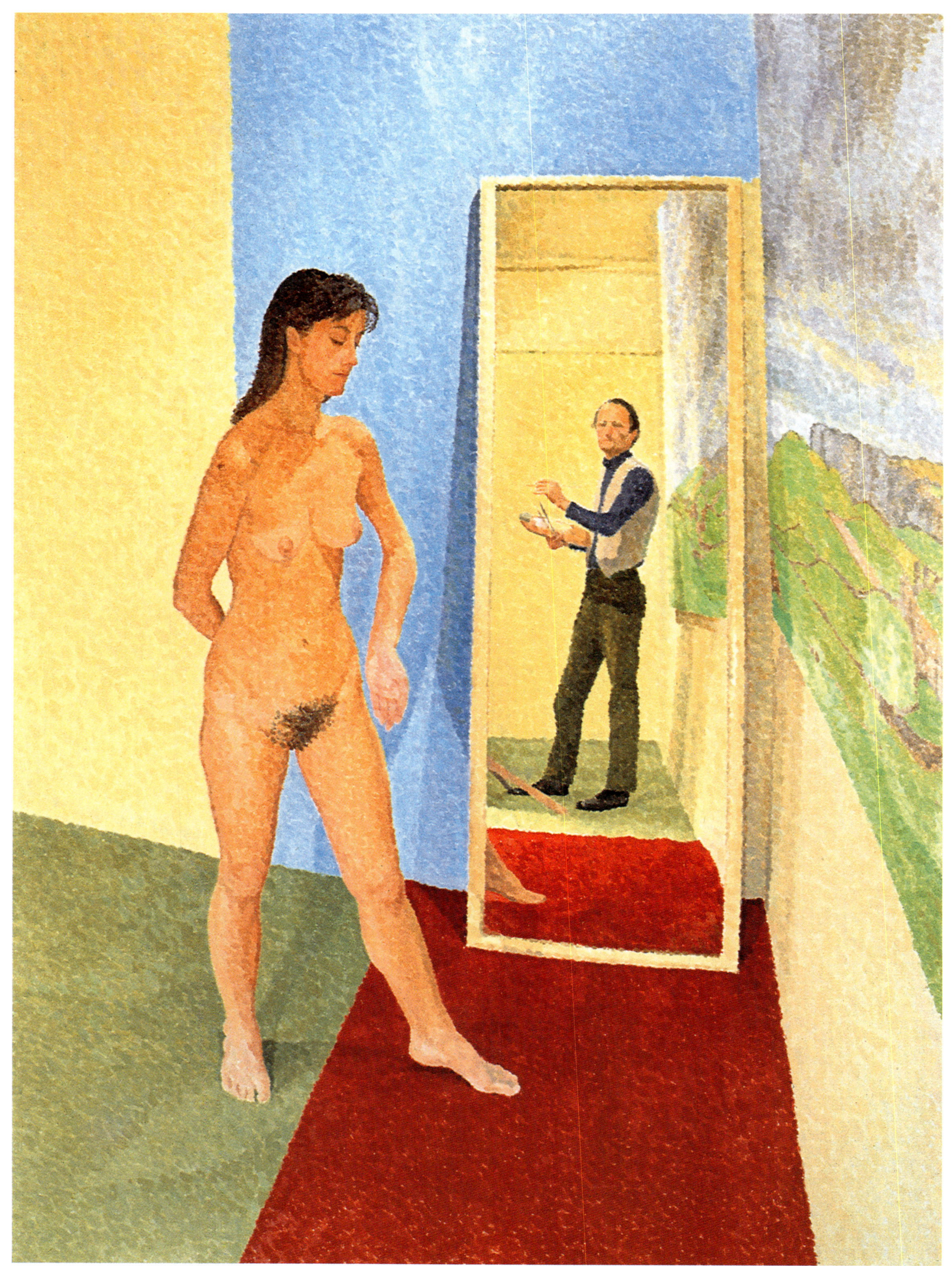

Two Standing Figures, 1984, oil on canvas, 76 x 55cm, Courtesy of the artist.

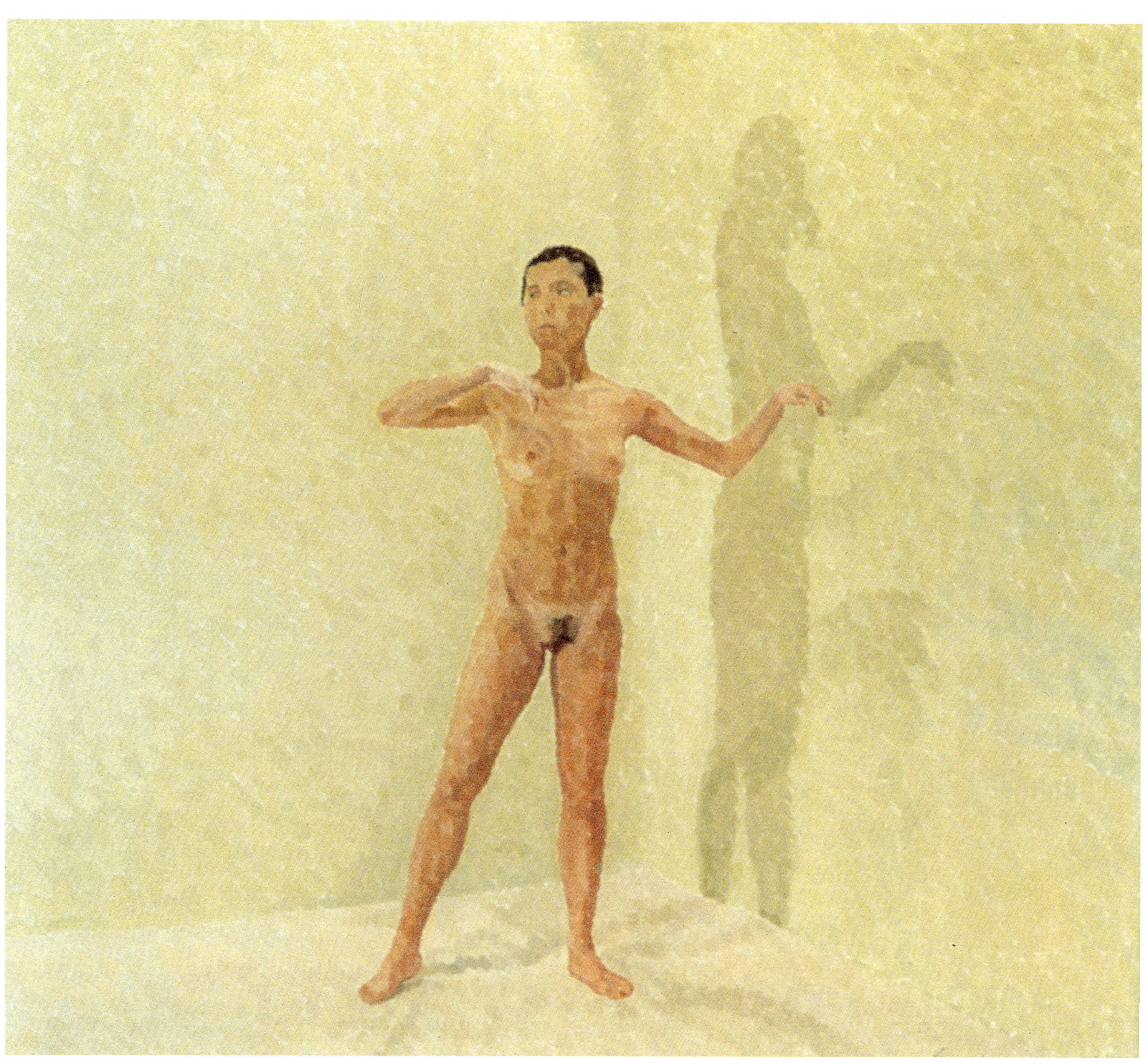

Standing Dancer, 1986, oil on canvas, 50 x 53cm, Courtesy of the artist.

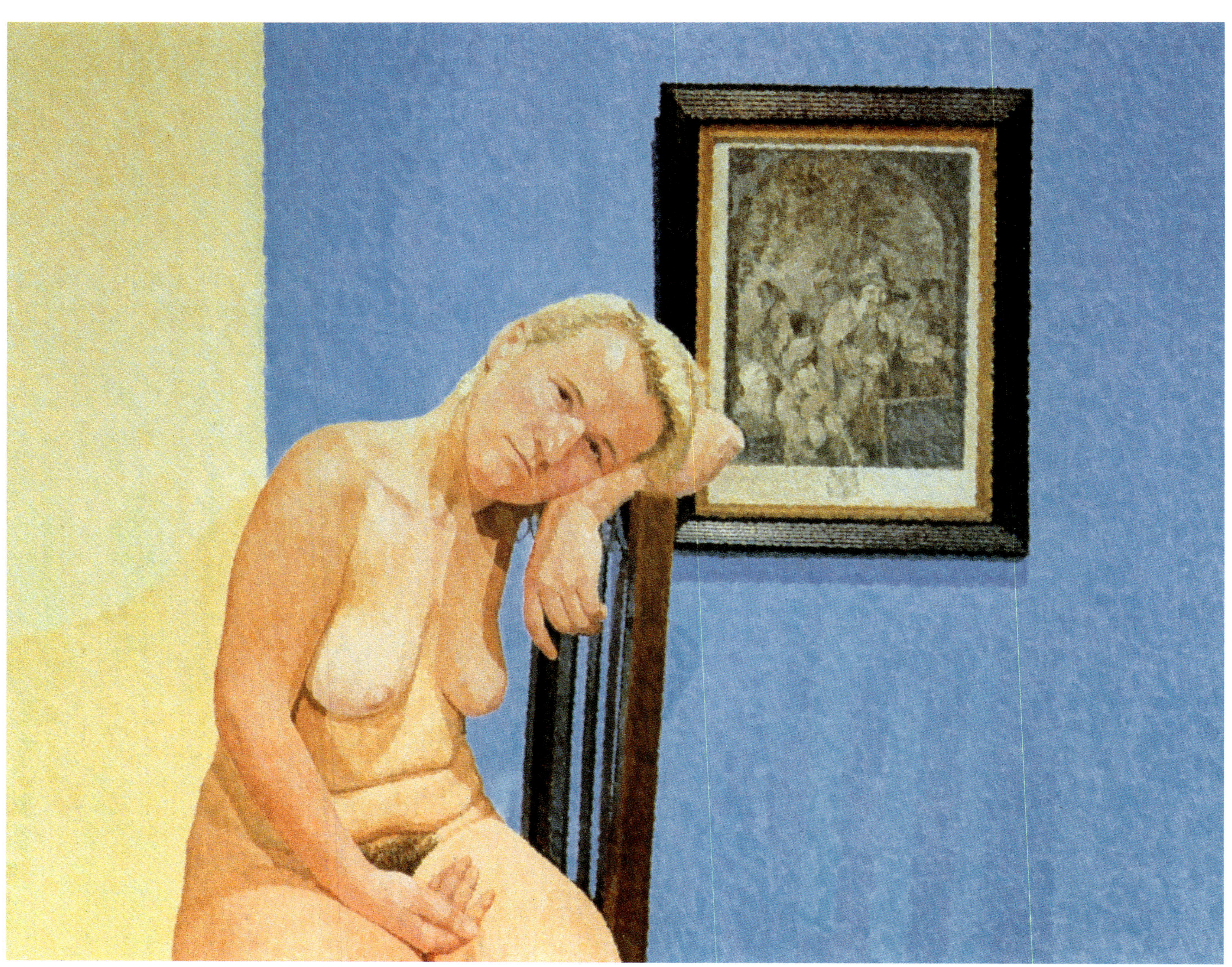

Seated Nude, 1984, oil on canvas, 63 x 88cm, Courtesy of the artist.

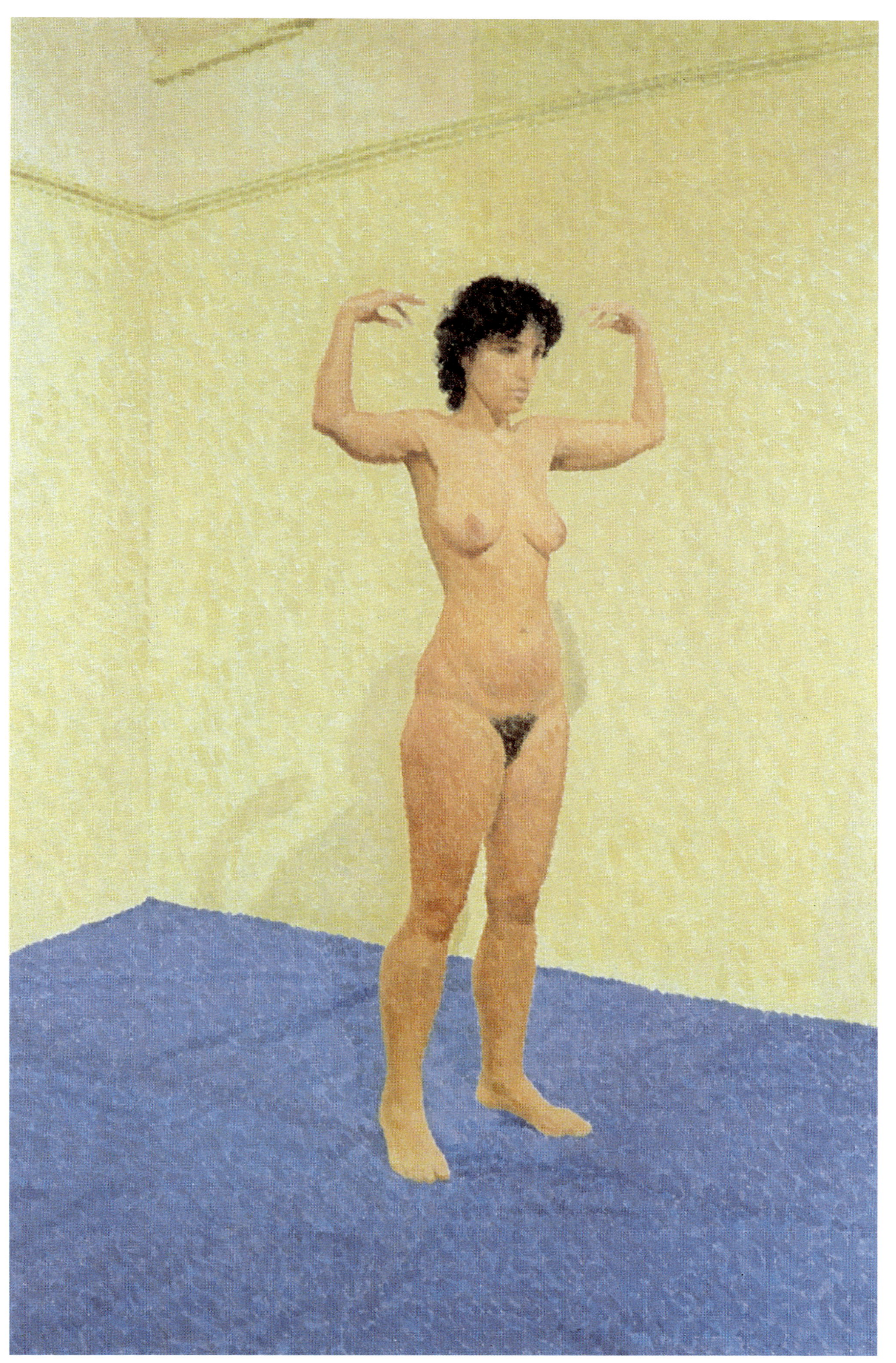

Rising Figure, 1983, oil on canvas, 58 x 40cm, Private collection.

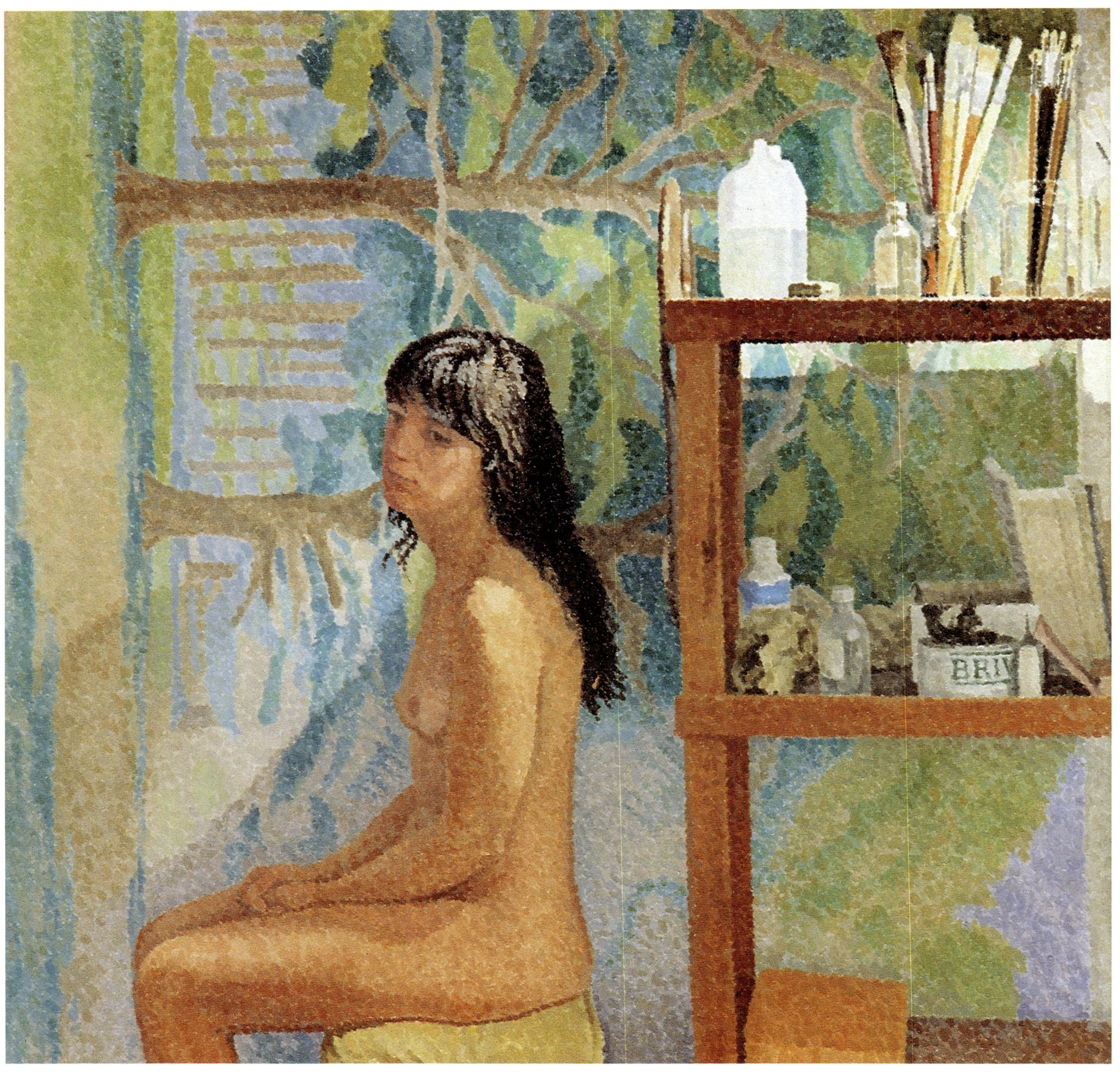

102   William Wilkins

Seated Girl, 1982, oil on canvas, 41 x 44cm, Private collection.

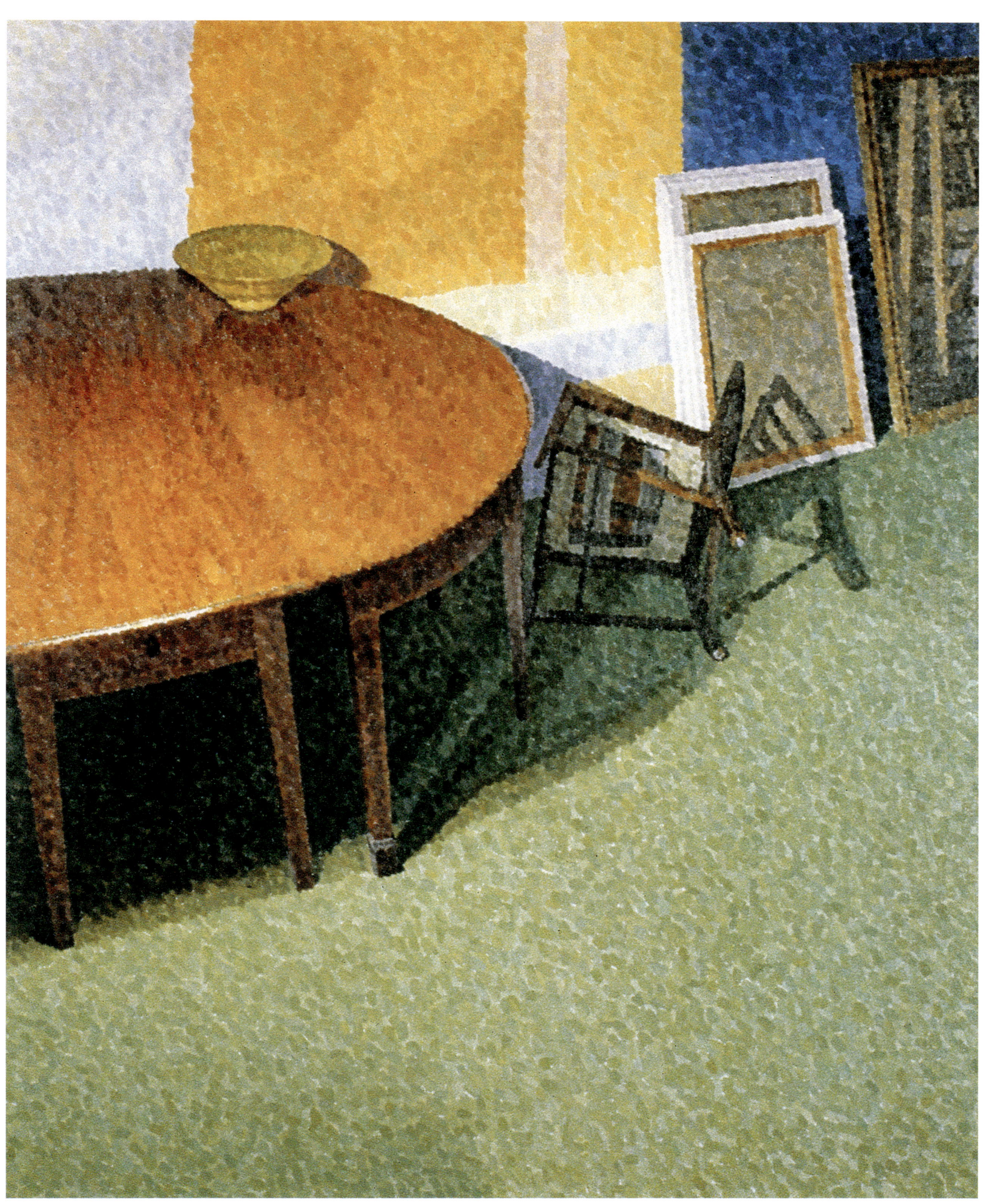

Still Life: Fallen Chair, 1989, oil on canvas, 78 x 66cm, Courtesy of the artist.

PAINTINGS
1991–2004

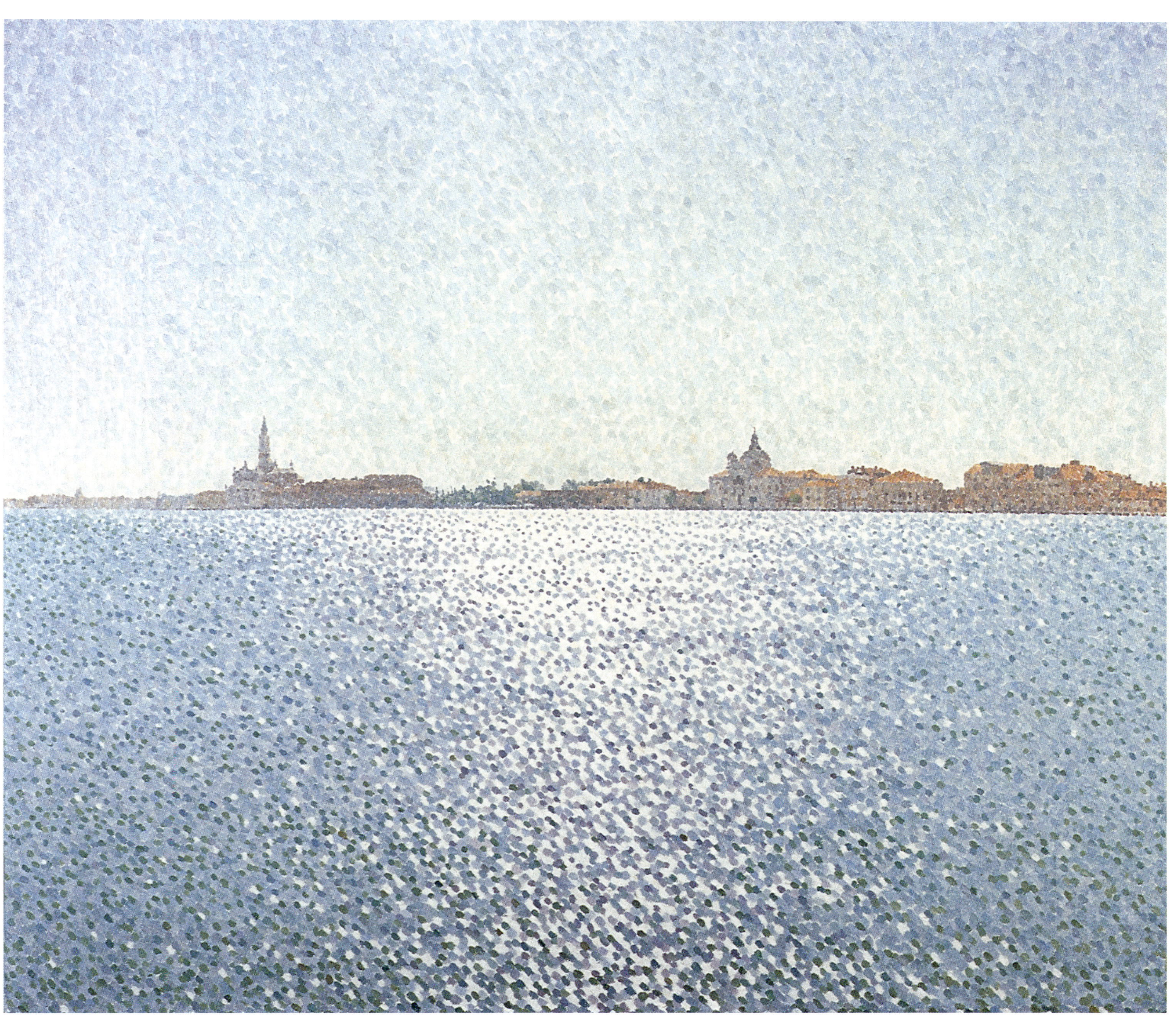

San Giorgio and the Zitelle, Venice, 1999, oil on canvas, 60 x 70cm, Private collection.

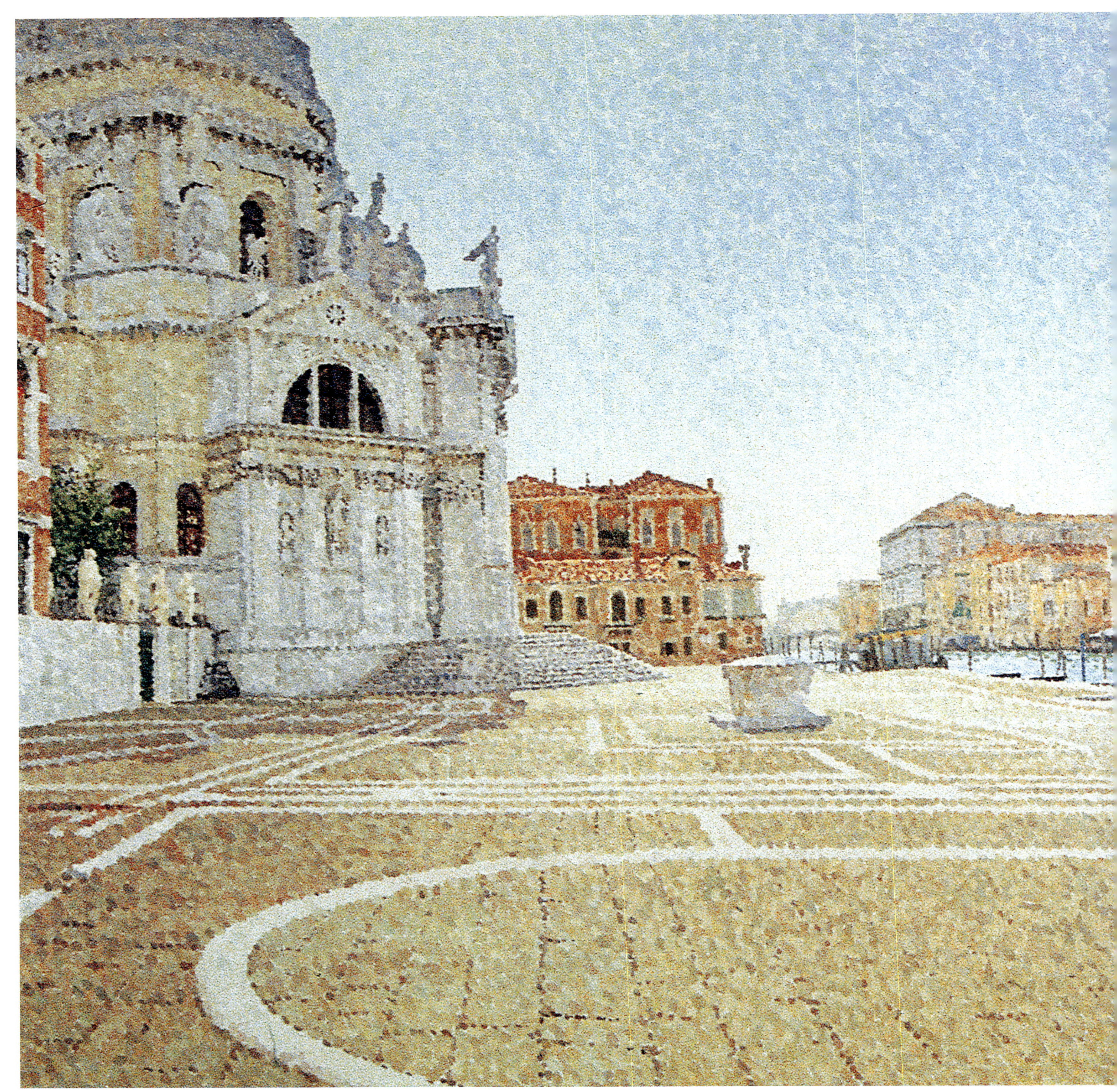

The Salute, Venice, 1991, oil on canvas, 40 x 58cm, Private collection.

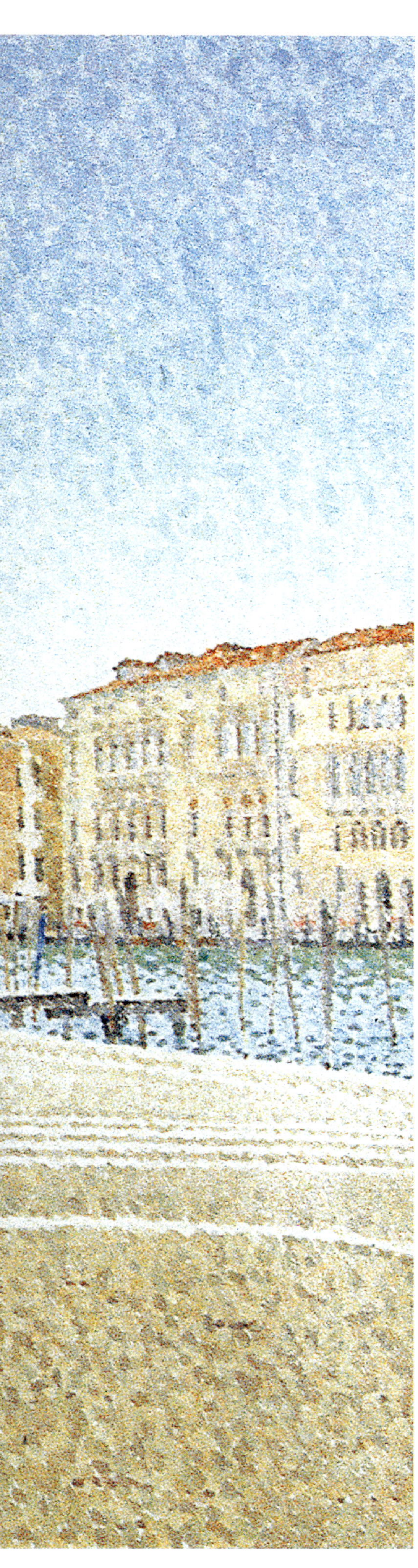

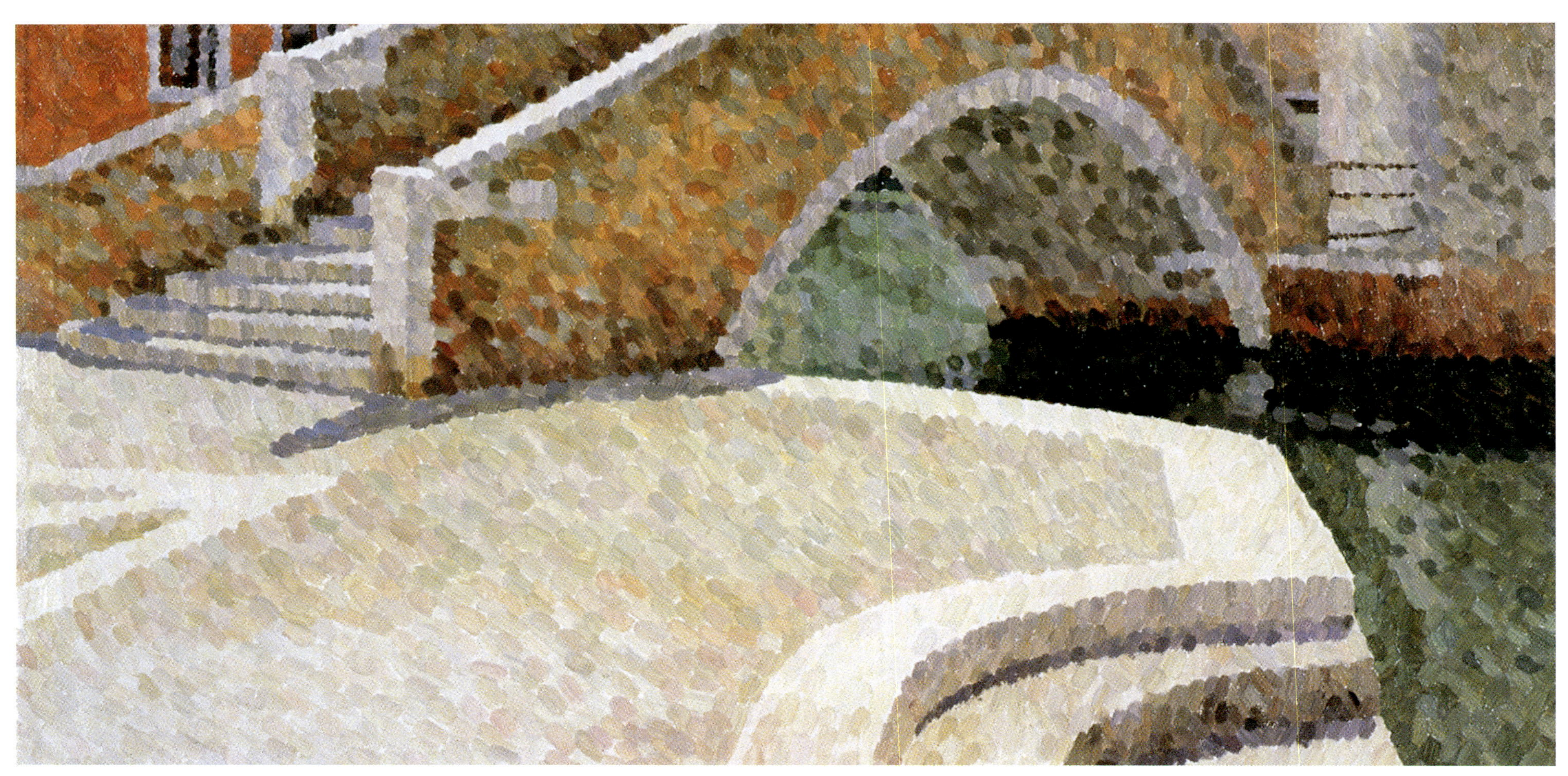

San Boldo, 2001, oil on canvas, 25 x 51cm, Private collection.

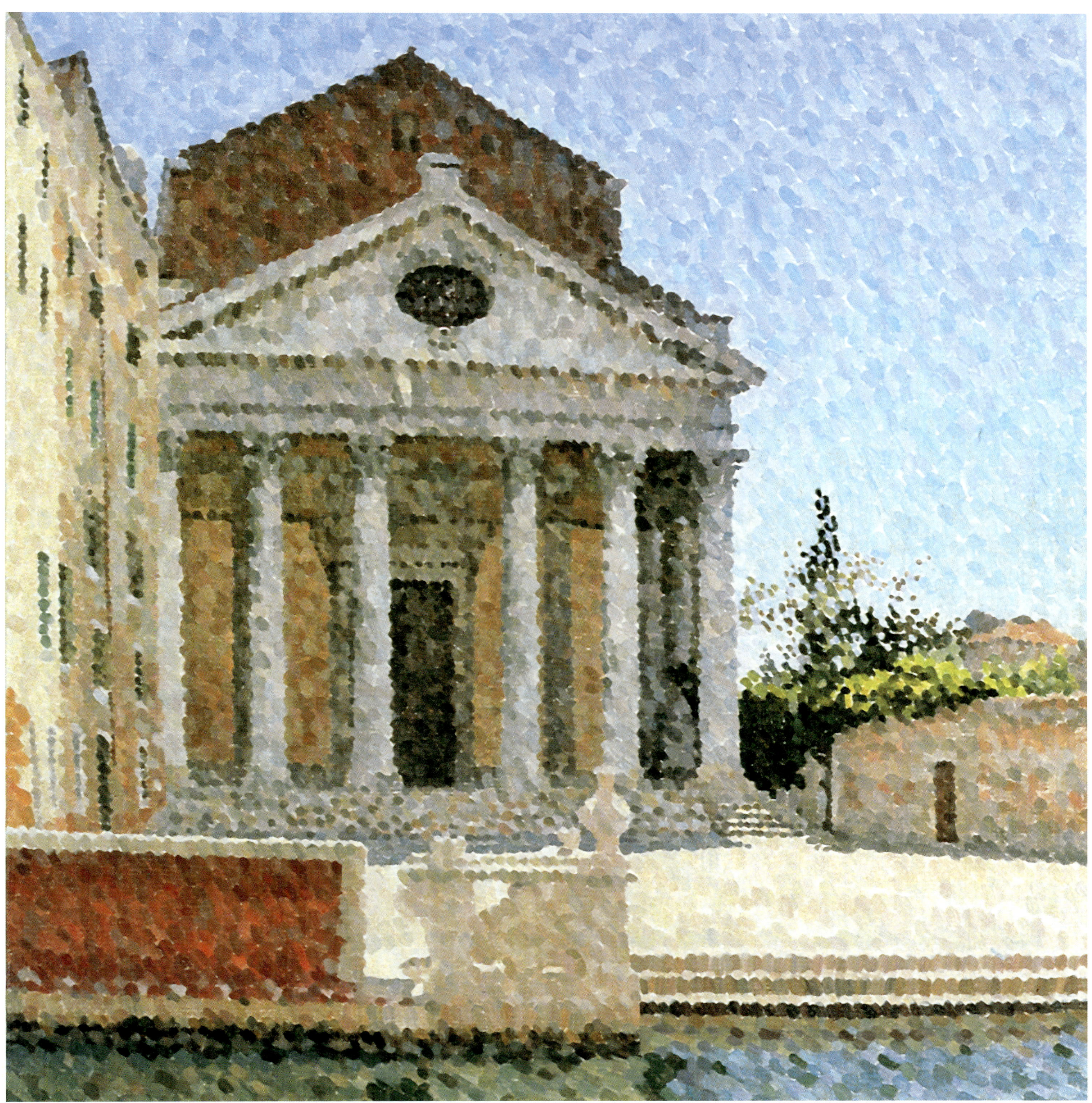

San Nicola dei Tolentiri, Venice, 2001, oil on canvas, 51 x 51cm, Private collection.

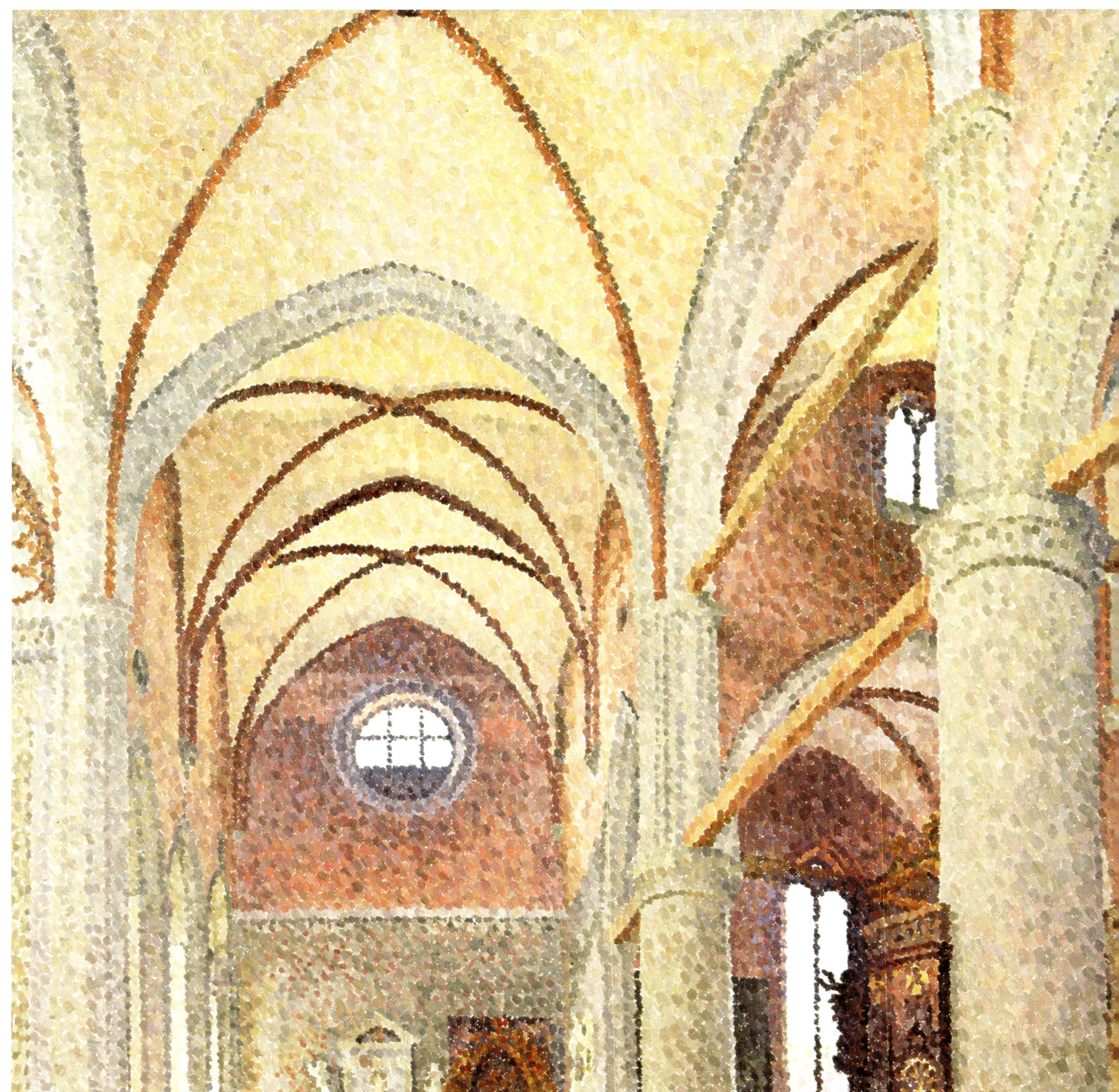

110   William Wilkins

Santa Maria Gloriosa dei Frari, Venice, 1994, oil on canvas, 47 x 66cm, Derek Williams Trust.

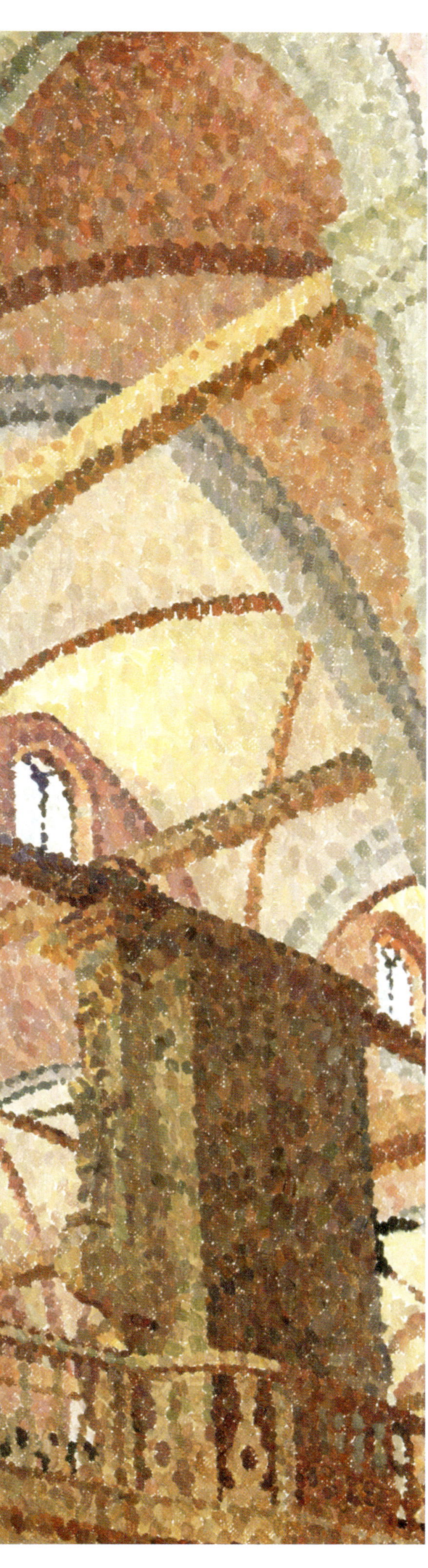

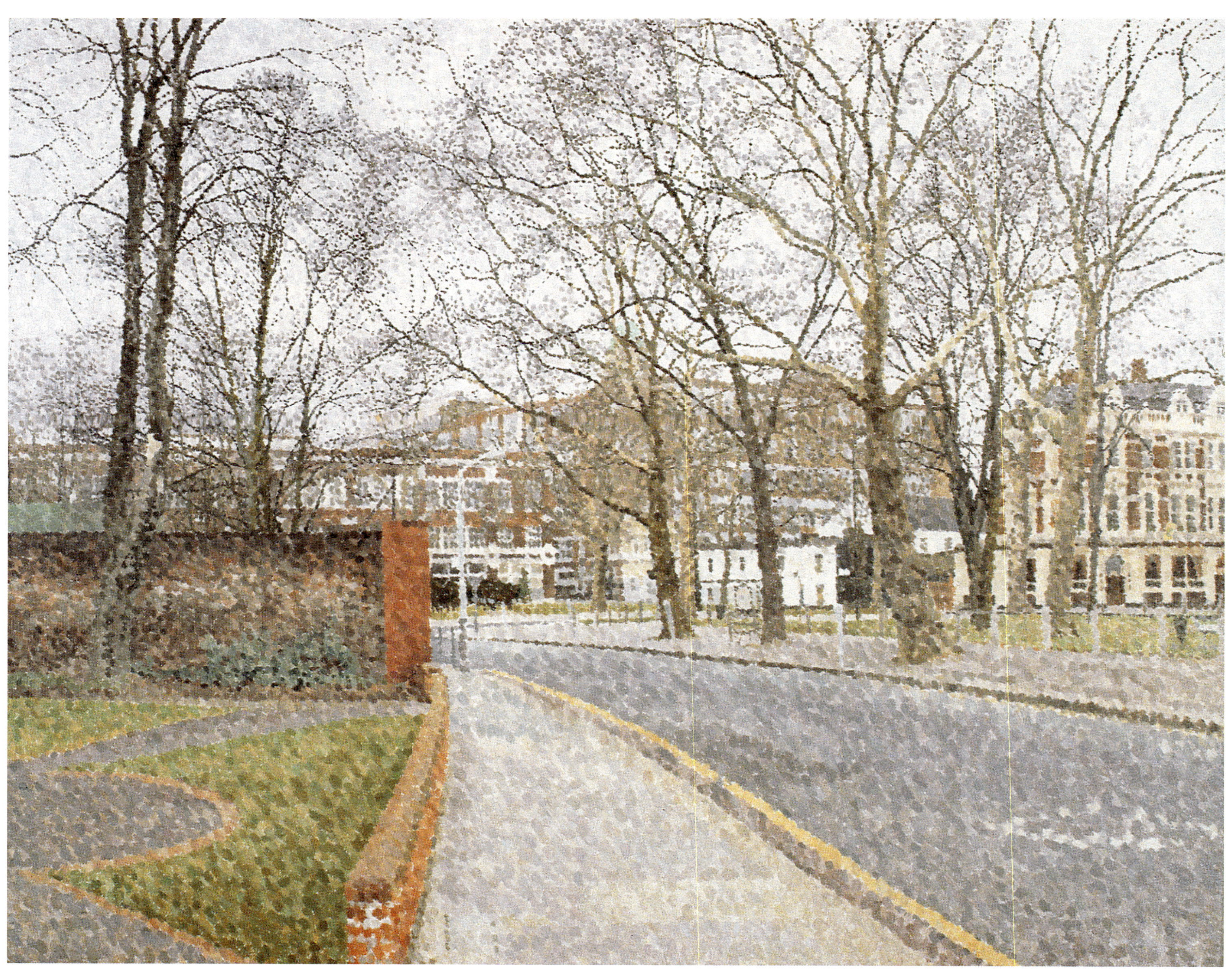

Brook Green, 1991, oil on canvas, 38 x 50cm, Private collection.

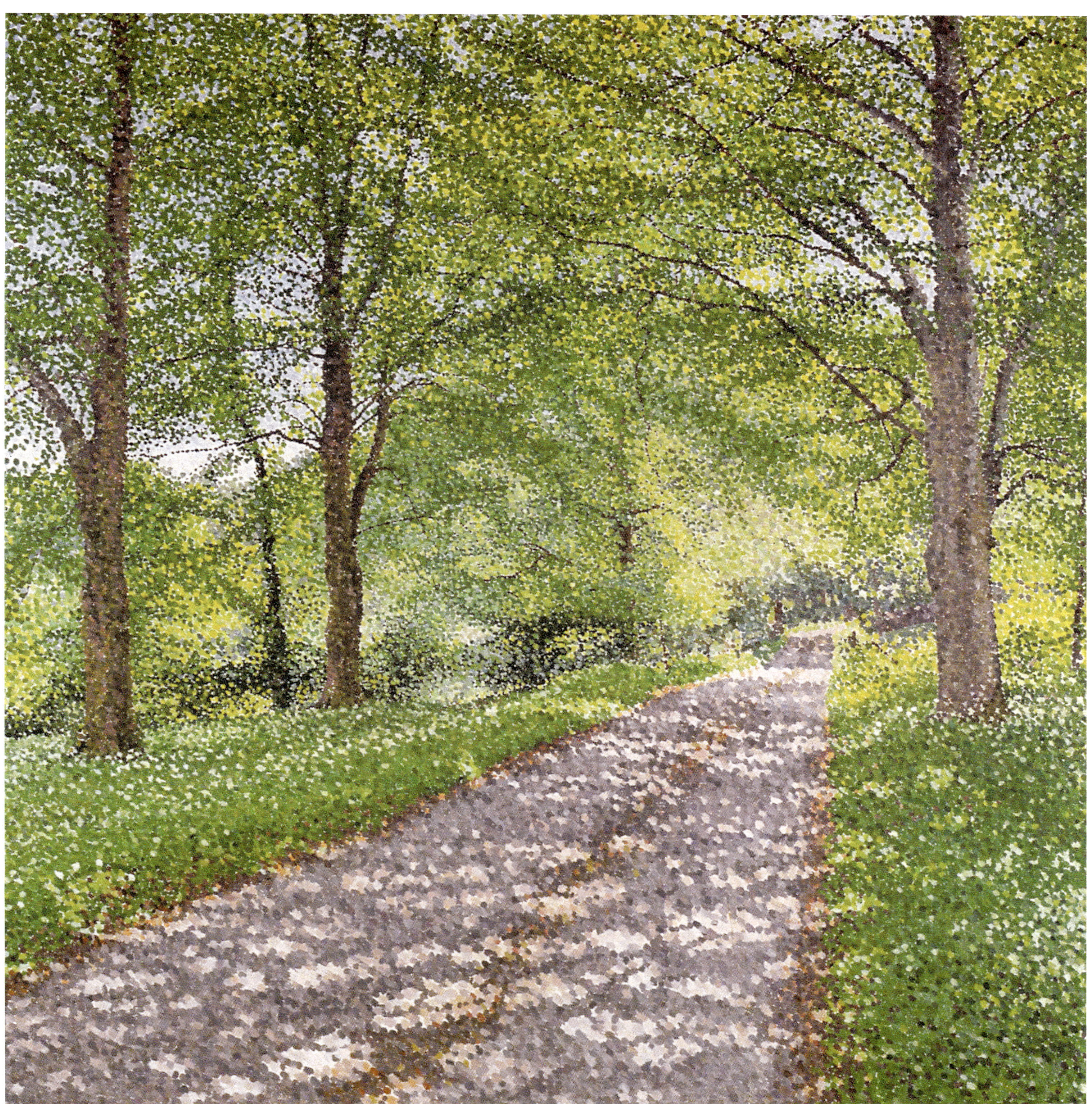

Avenue, Summer, 2003, oil on canvas, 58 x 61cm, Private collection.

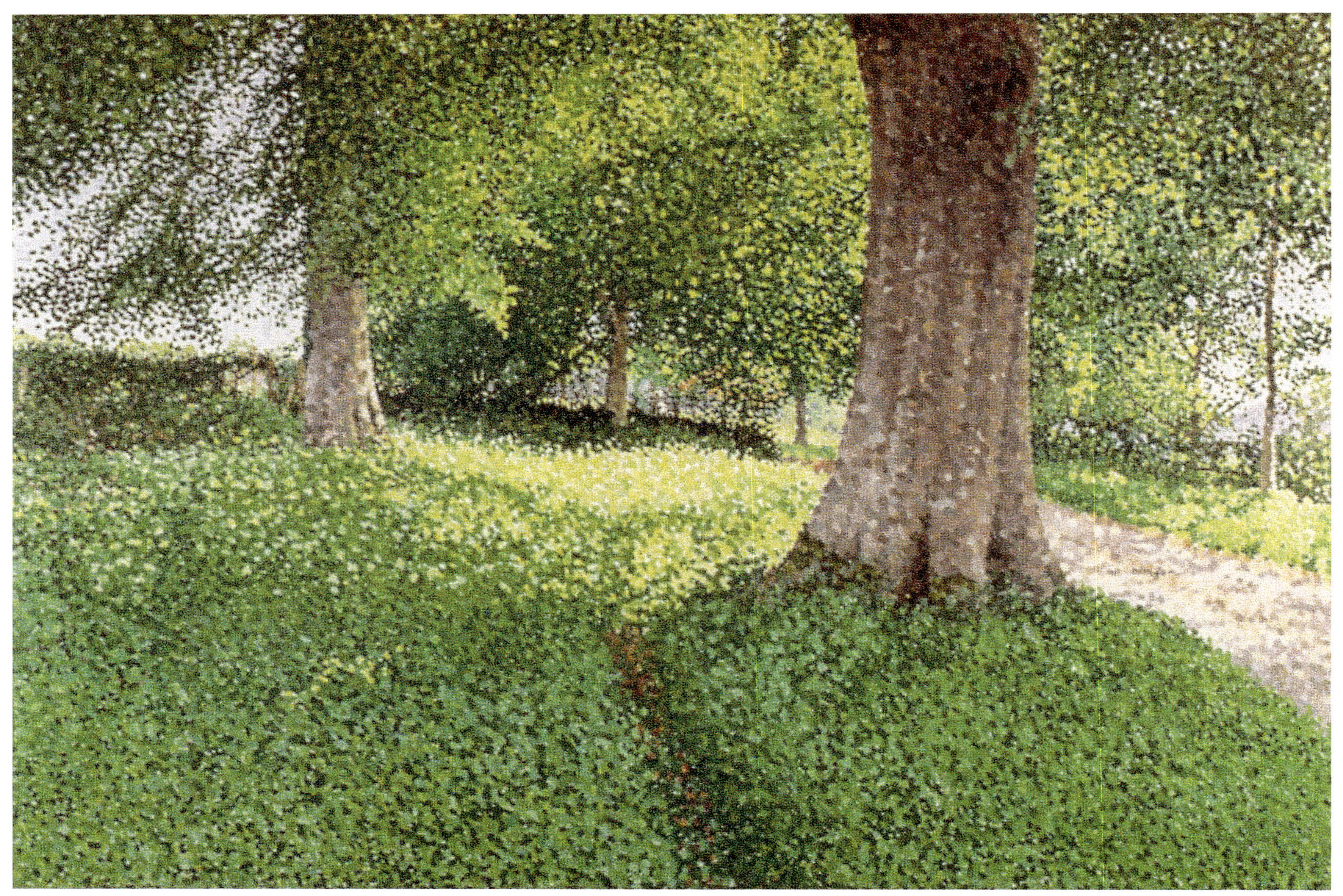

The Avenue, 1993, oil on canvas, 33 x 50cm, Private collection.

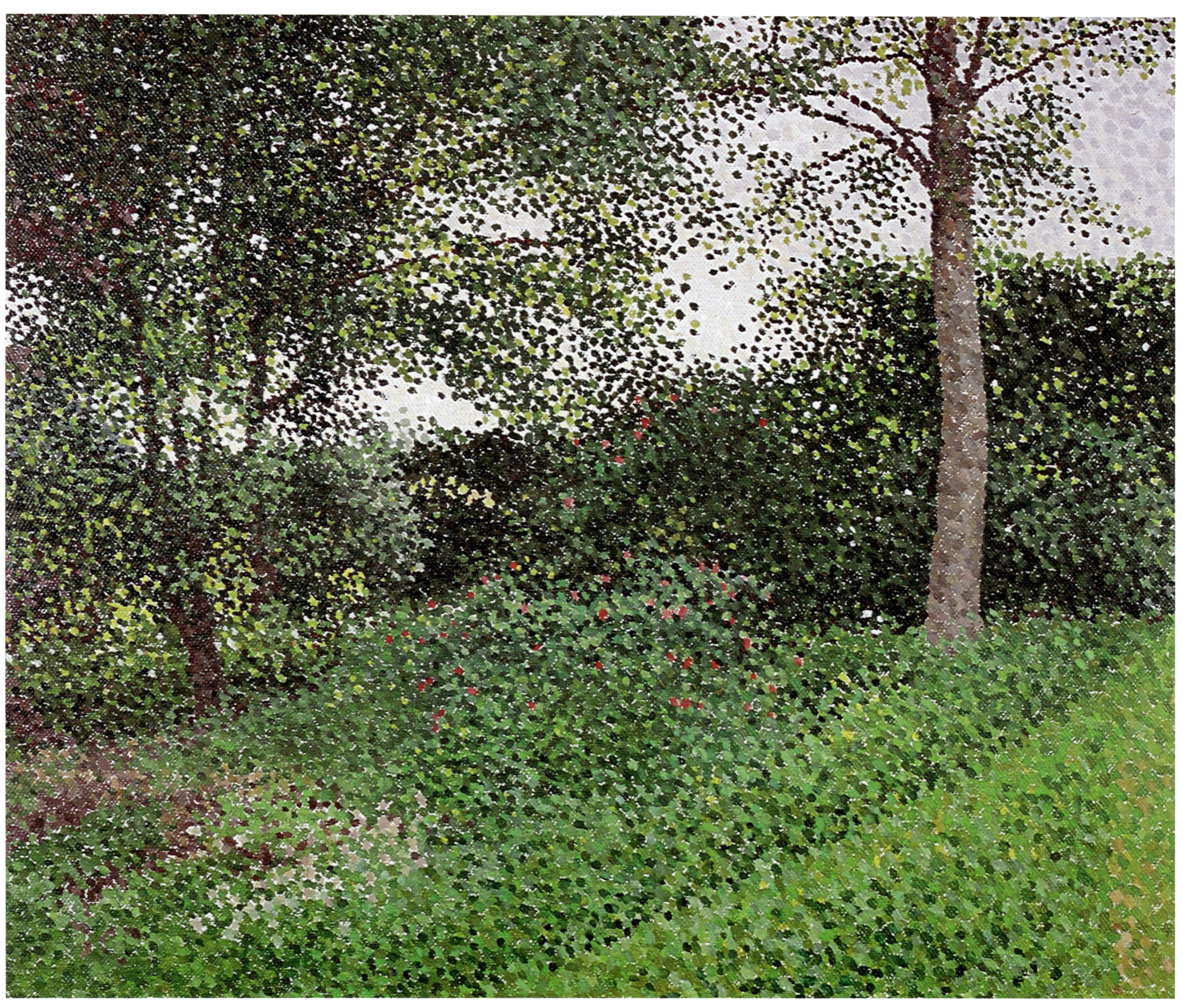

Evening Light: Young Ash, 1998, oil on canvas, 30 x 35cm, Private collection.

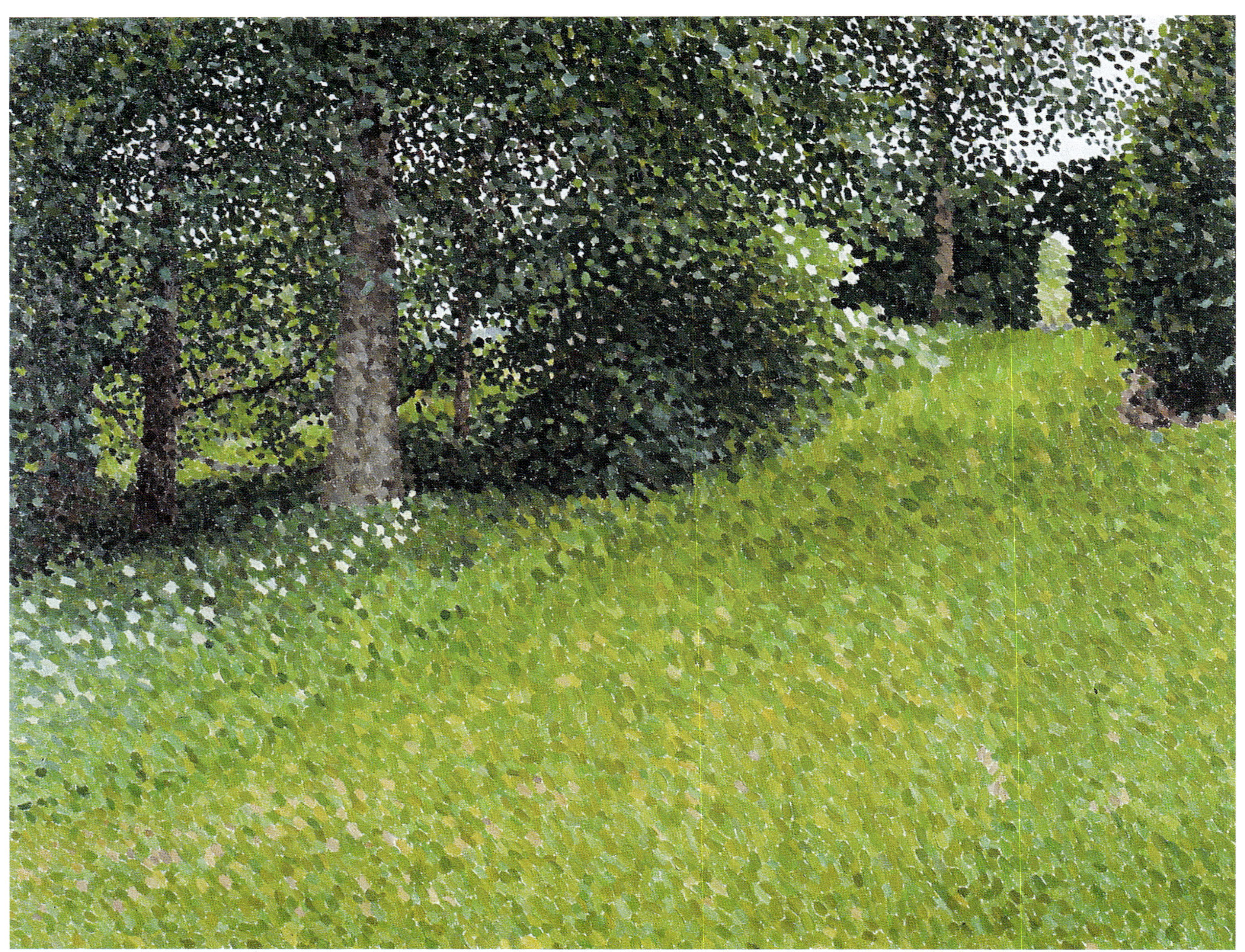

Garden, Grey Day, 2003, oil on canvas, 53 x 70cm, Private collection.

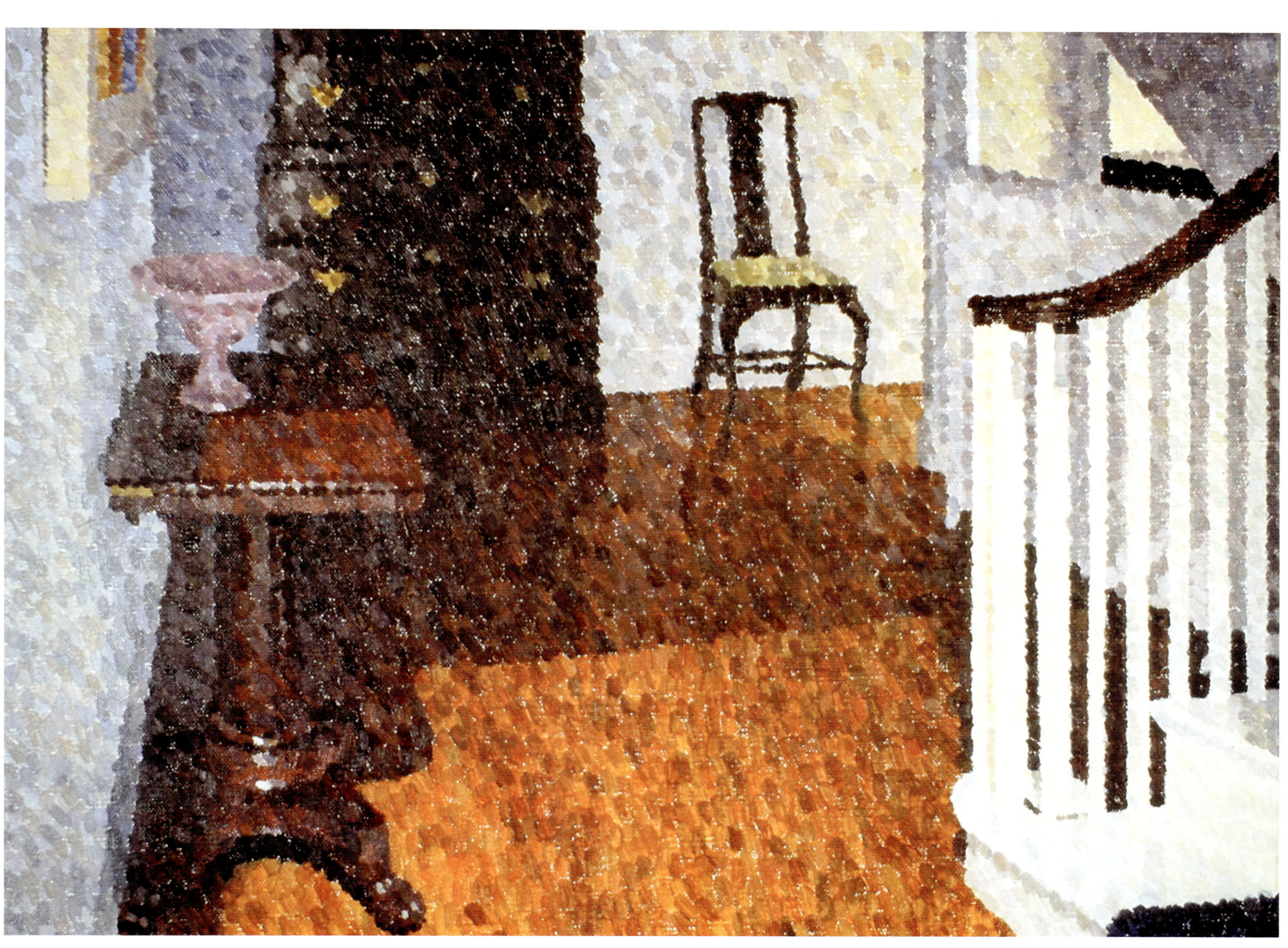

Hallway, 1998, oil on canvas, 34 x 47cm, Private collection.

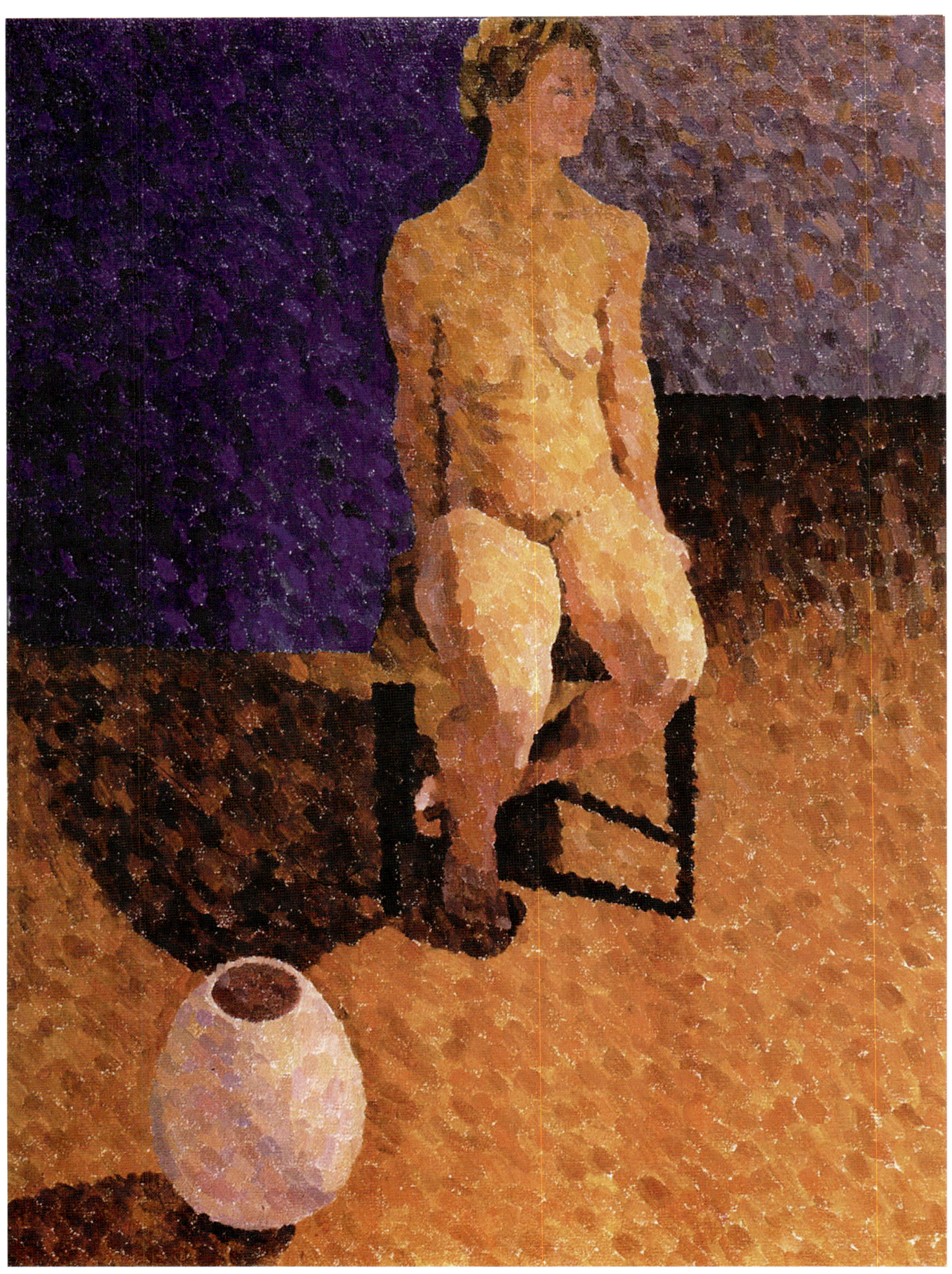

   Seated Nude with Bowl, 2004, oil on canvas, 51 x 38cm, Courtesy of the artist.

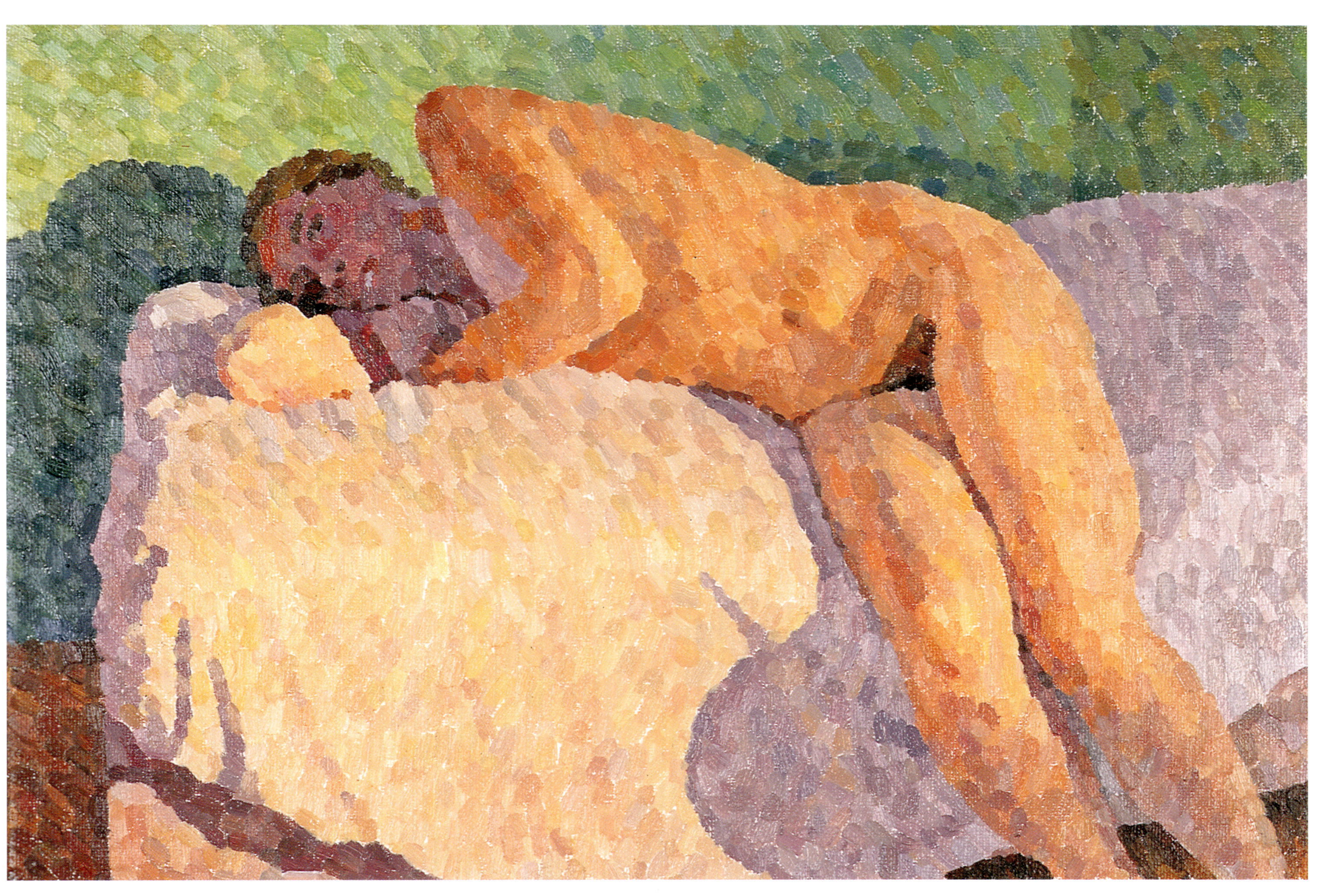

Nude with Face in Shadow, 2000, oil on canvas, 28 x 43cm, Private collection.

RECENT DRAWINGS

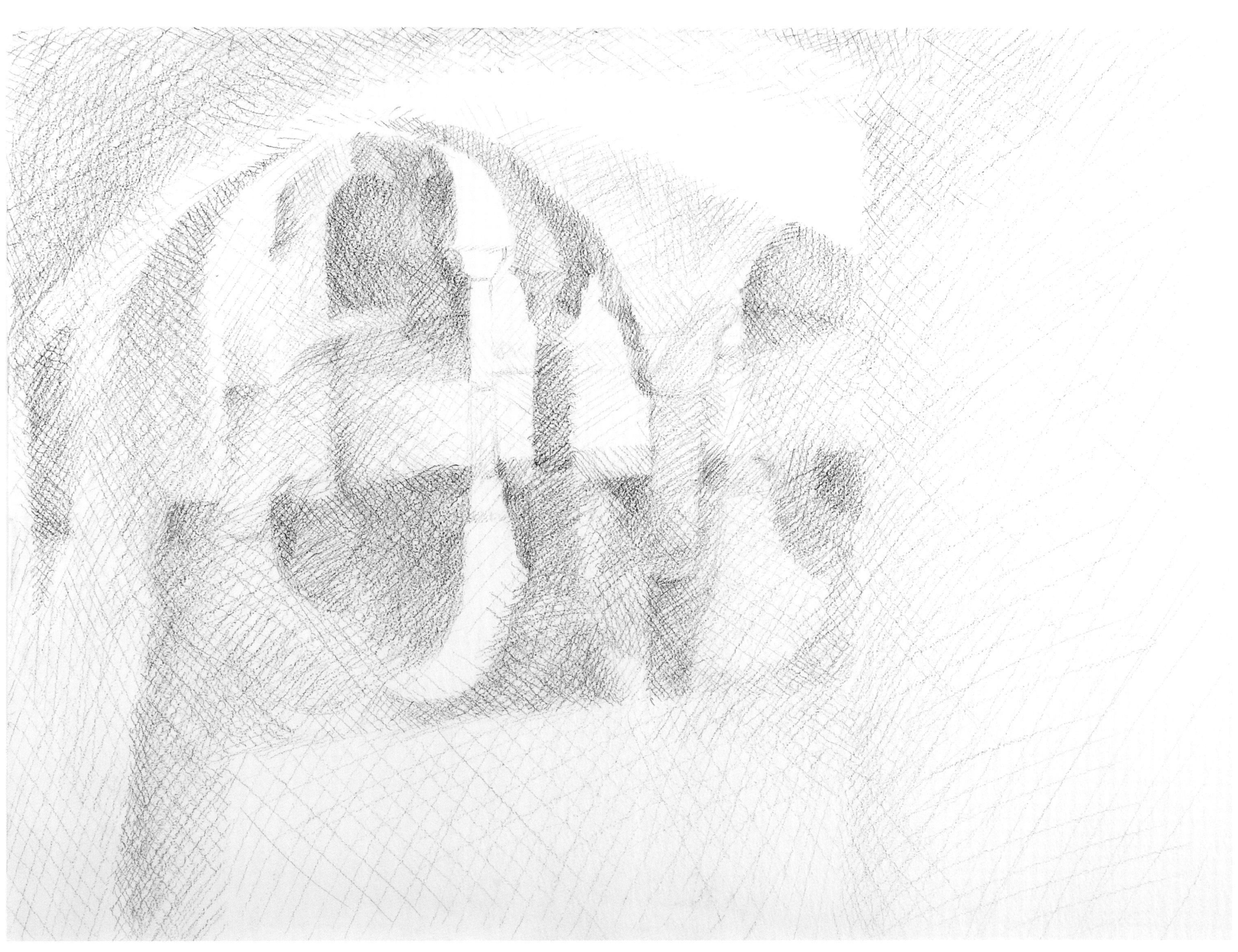

Flooded Crypt, San Zaccaria, Venice, 2006, pencil on paper, 45 x 61cm, Courtesy of the artist.

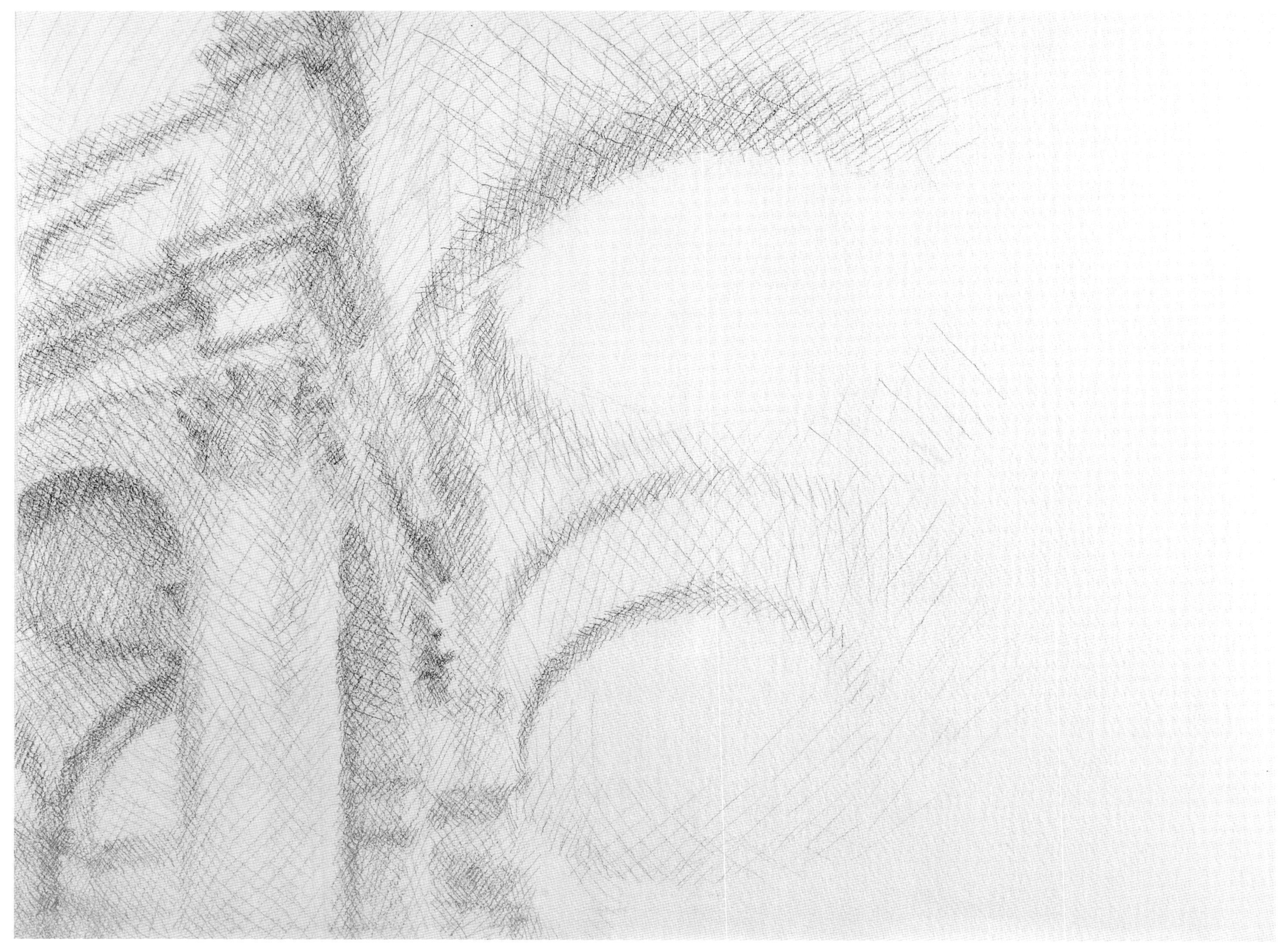

San Salvador, Venice, 2007, pencil on paper, 45 x 61cm, Private collection.

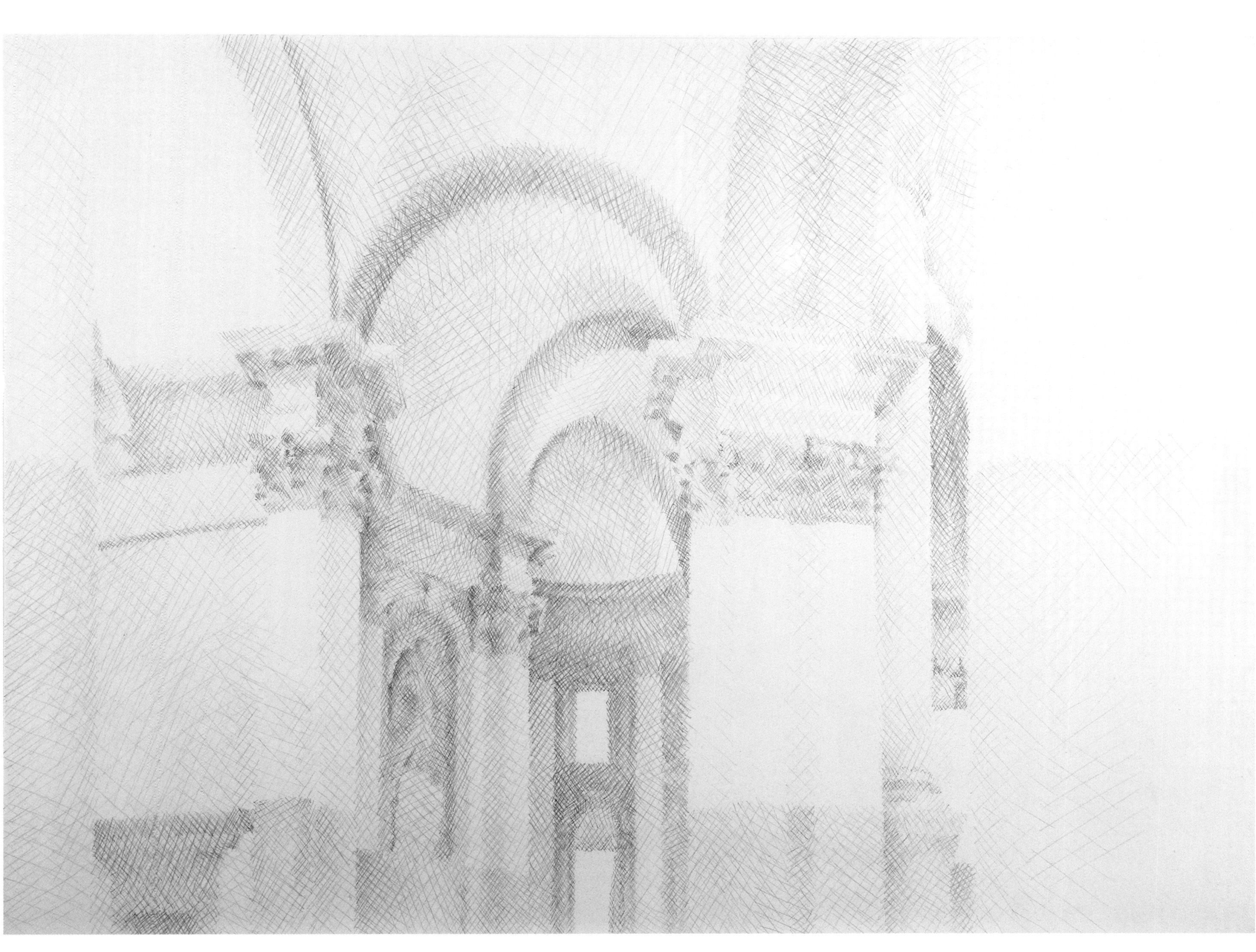

The Salute, Venice, 1996, pencil on paper, 45 x 61cm, Private collection.

The Salute, Venice, 2007, pencil on paper, 45 x 61cm, Courtesy of the artist.

Archway to Rio Terra, Venice, 2008, pencil on paper, 45 x 30cm, Private collection.
Sotoportego with Figure, Venice, 2008, pencil on paper, 45 x 30cm, Courtesy of the artist.

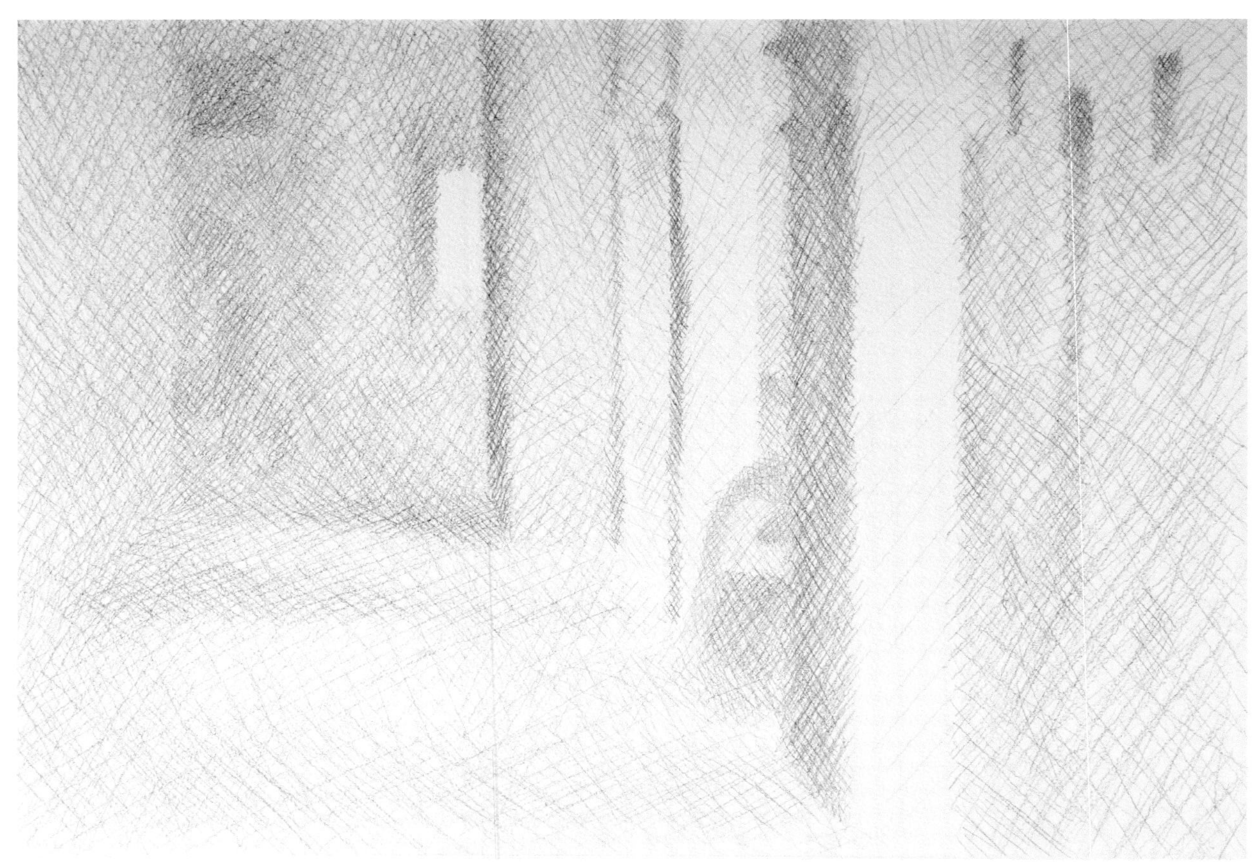

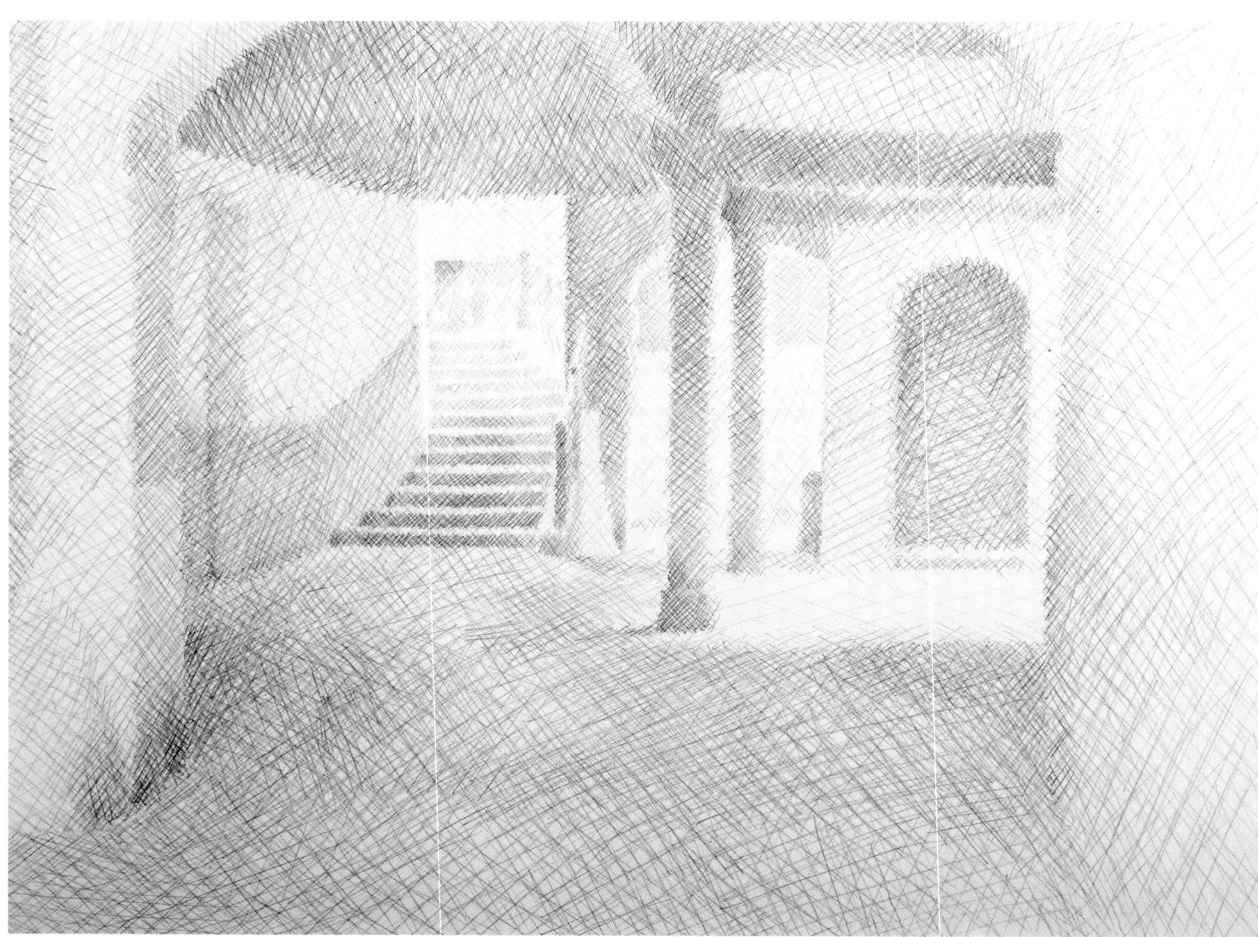

Sotoportego Salviati, Venice, 2009, pencil on paper, 30 x 45cm, Courtesy of the artist.
Sotoportego de la Malvazia Vecchia, Venice, 1998, pencil on paper, 30 x 40cm, Private collection.

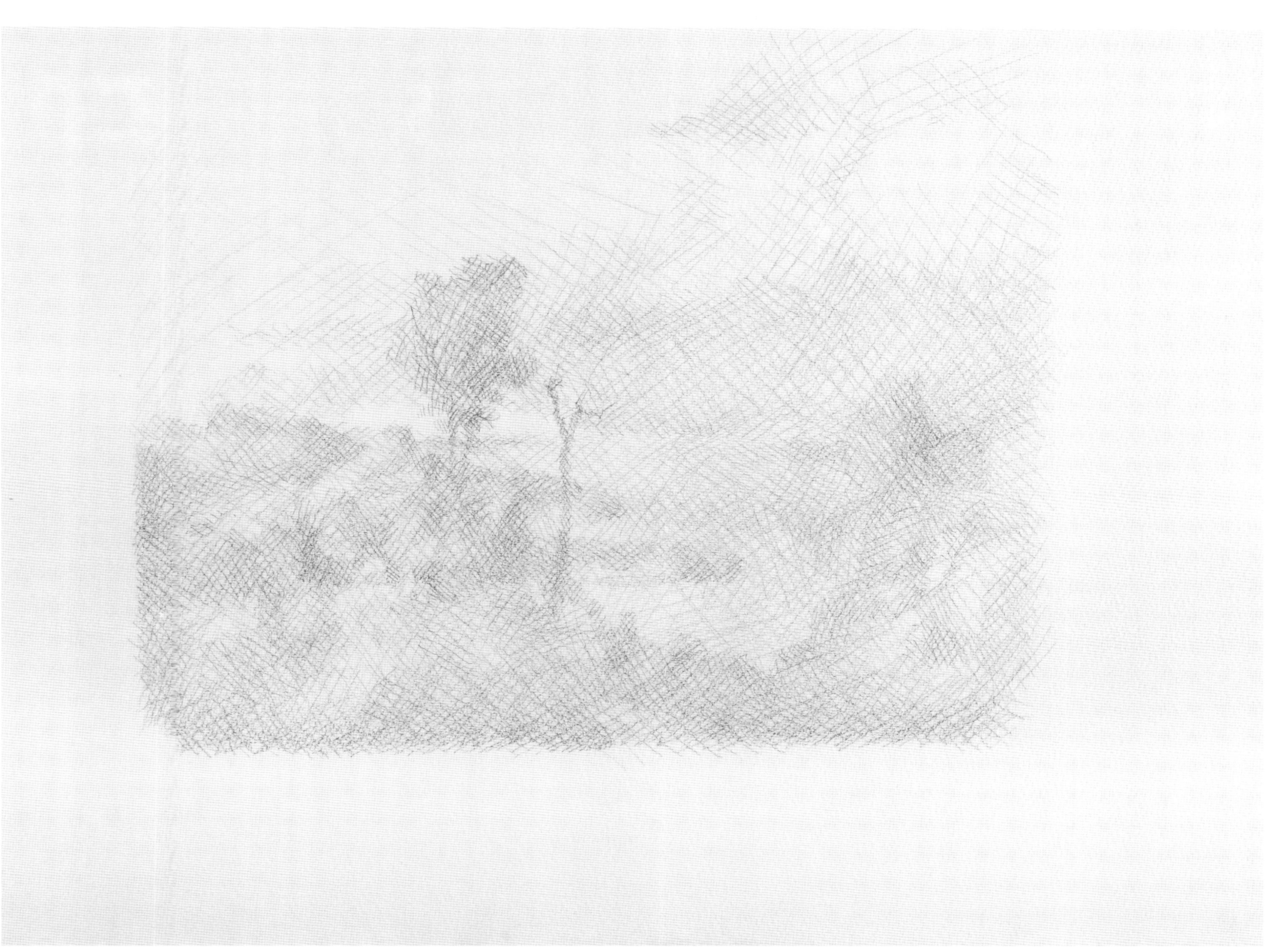

RECENT PAINTINGS

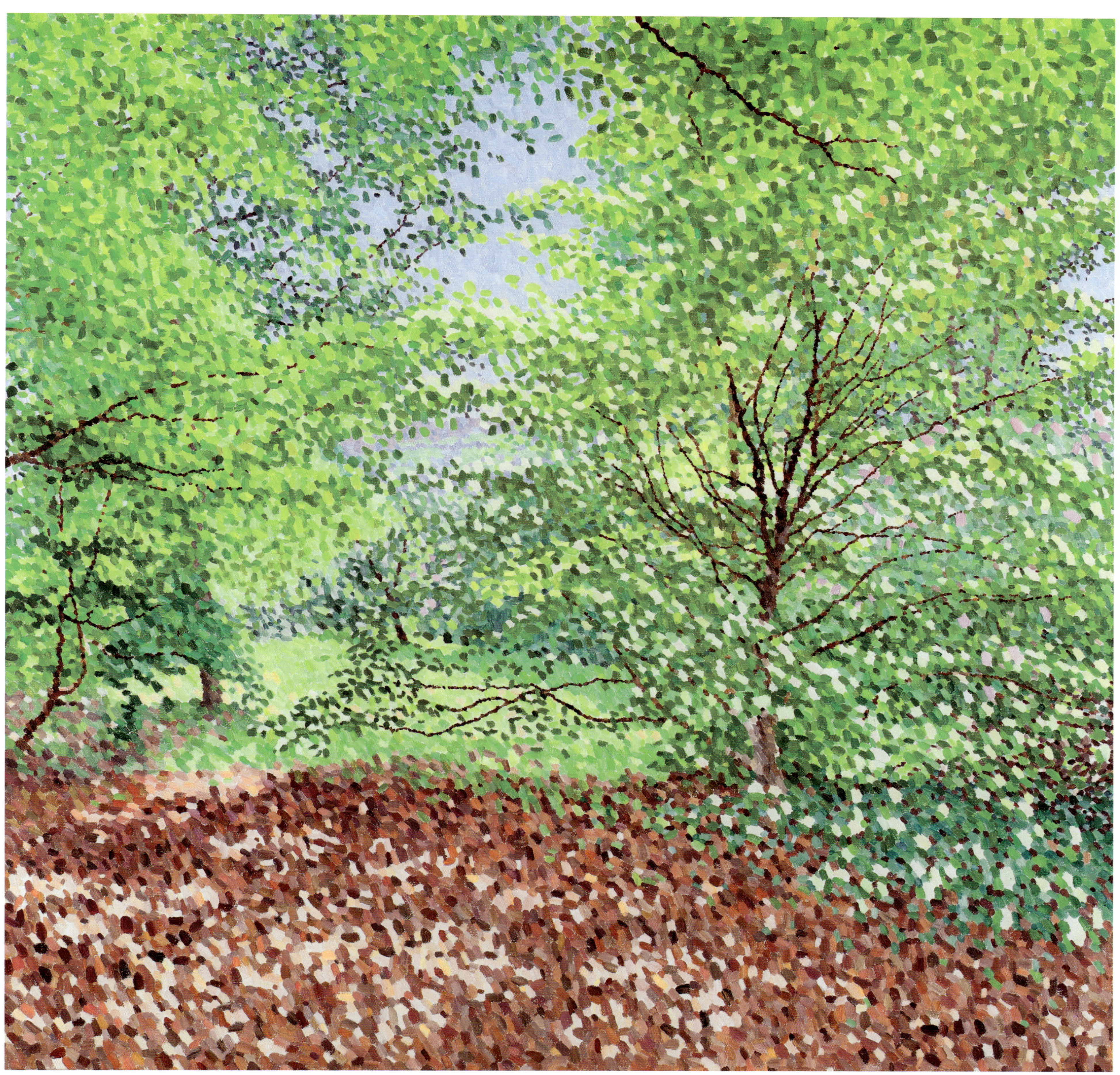

Sunlight, Cornus Florida 2014, oil on canvas, 86 x 92cm, Courtesy of the artist.

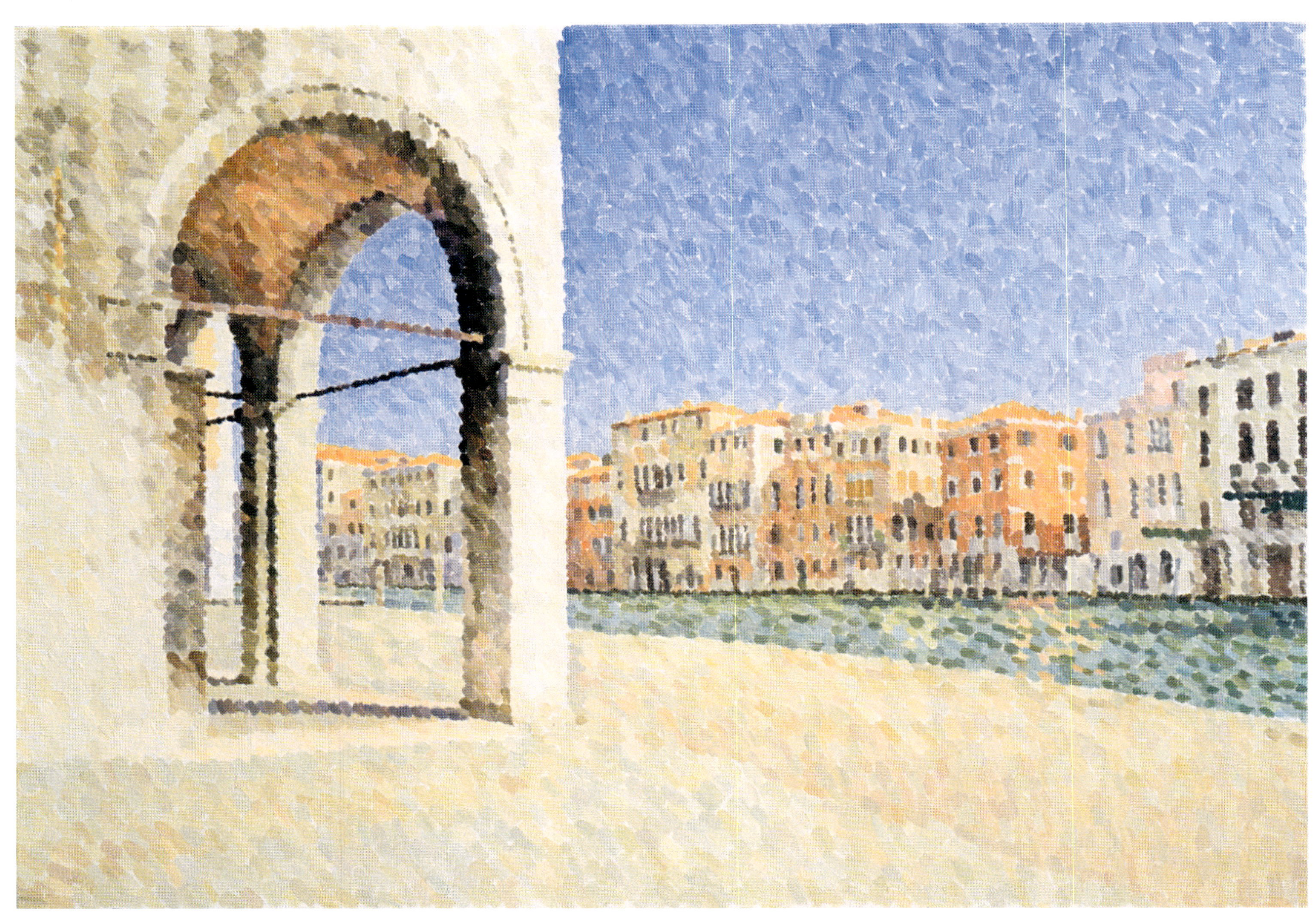

'In the South', The Grand Canal, 2006, oil on canvas, 50 x 74cm, Private collection.

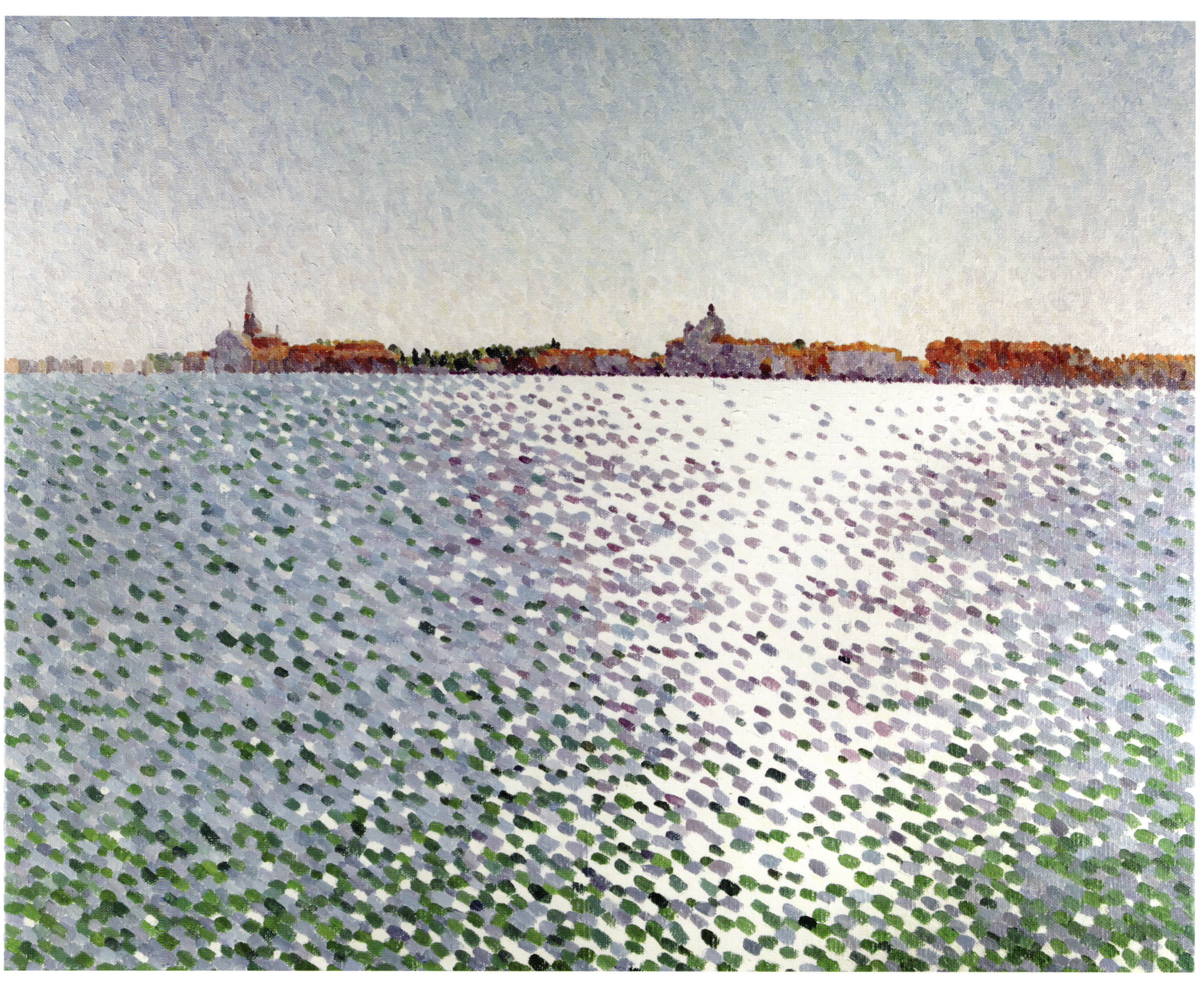

San Giorgio Maggiore and the Guidecca, Venice, 2013, oil on canvas, 60 x 75cm, Courtesy of the artist.

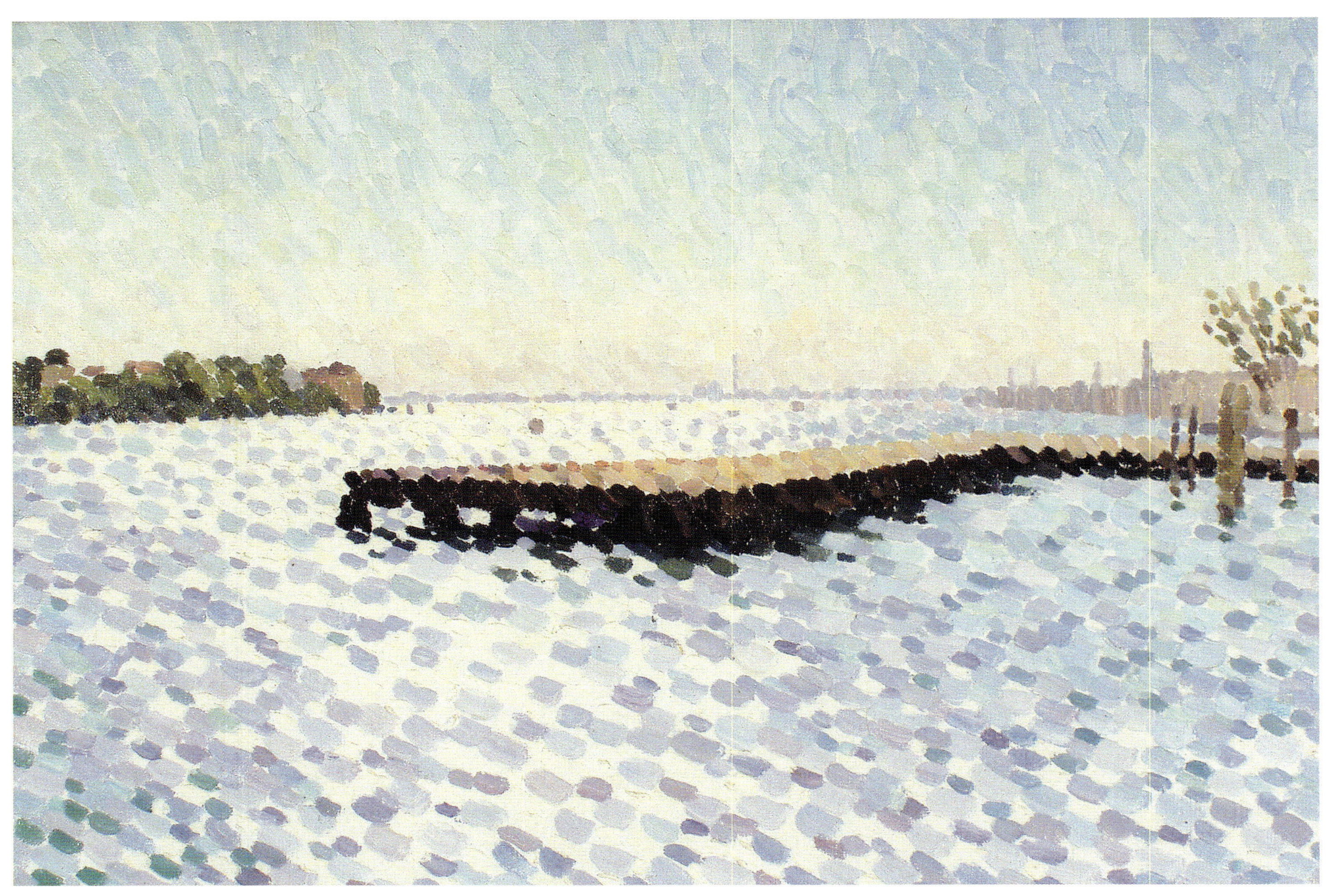

The Guidecca Canal, Venice, 2006, oil on canvas, 28 x 42cm, Private collection.

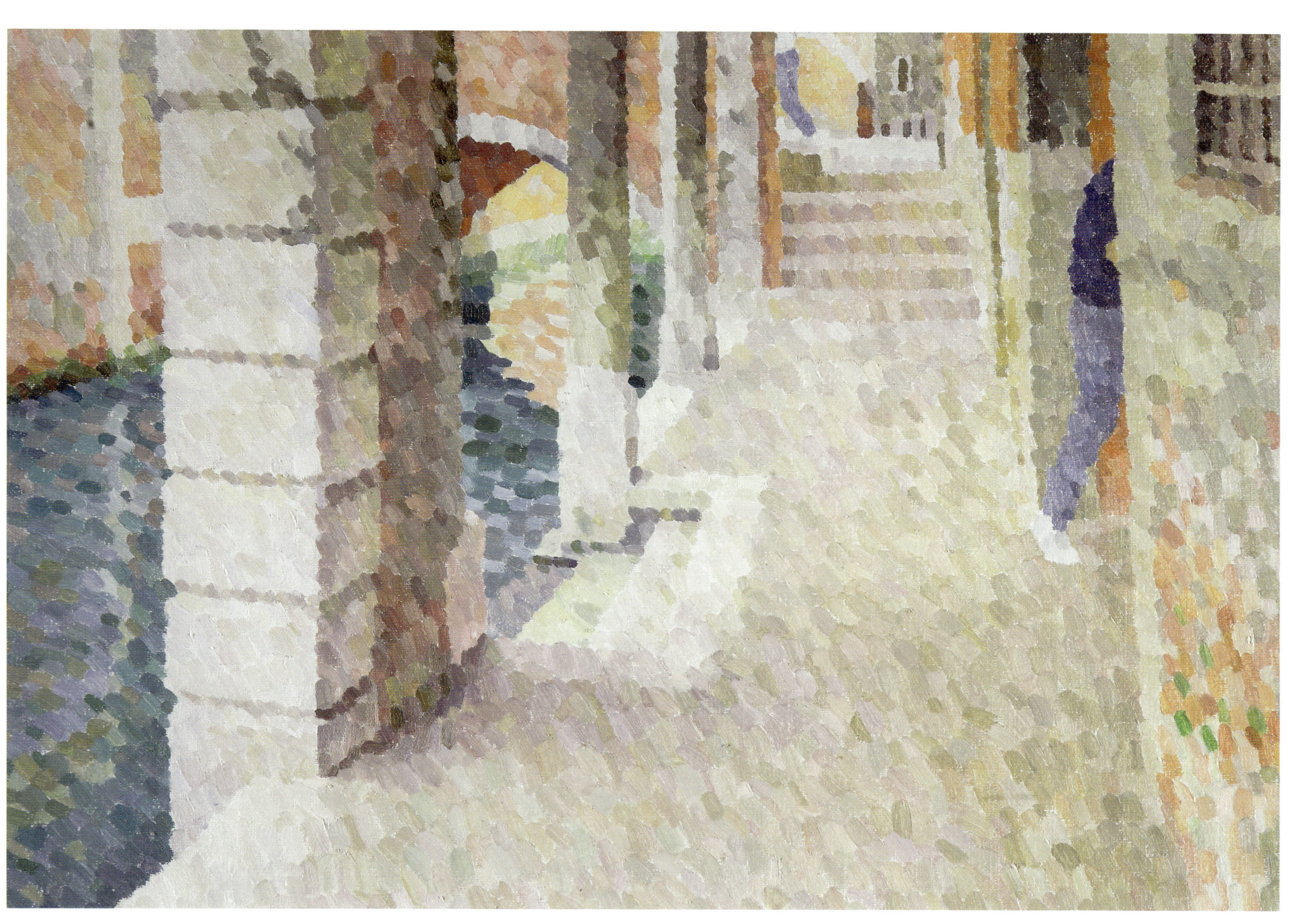

Sotoportego Panada, Venice, 2011, oil on canvas, 35 x 50cm, Courtesy of the artist.

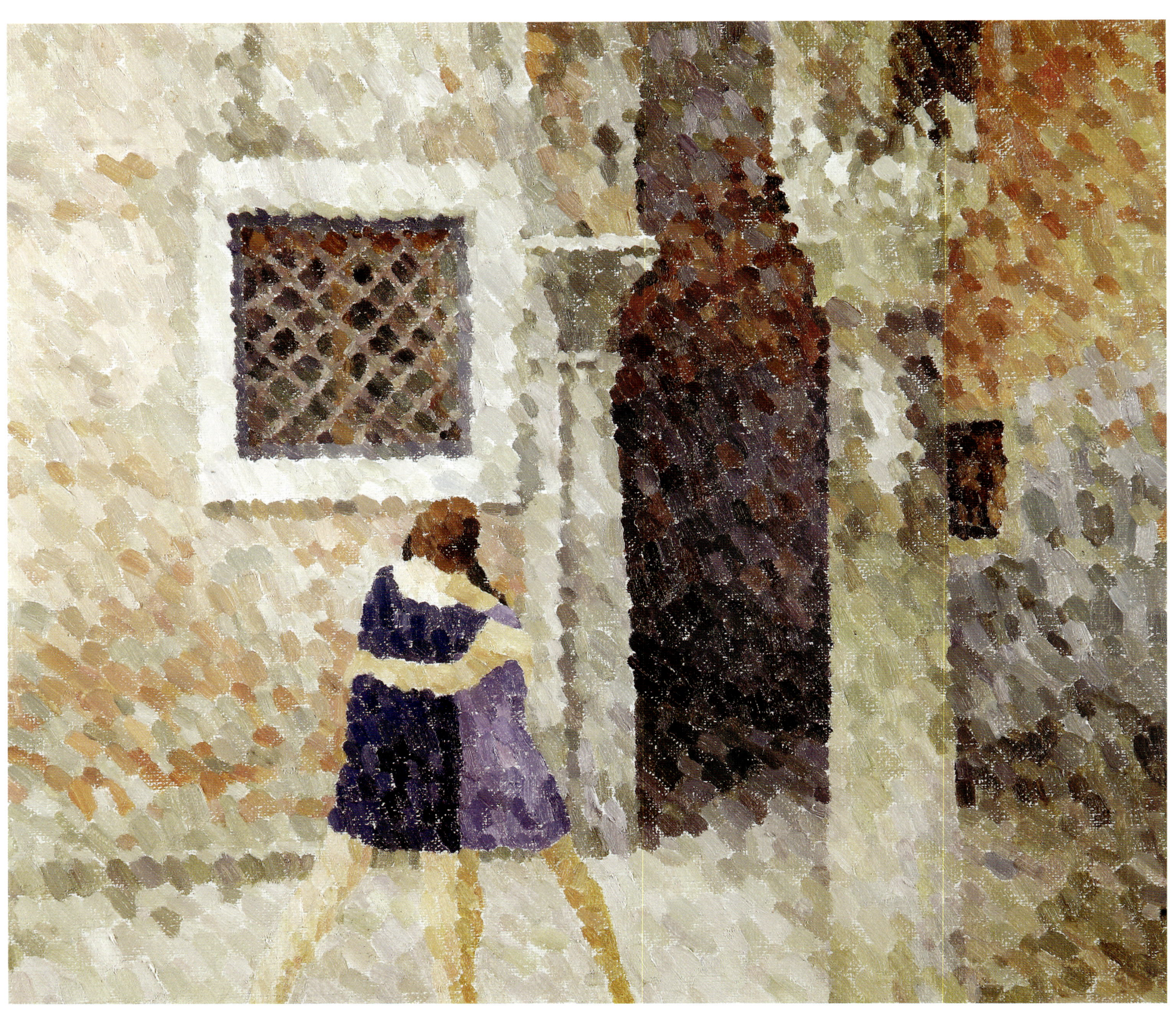

A Meeting, Venice, 2011, oil on canvas, 28 x 33cm, Courtesy of the artist.

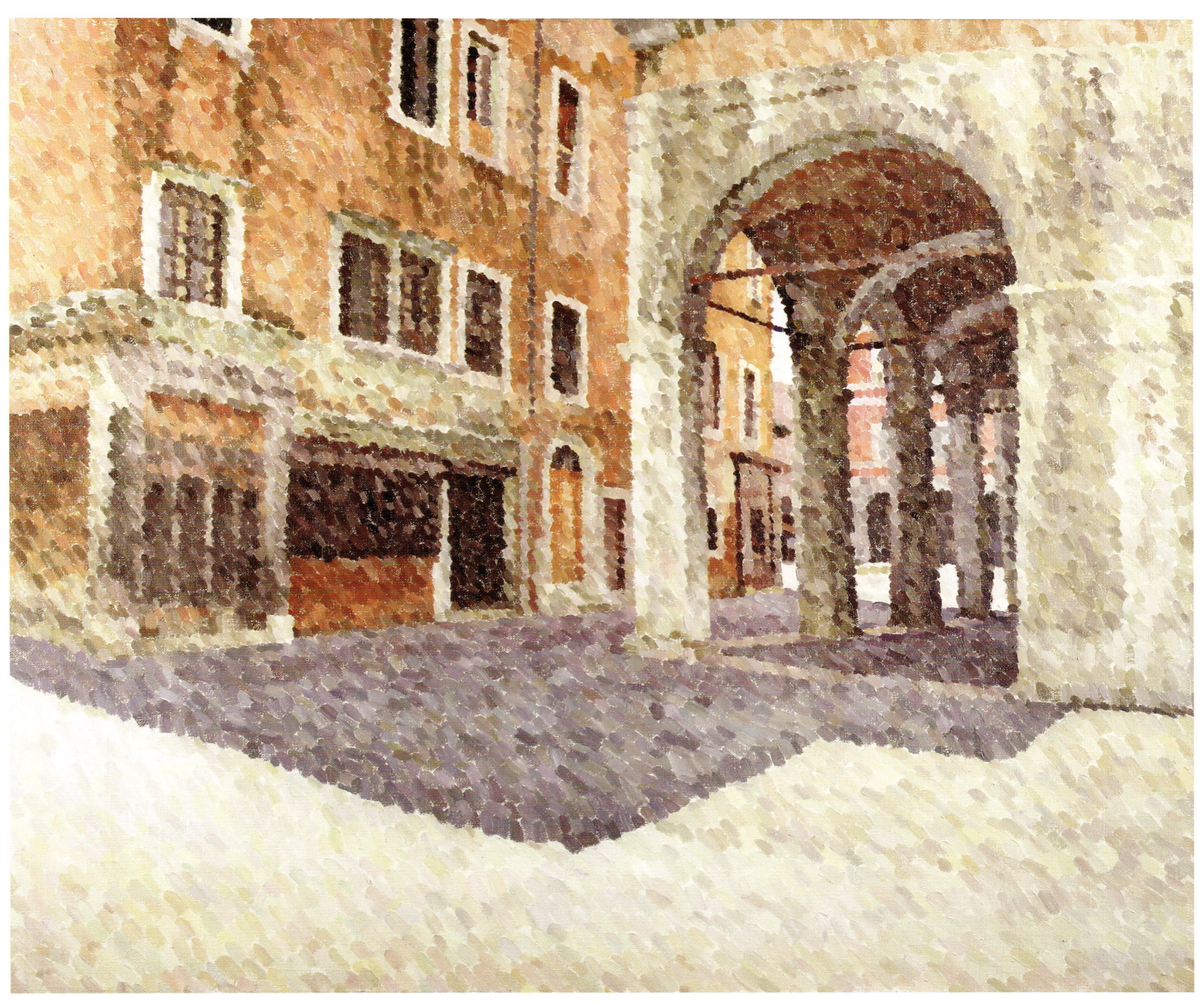

The Naranzaria, Venice, 2009, oil on canvas, 65 x 80cm, Private collection.

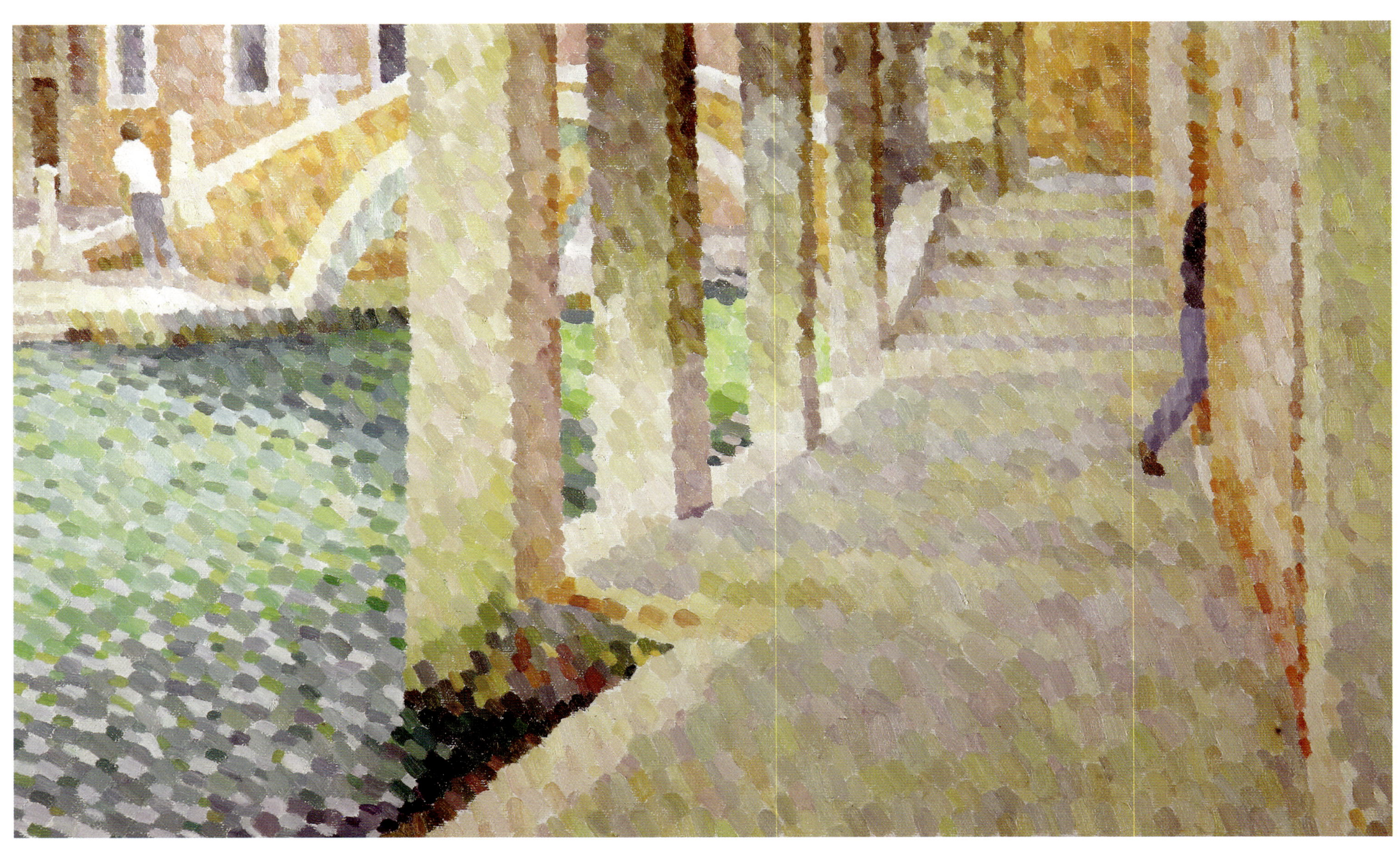

Sotoportego del Traghetto, Venice, 2011, oil on canvas, 35 x 55cm, Courtesy of the artist.

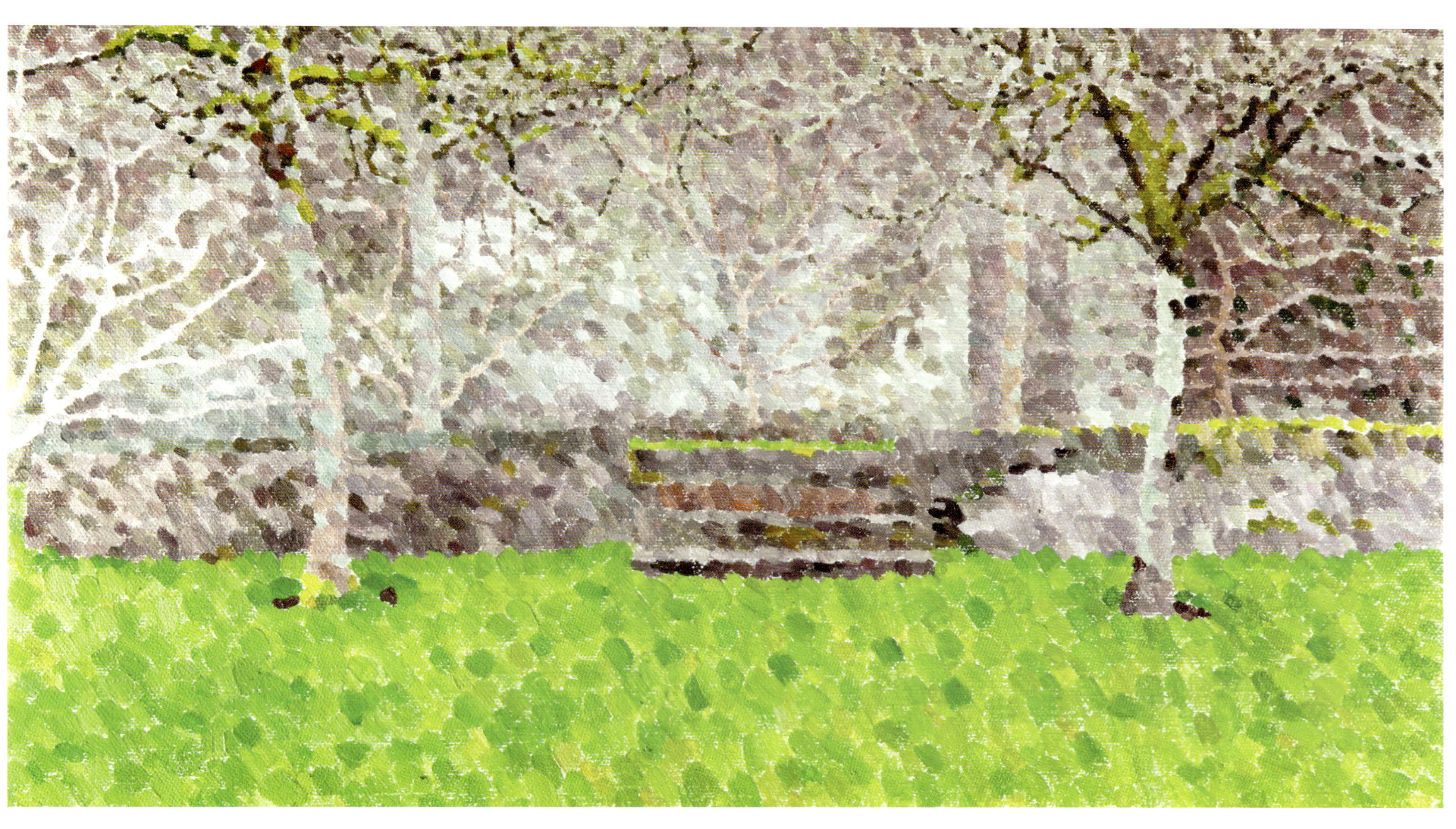

Orchard in Winter, 2014 oil on canvas, 25 x 45, Courtesy of the artist.

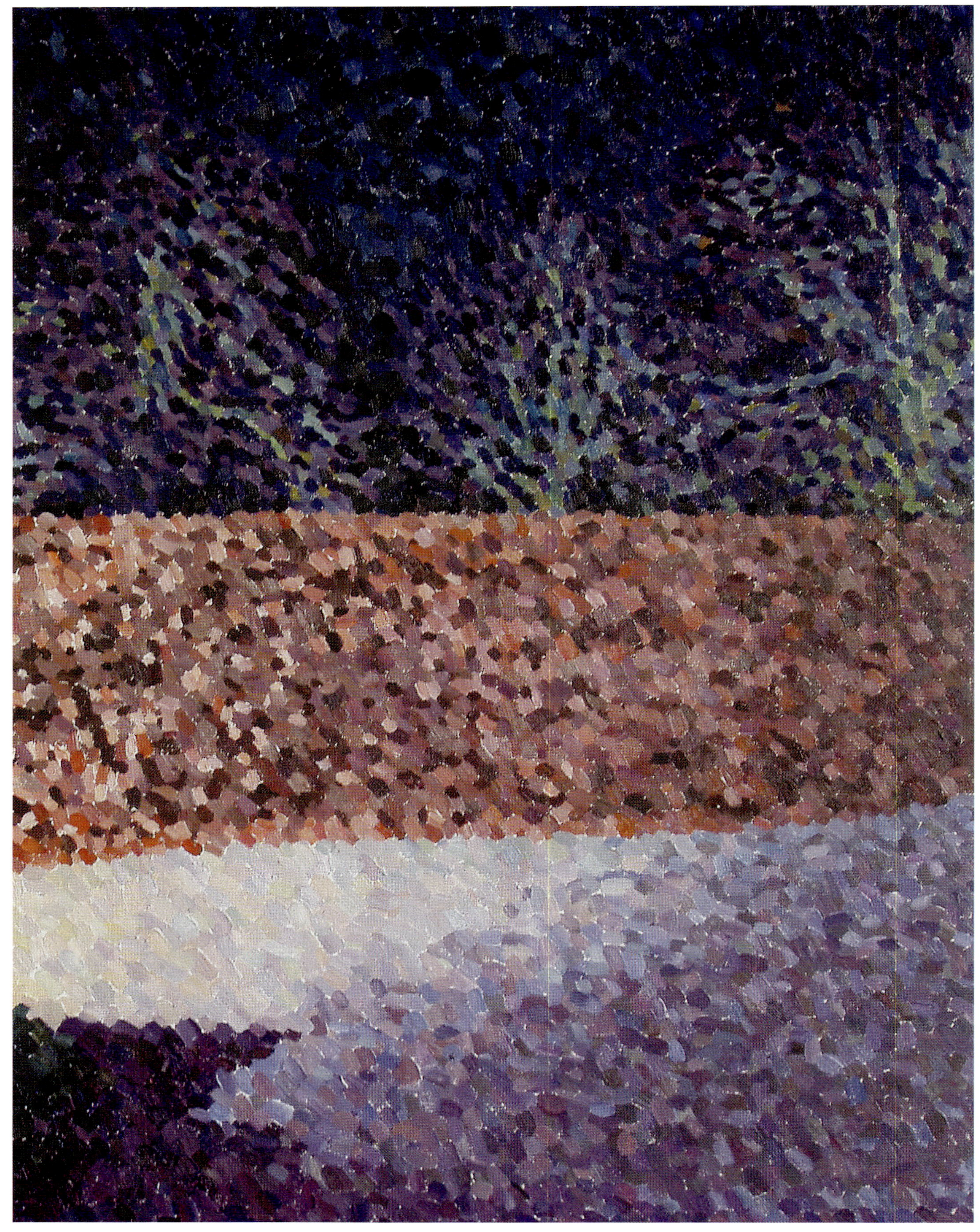

Night Landscape, 2009, oil on canvas, 57 x 46cm, Private collection.

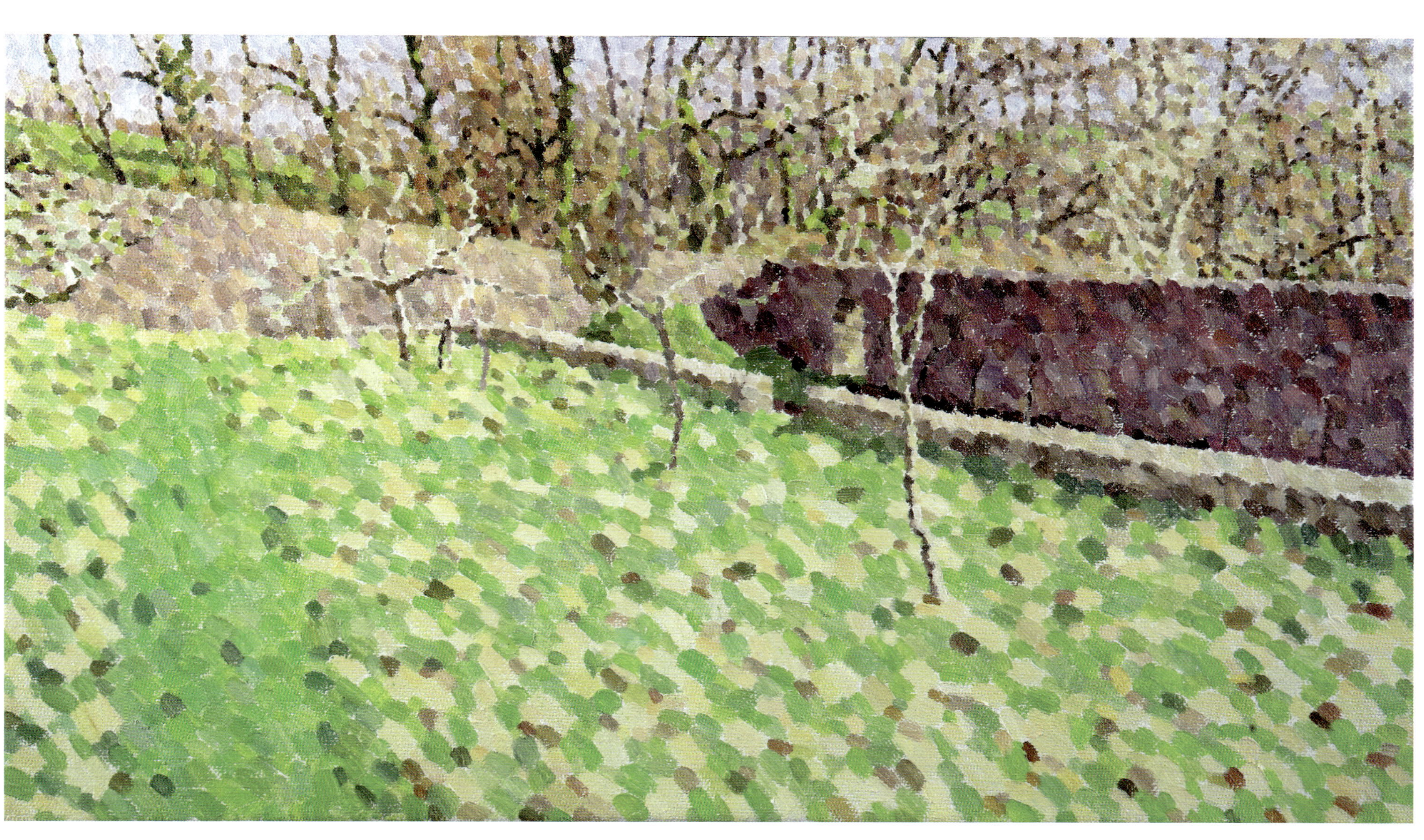

Orchard in Winter Sun, 2011, oil on canvas, 26 x 46cm, Private collection.

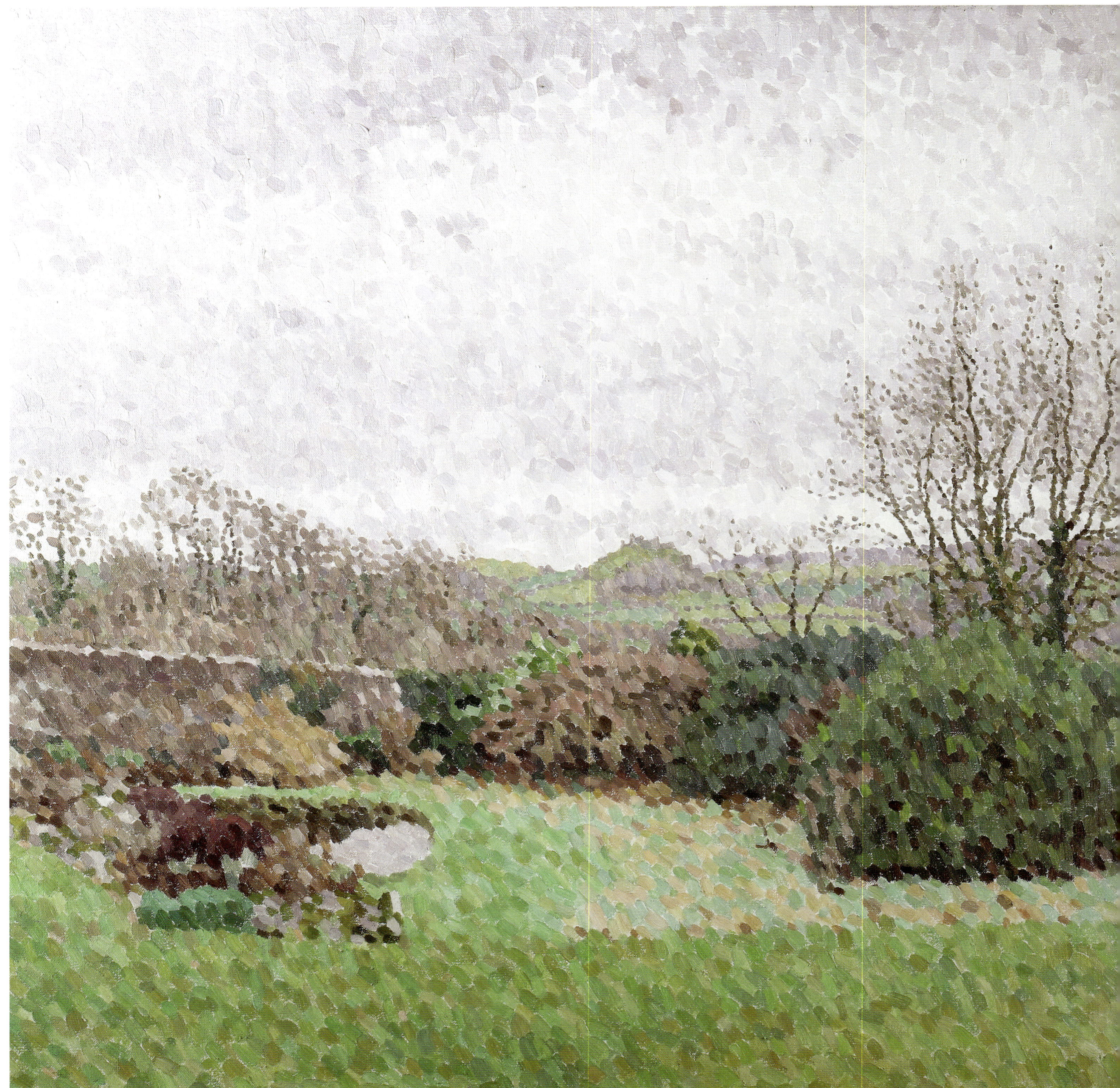

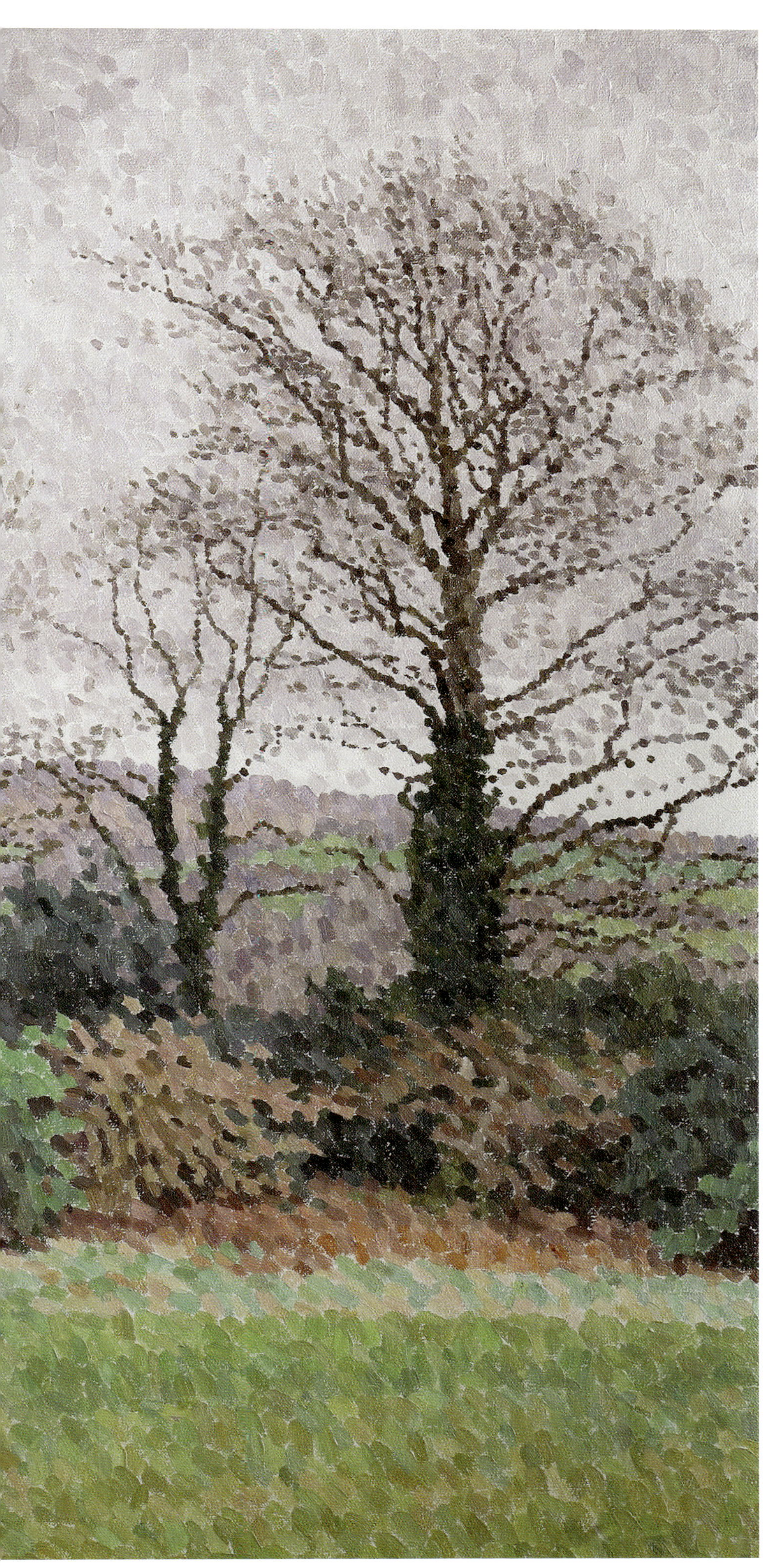

The Castle in Winter, 2011, oil on canvas, 64 x 102cm, Private collection.

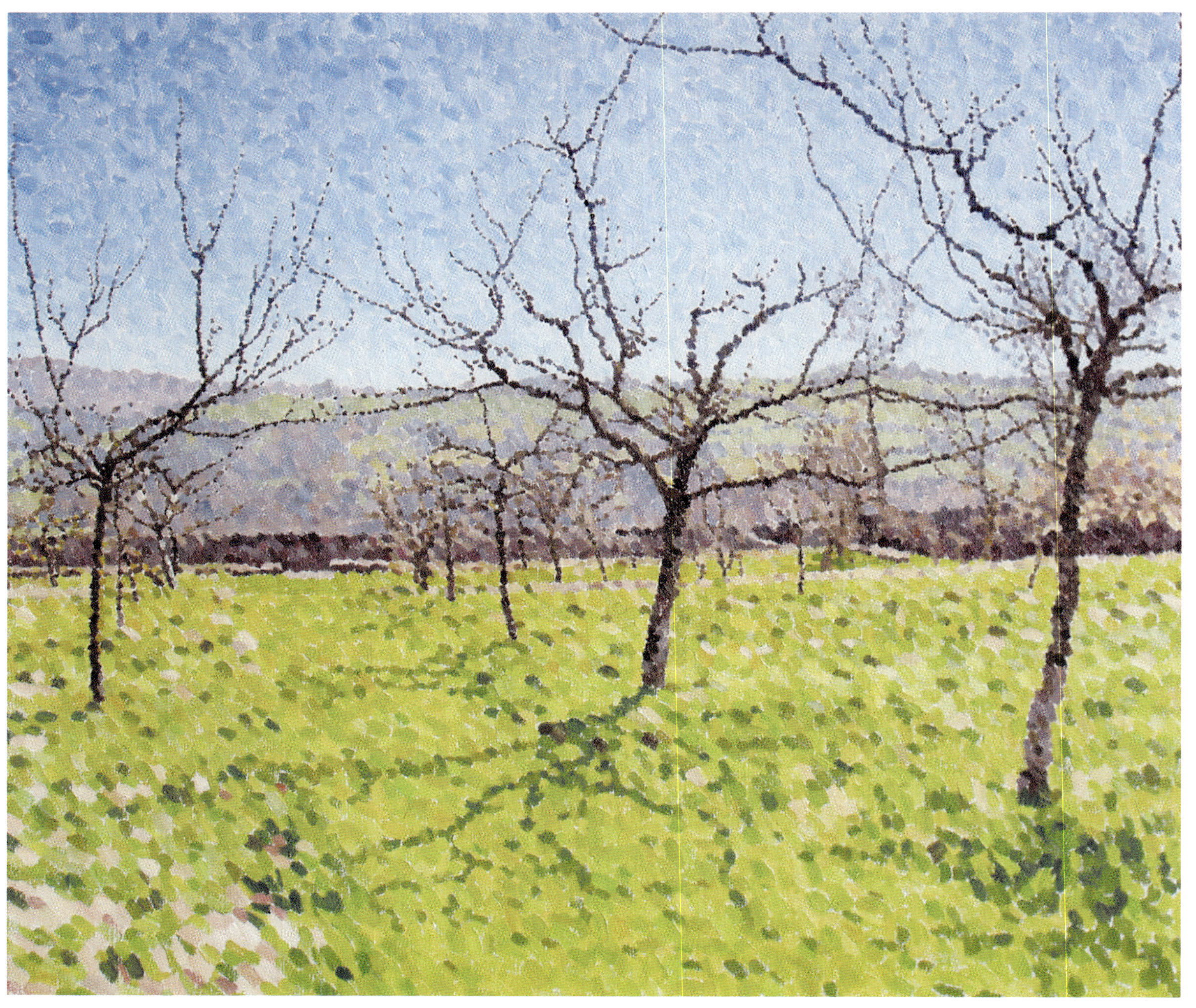

Spring Morning, 2007, oil on canvas, 50 x 61cm, Private collection.

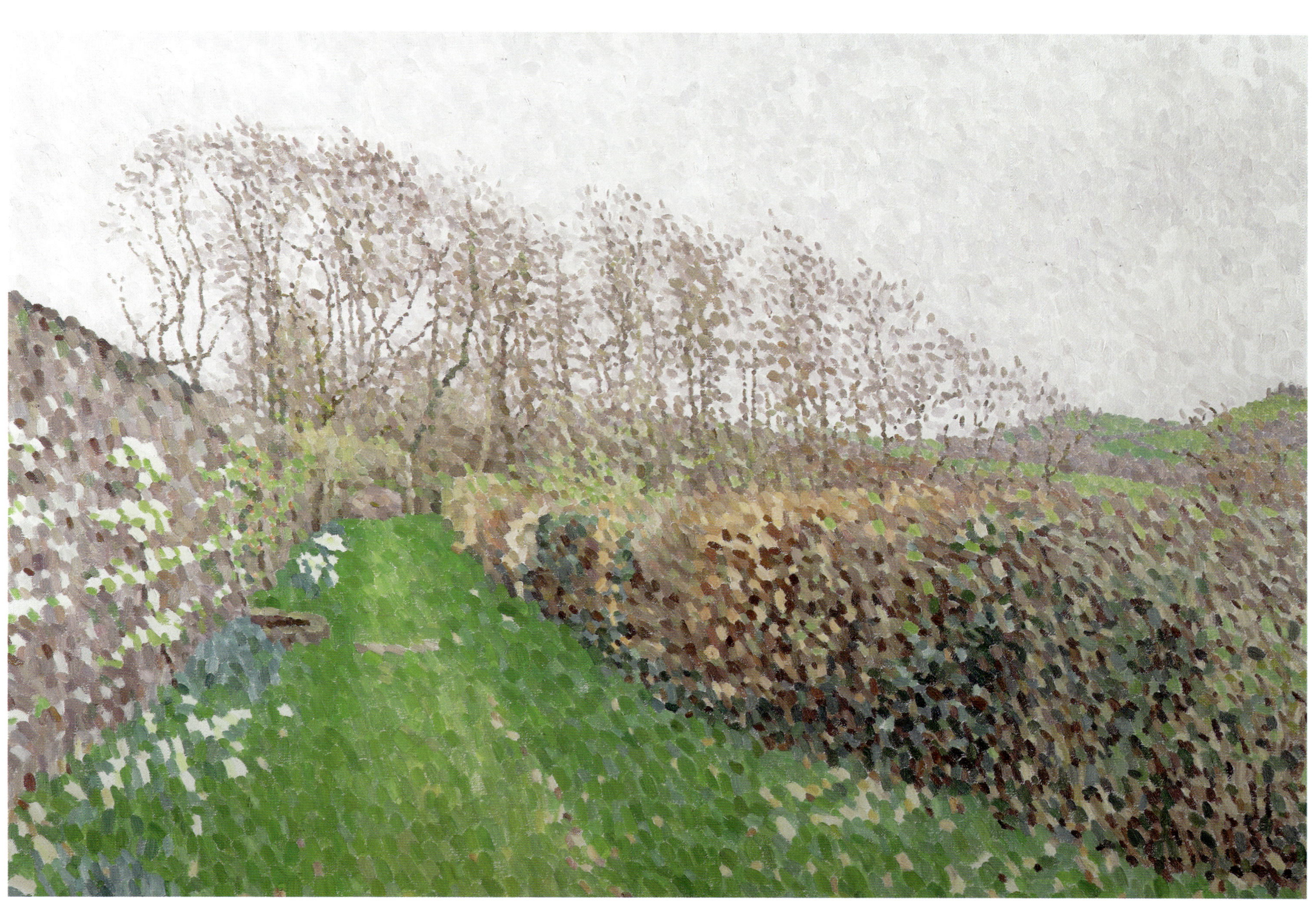

Pear Blossom, 2011, oil on canvas, 51 x 76cm, Private collection.

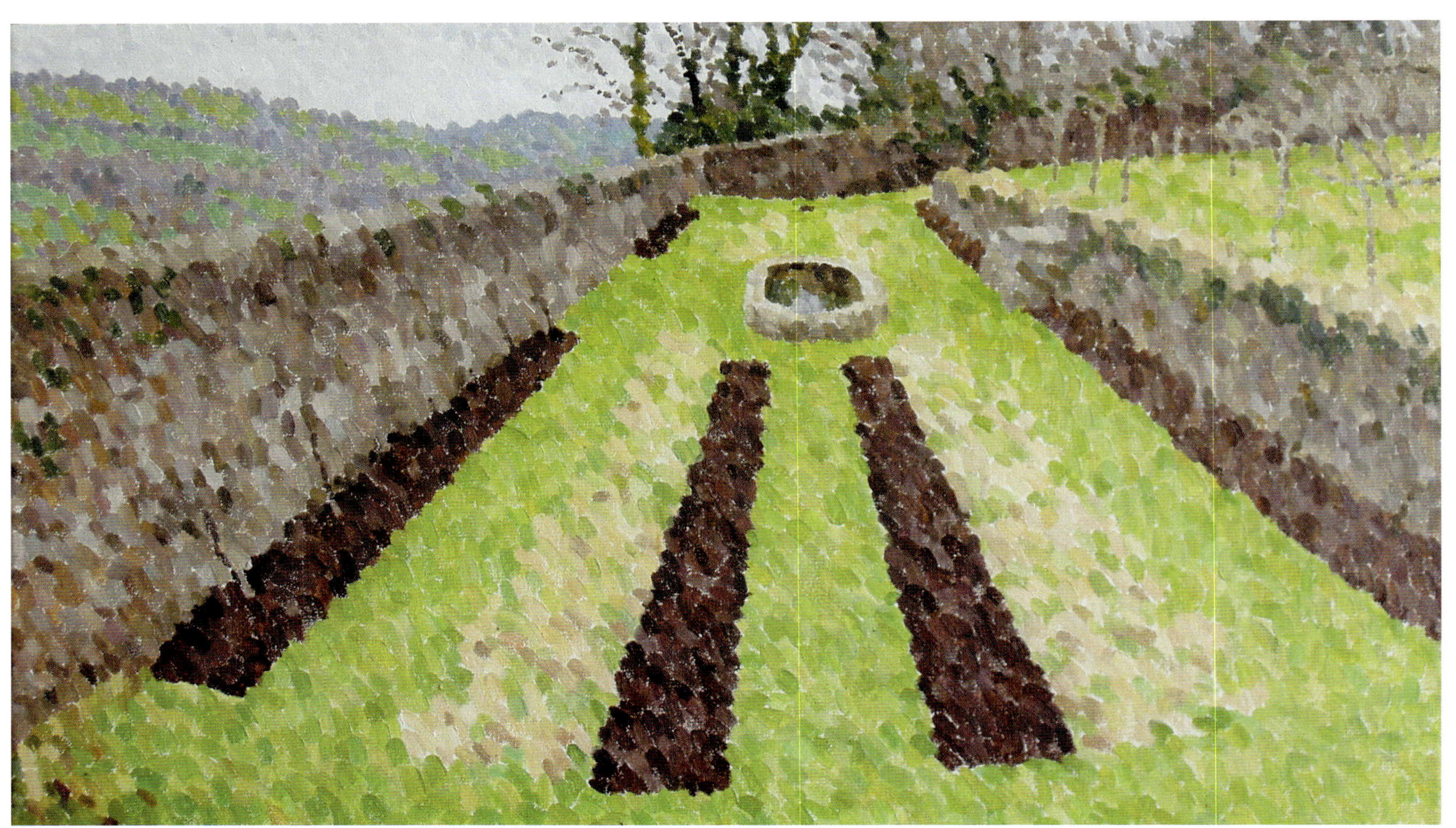

The Pool Garden (Winter), 2008, oil on canvas, 35 x 63cm, Courtesy of the artist.

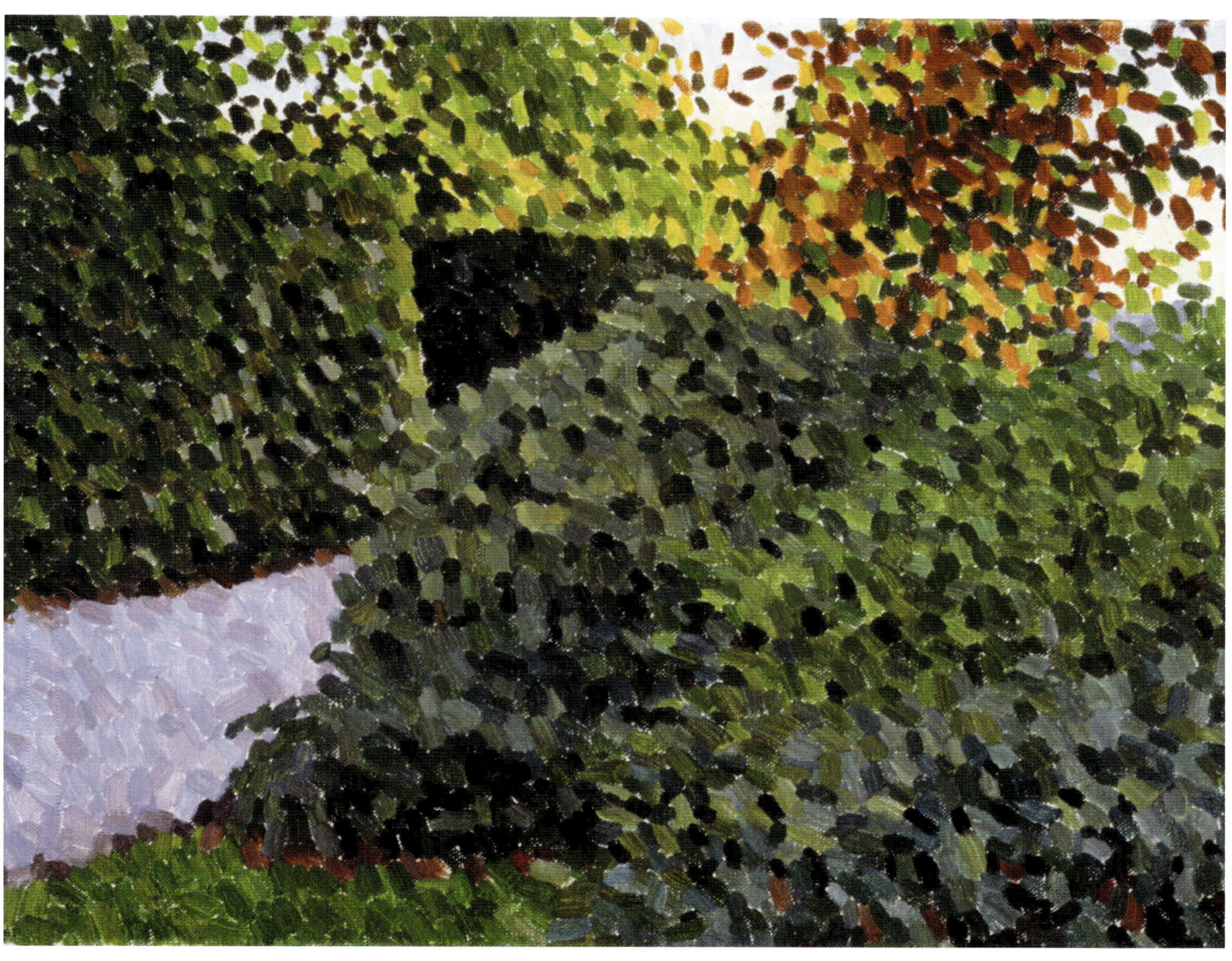

Autumn Landscape, Evening Light, 2007, oil on canvas, 30 x 41cm, Courtesy of the artist.

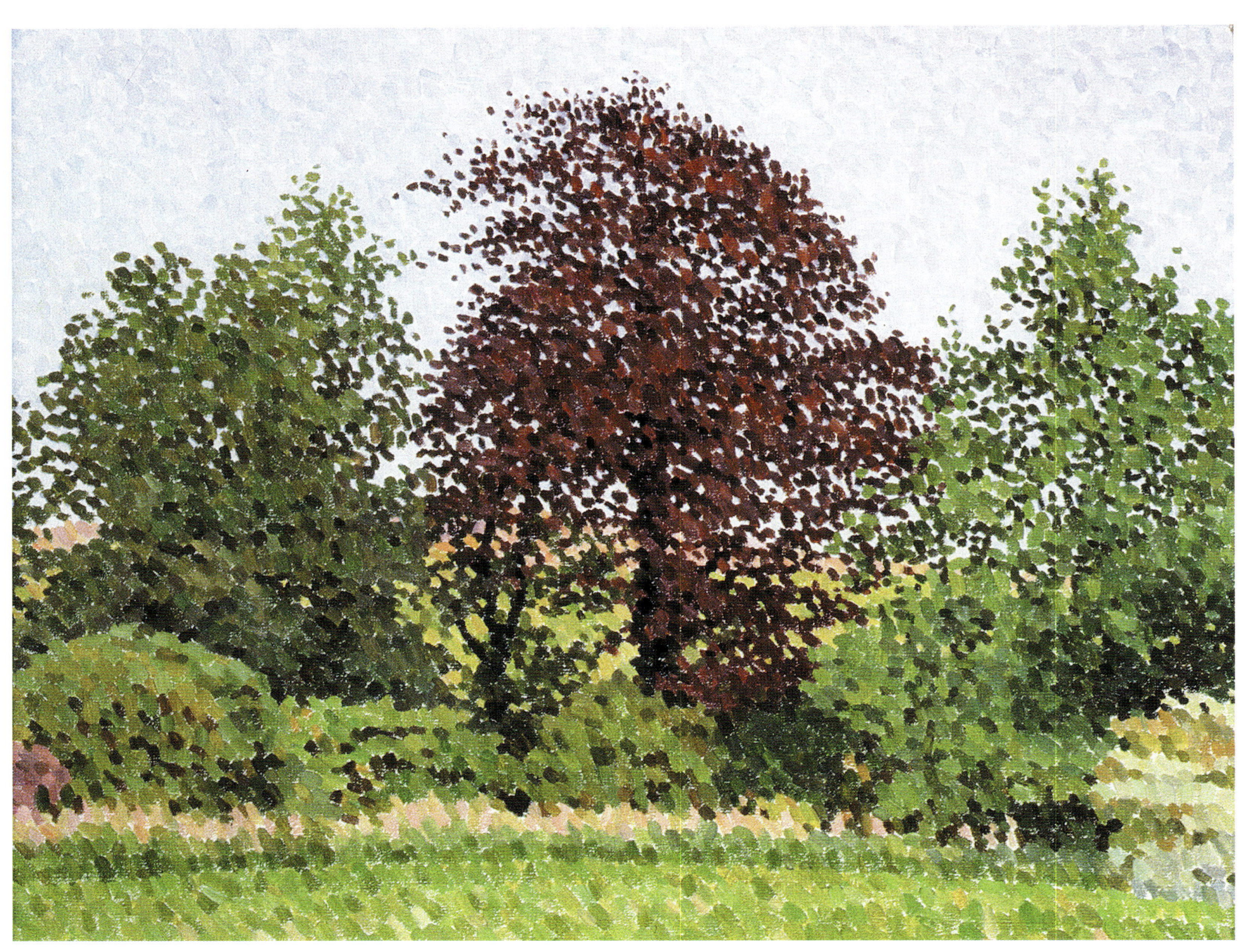

Landscape, Light Leaving, 2007, oil on canvas, 45 x 60cm, Private collection.

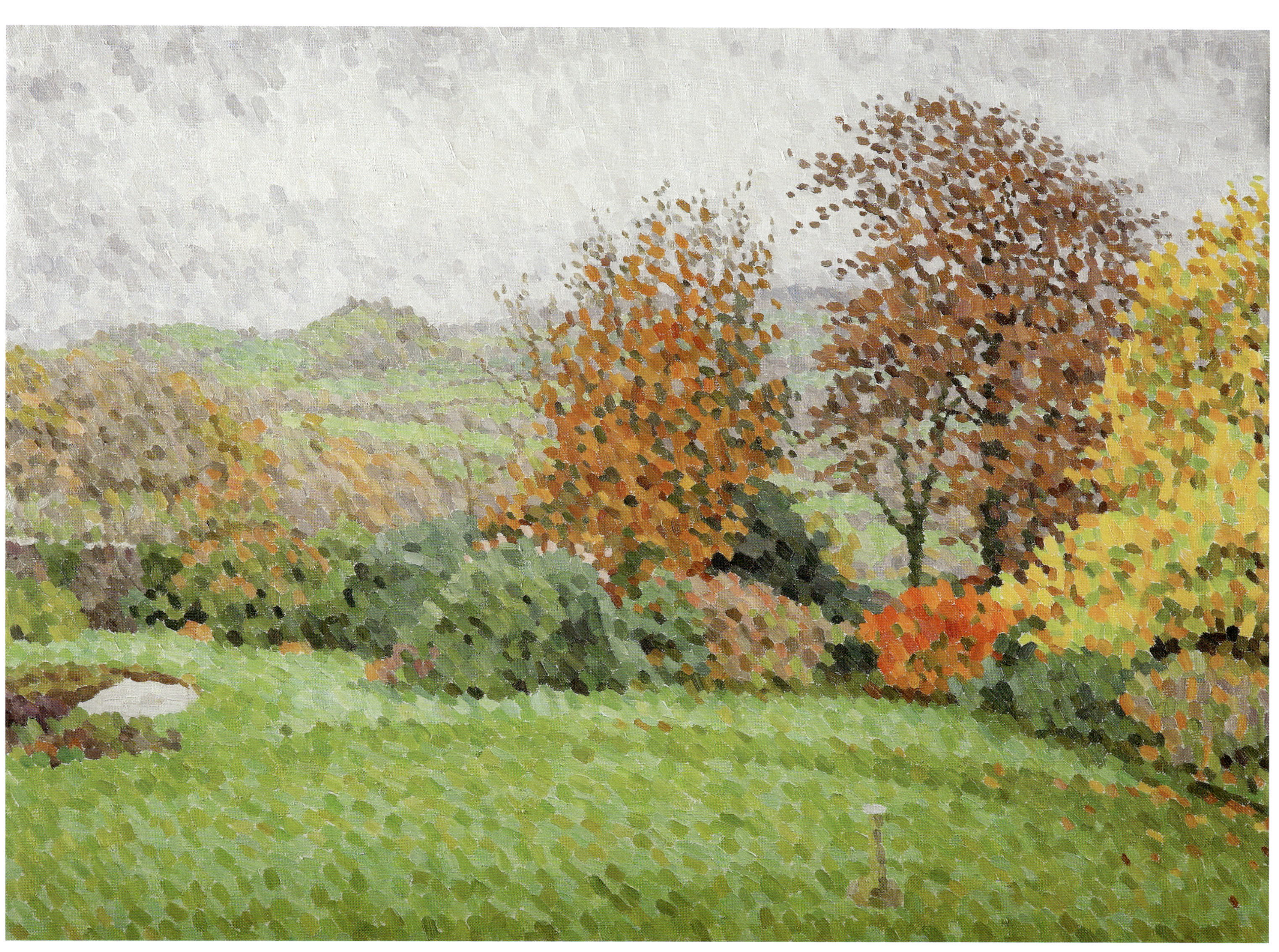

Autumn Landscape, Rain, 2007, oil on canvas, 44 x 60cm, Private collection.

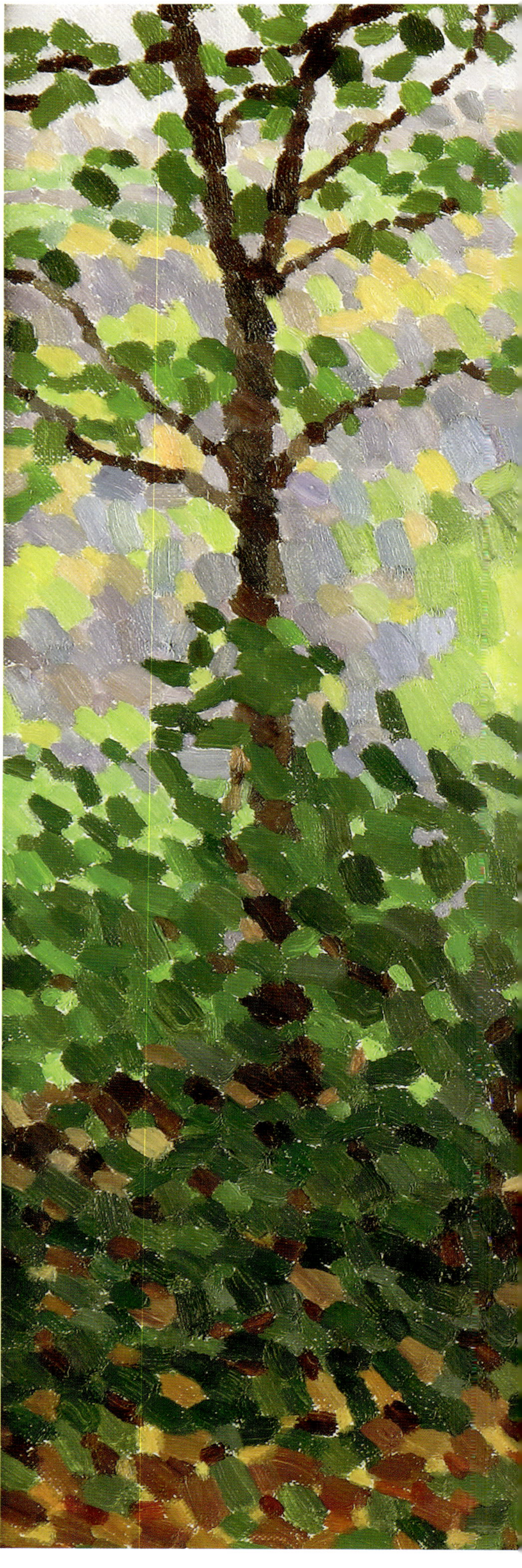

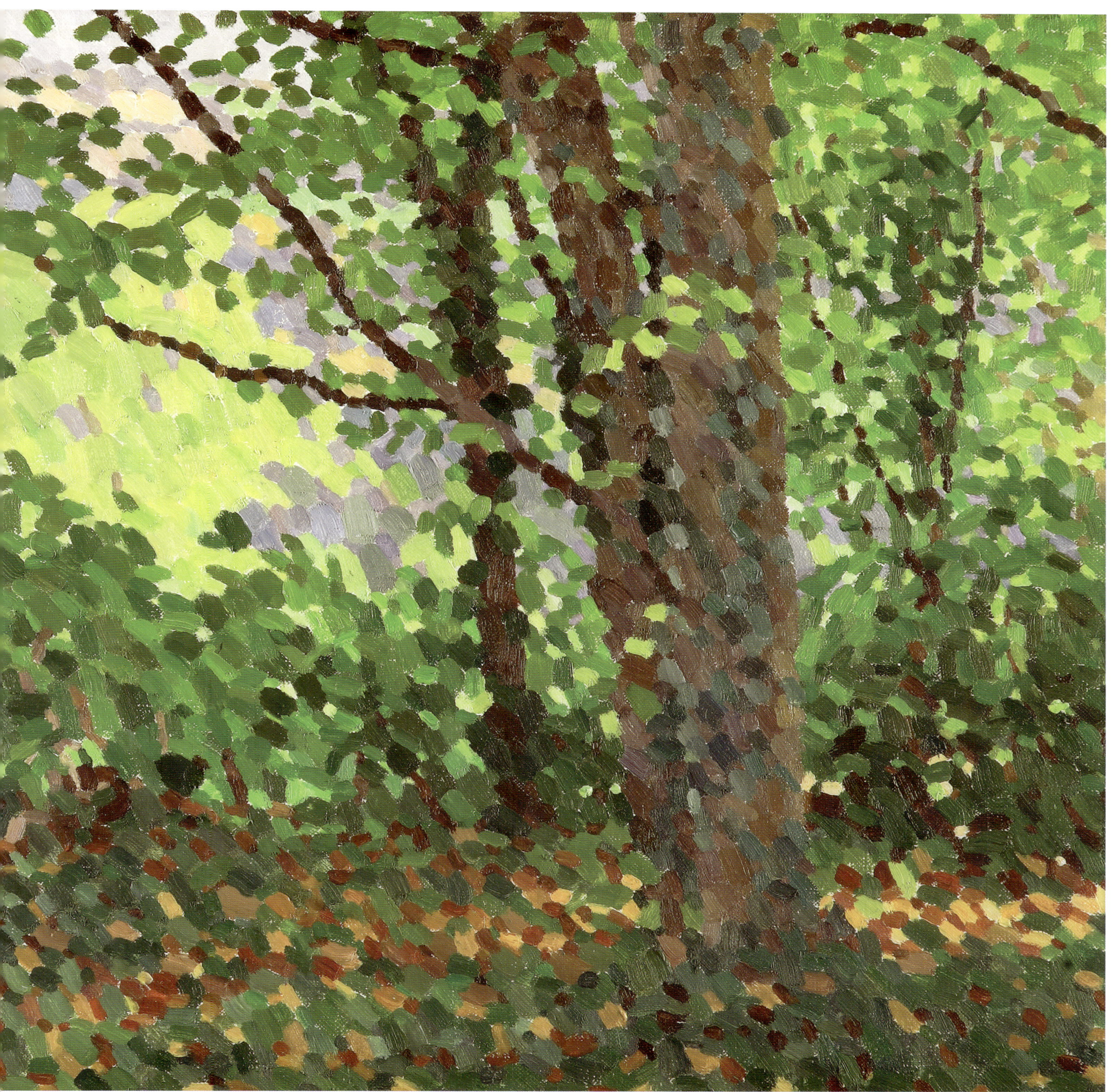

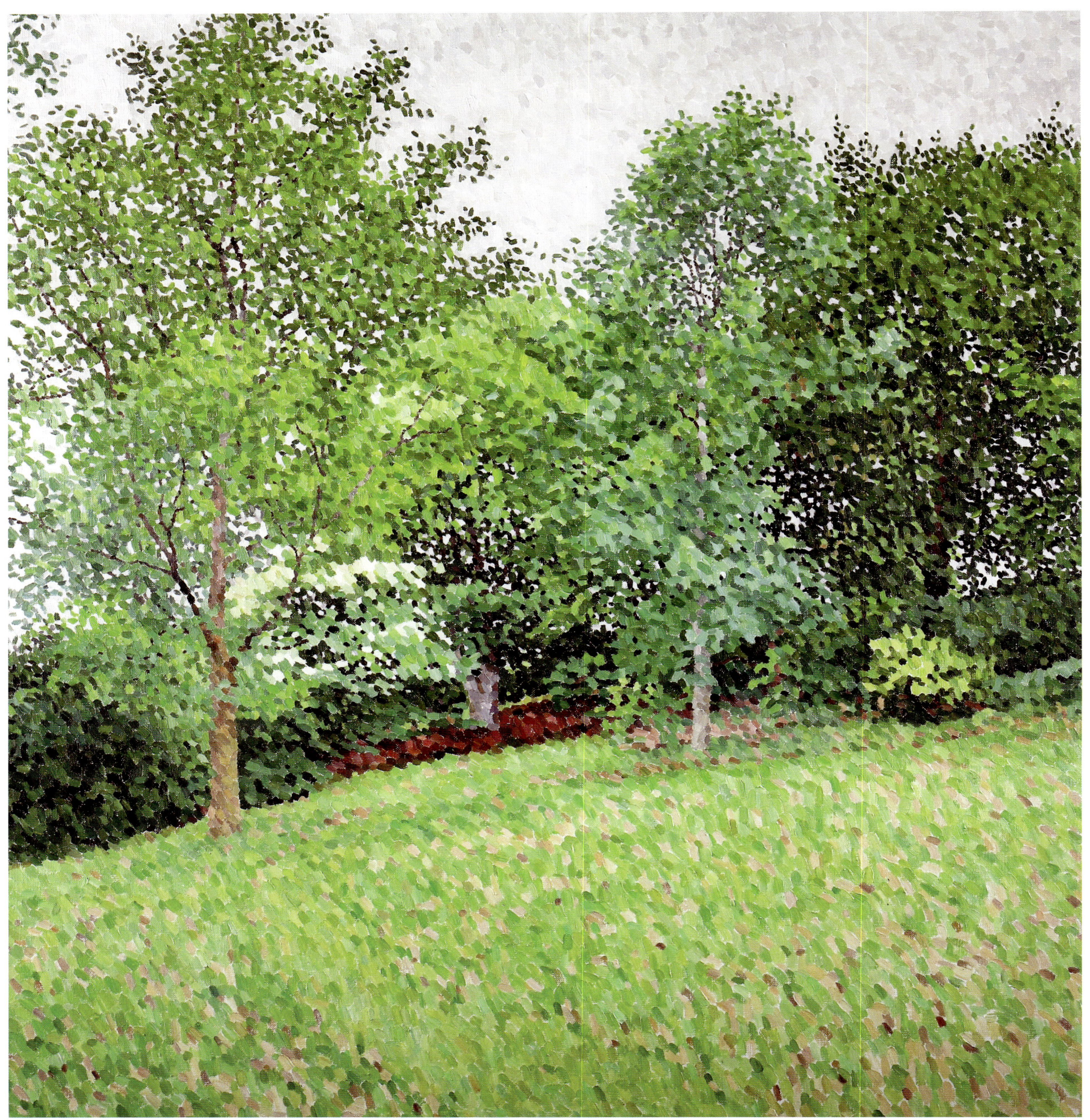

Trees and Cornus Florida, 2011, oil on canvas, 87 x 85cm, Private collection.

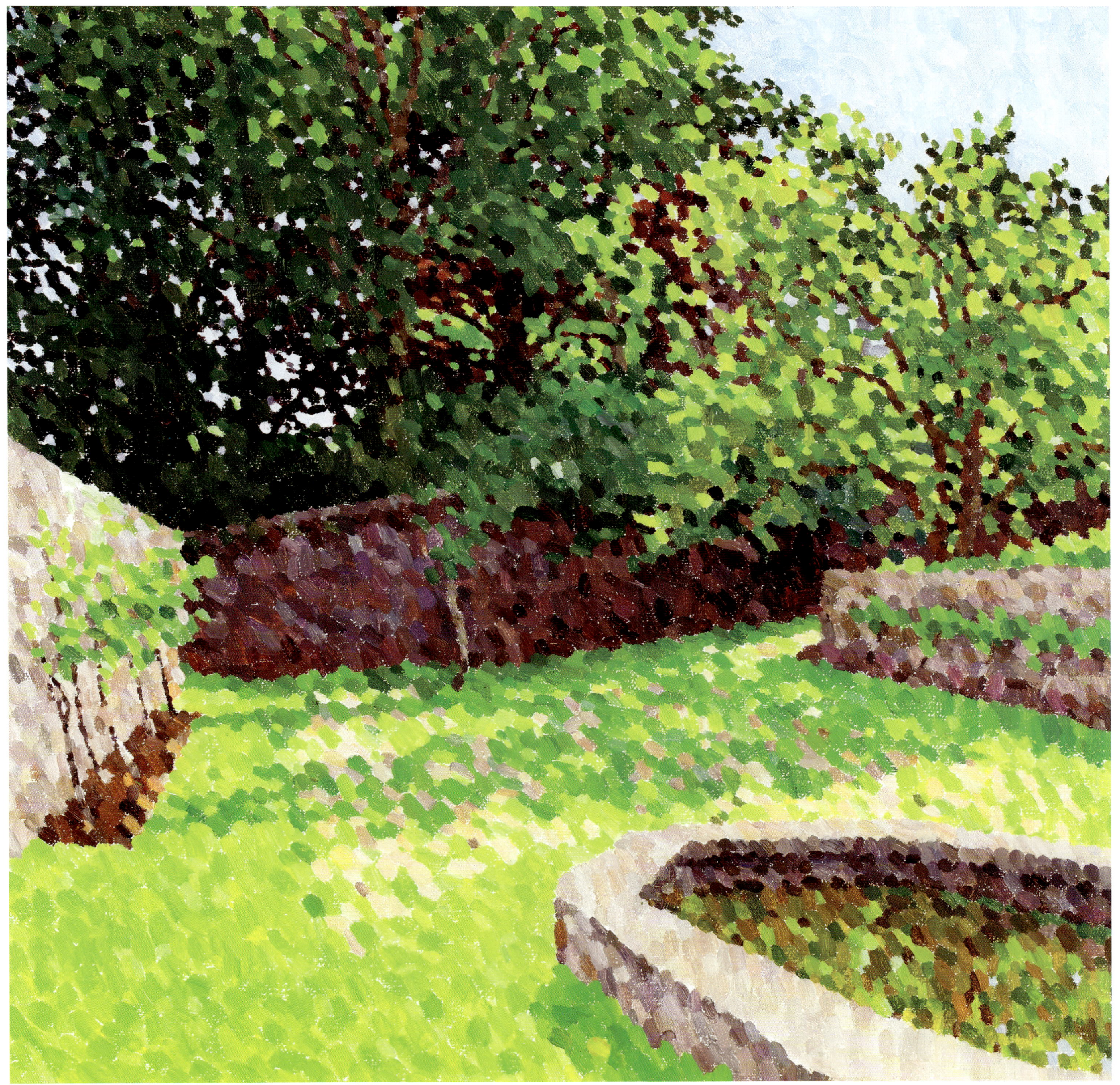

Pool Garden, Evening Light, 2014, oil on canvas, 39 x 41cm, Courtesy of the artist.

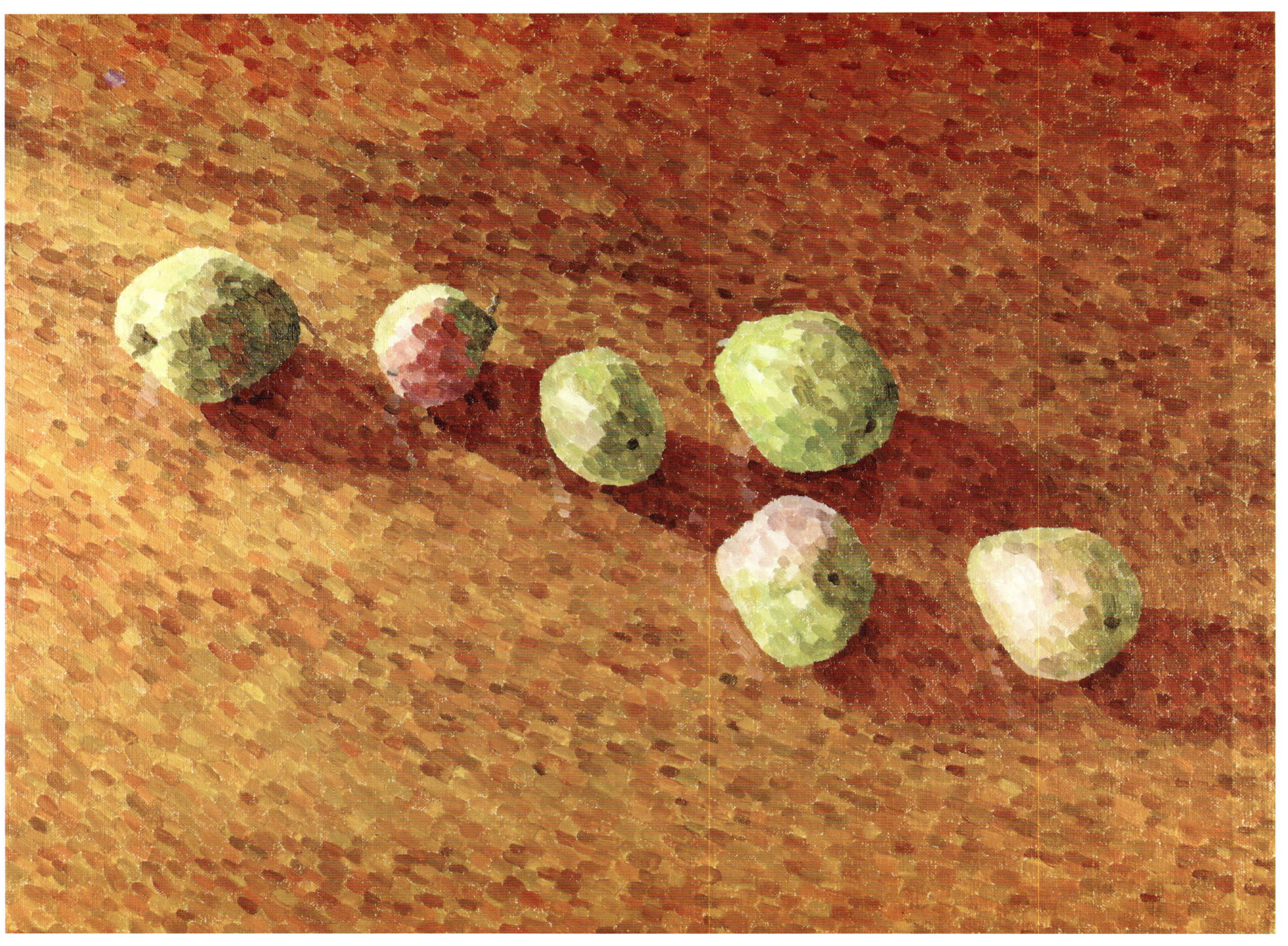

Still Life, Black Worcesters, 2013, oil on canvas, 45 x 63cm, Courtesy of the artist.

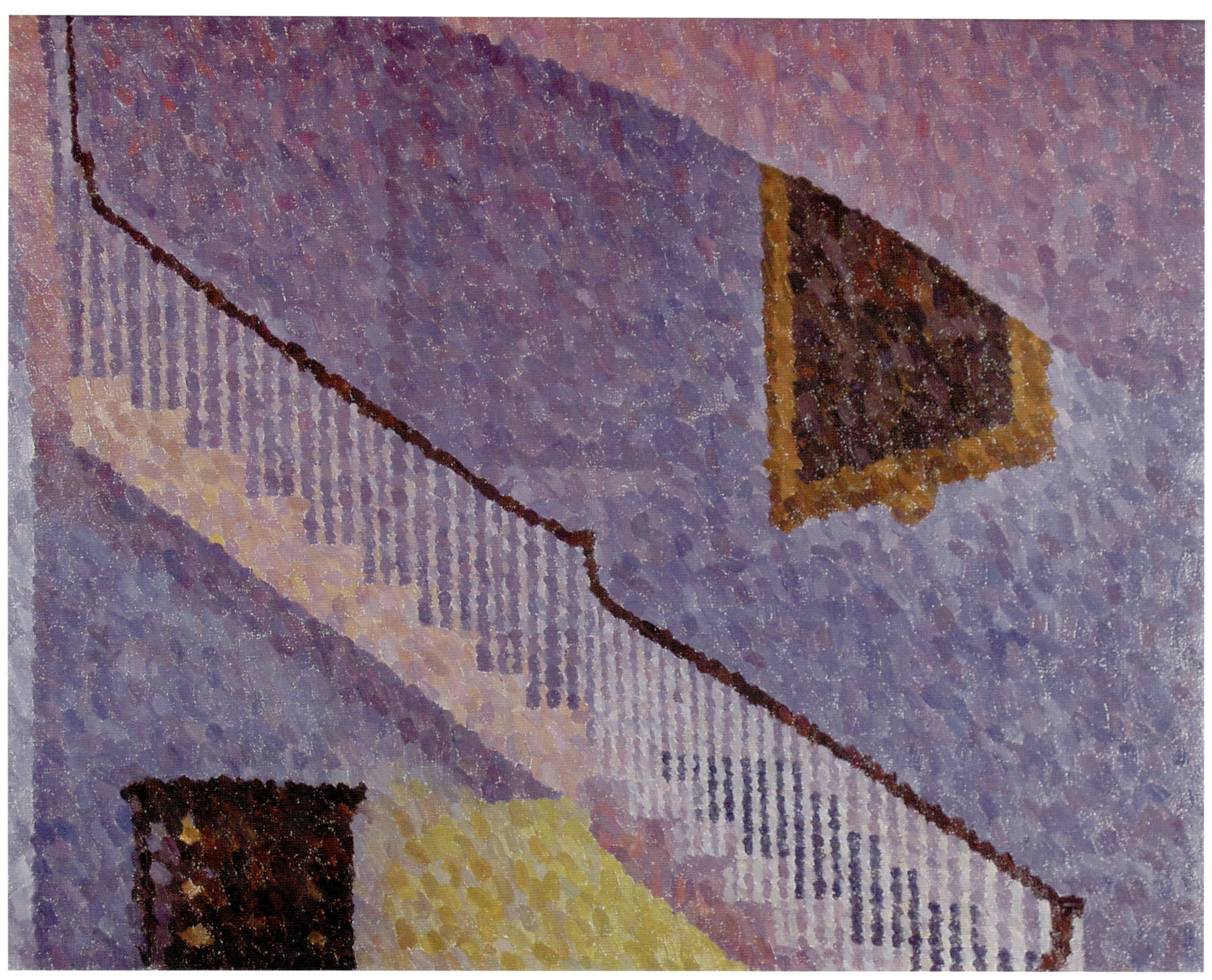

Stairwell at Night, 2007, oil on canvas, 43 x 55cm, Courtesy of the artist.

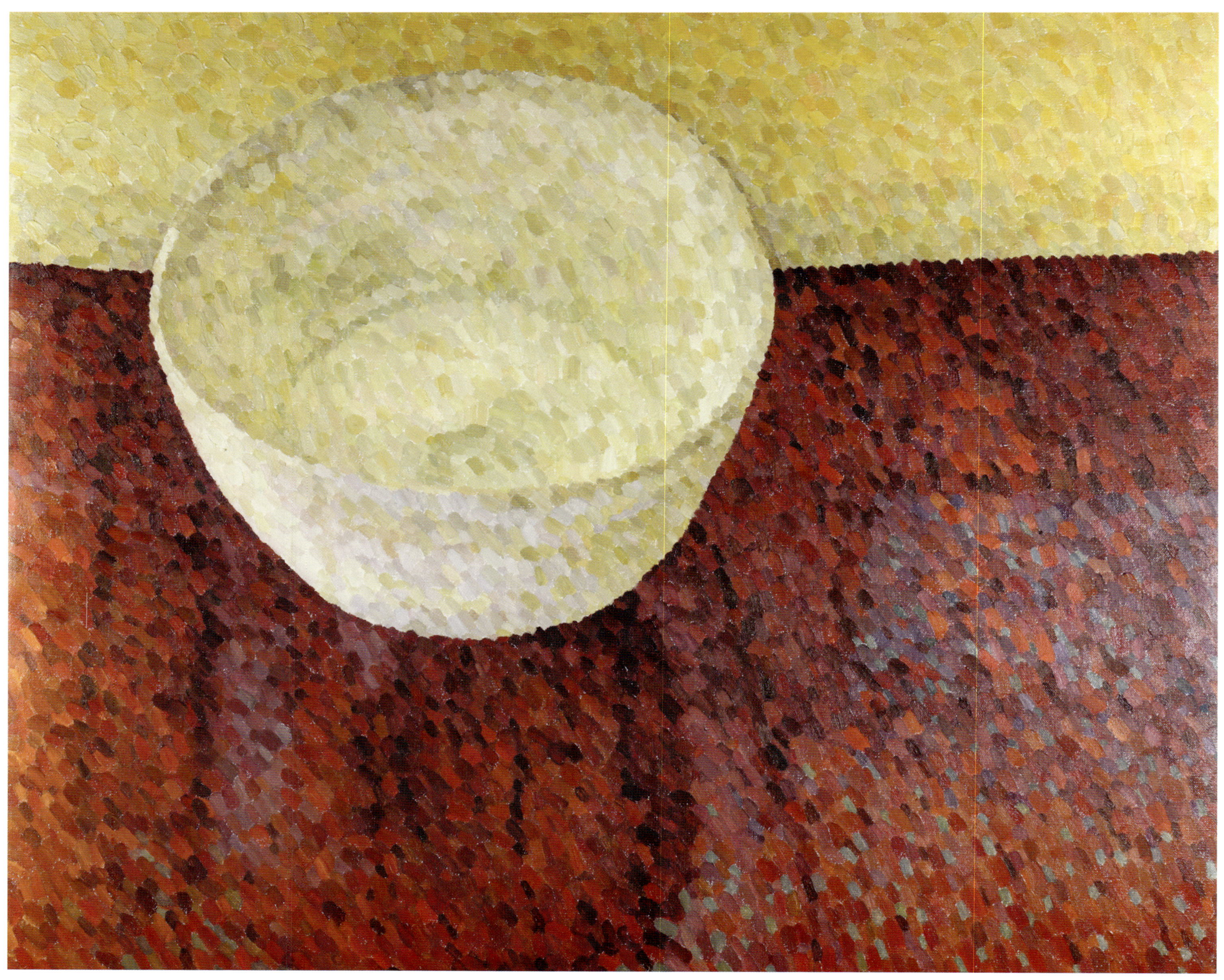

154   William Wilkins

Still Life, Lucie Rie Bowl, 2013, oil on canvas, 60 x 76cm, Courtesy of the artist.

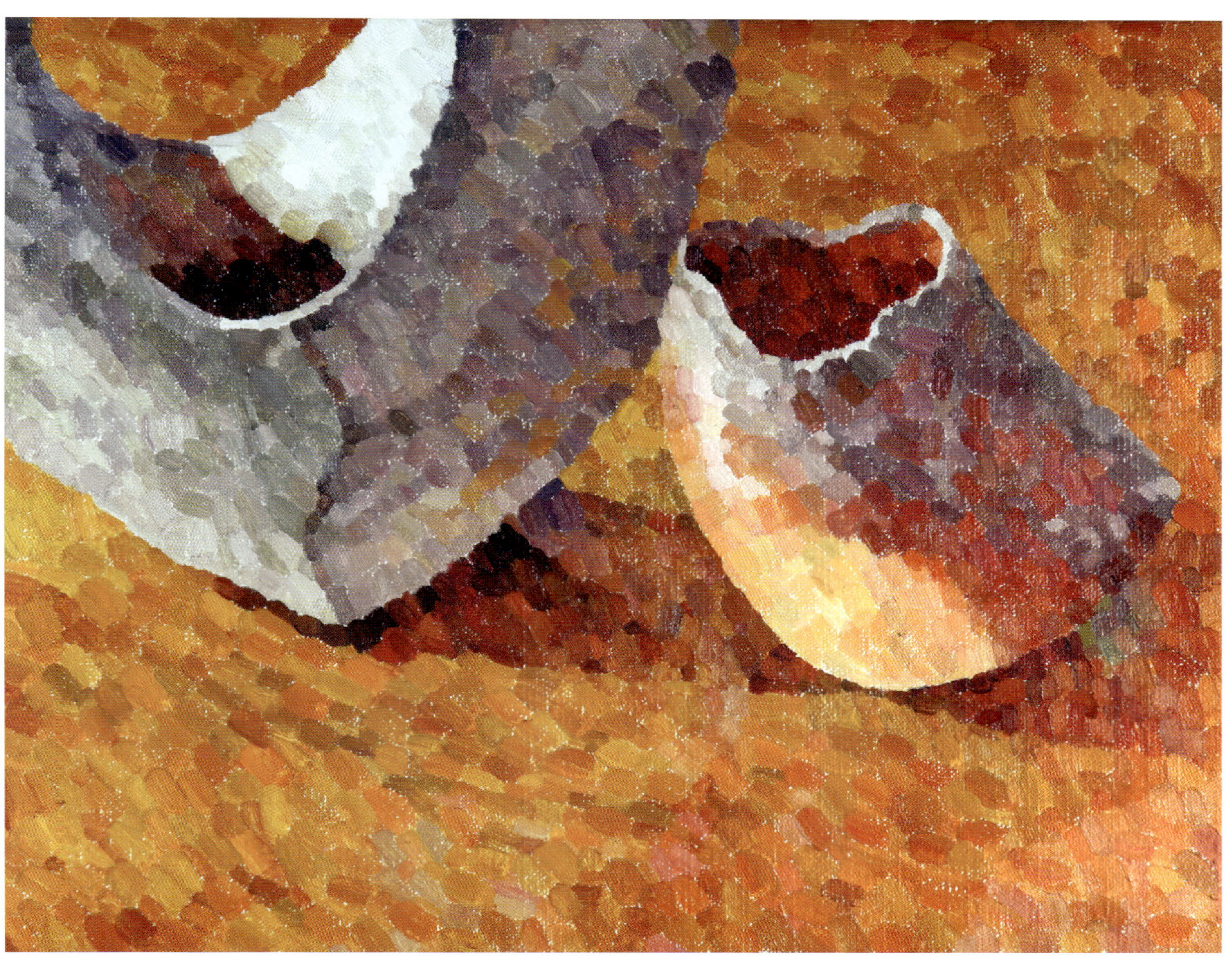

Still Life, Koyama Vessels, 2014, oil on canvas, 27 x 36cm, Courtesy of the artist.

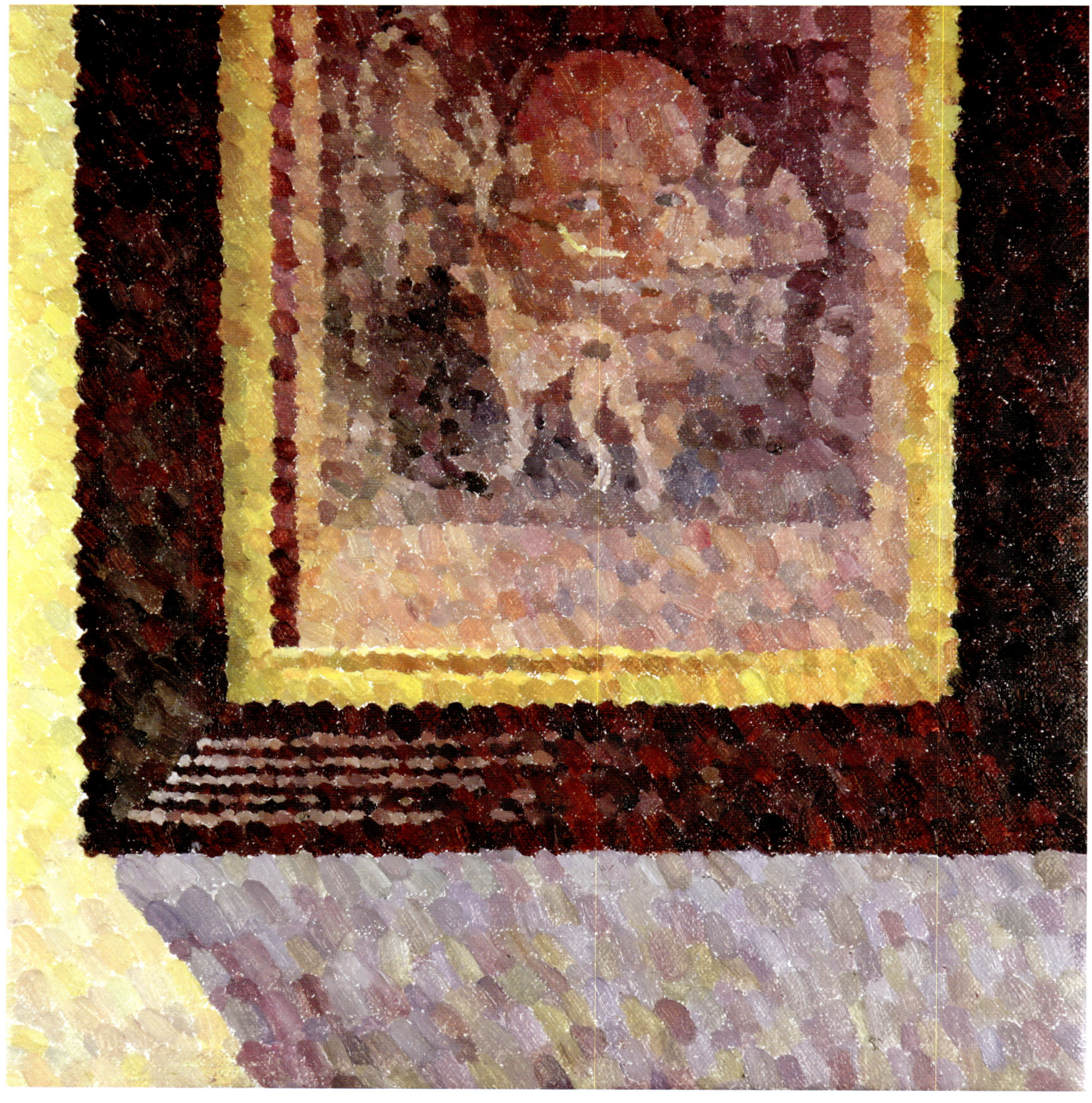

The Trumpeter's Dog, 2014, oil on canvas, 26 x 26cm, Courtesy of the artist.

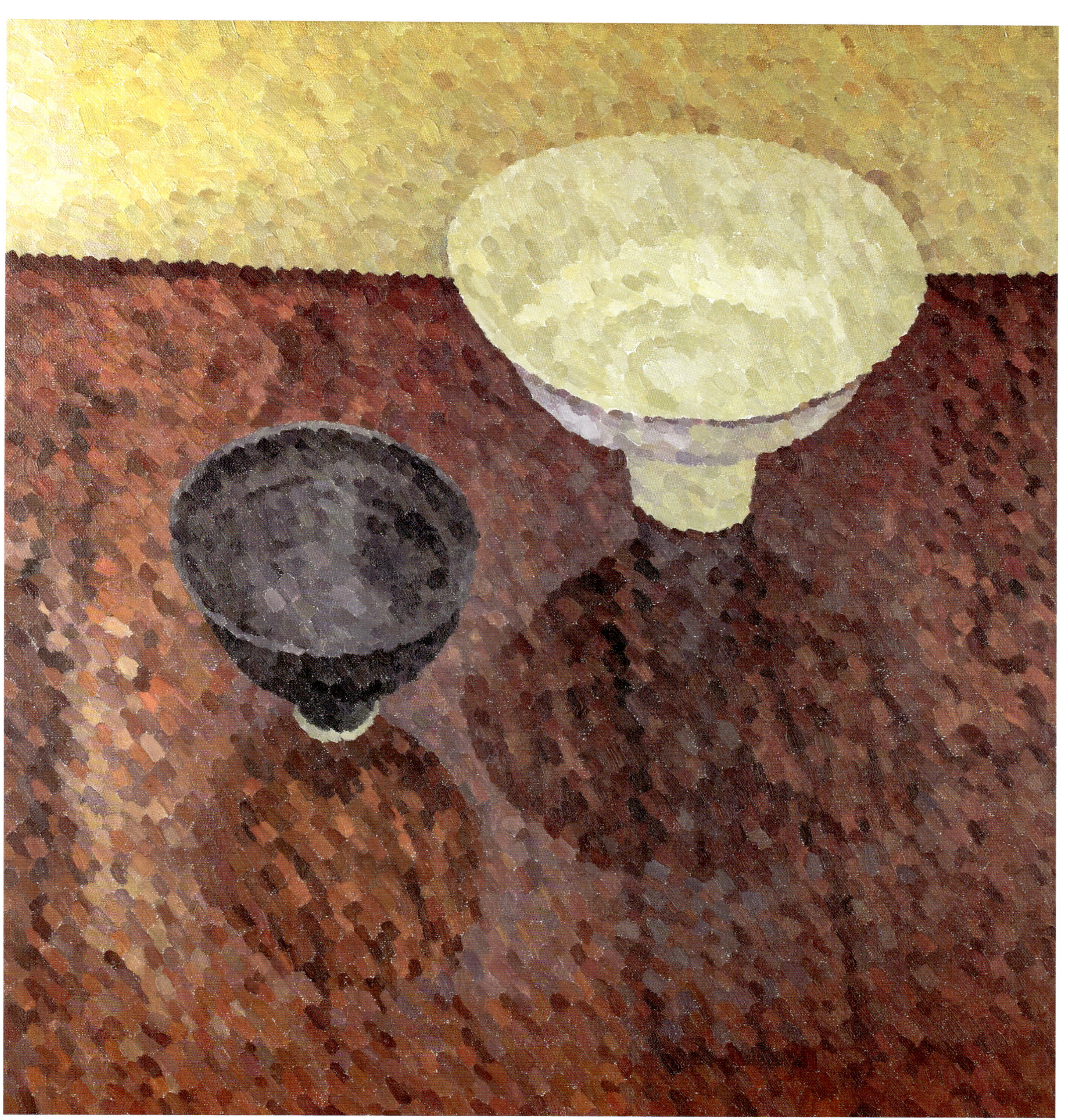

Two Lucie Rie Bowls, 2011, oil on canvas, 51 x 51cm, Courtesy of the artist.

William Powell Wilkins

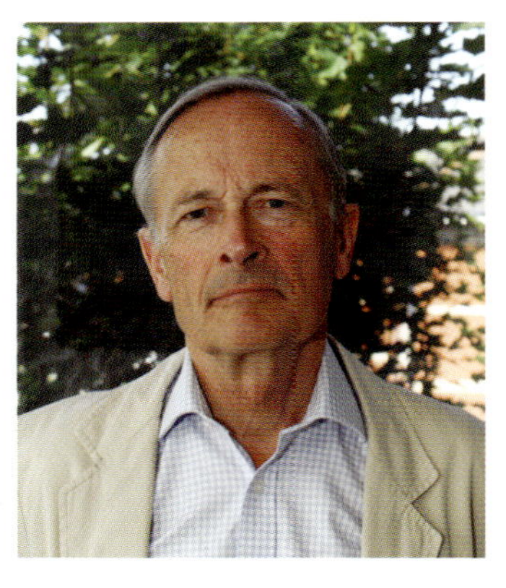

Born in Kersey, Suffolk	1938
Moved to Llandeilo, Carmarthenshire	1940
Swansea College of Art	1955-57
Royal College of Art	1957-60

One-Man Exhibitions

University College of Wales, Aberystwyth	1970
University College, Cardiff	1971
Covent Garden Gallery, London	1972
Welsh Arts, Council, Cardiff	1972
British Institute, Warsaw	1973
Langton Gallery, London	1975
University College, Swansea	1975
Robert Schoelkopf Gallery, New York	1977
Robert Schoelkopf Gallery, New York	1979
Robert Schoelkopf Gallery, New York	1981
12 Duke Street Gallery, London	1983
Barbara Mathes Gallery, New York	1984
Barbara Mathes Gallery, New York	1985
Helander Gallery, Palm Beach, Florida	1986
John Berggruen Gallery, San Francisco	1987
Albemarle Gallery, London	1988
Glynn Vivian Art Gallery, Swansea	1989
Piccadilly Gallery, London	1991

Maxwell Davidson Gallery, New York	1994
Martin Tinney Gallery, Cardiff	2000
Martin Tinney Gallery, Cardiff	2004
Piccadilly Gallery, London	2006
National Botanic Garden of Wales	2007
Martin Tinney Gallery, Cardiff	2008
50 Albemarle Street, London	2011
Martin Tinney Gallery, Cardiff	2011
Martin Tinney Gallery, Cardiff	2014
Erskine, Hall & Coe, London	2014

Group Exhibitions

Covent Garden Gallery, London	1973
Agnews, London – summer and winter exhibitions	1974
Roland, Browse, Delbanco, London	1974
Member of 56 Group Wales	
Exhibitions in England, Scotland, Ireland, Wales, France, Italy and Czechoslovakia	1975-98
Allan Stone Gallery, New York	1976
Welsh Arts Council, Cardiff, 'The Probity of Art'	1976
Leinster Gallery, London, 'Critics Choice'	1985
'Painting in Wales: 1850-1980', Andrew Knight Gallery, Cardiff	1985
'Intimate and Intense – The New Genre of Painting', Payne Gallery, Moravian College, Bethlehem, Penna	1986
Gruenebaum Gallery, New York	1987
'The Self-Portrait: A Modern View', Artsite, Bath and elsewhere	1987-88

Awards

Welsh Arts Council Bursary	1971
Welsh Arts Council Grant	1978
First International Artist in Residence, Artists for the Environment Foundation, Delaware Water Gap National Park, New Jersey, U.S.A.	1980
Ingram Merrill Foundation Award	1980
Royal Cambrian Academician	1993
Honorary Fellow, Royal Institute of British Architects	2001
Honorary Fellow, Trinity College Carmarthen	2001
Honorary Fellow, Swansea Metropolitan University	2002
Honorary Fellow, UWIC	2003
Chancellor's Medal, University of Glamorgan	2003
CBE for services to the environment	2003
Honorary Fellow, Cardiff University	2007

Public Collections

National Museum of Wales

Hirshhorn Museum and Sculpture Garden, Washington DC

Welsh Arts Council, Cardiff

University College of Wales, Aberystwyth

University College, Swansea

Contemporary Arts Society of Wales

Glynn Vivian Art Gallery, Swansea

Private Collections

Britain, USA, Germany, Holland, Switzerland, Australia, Canada and France

Selected Bibliography

Hilton Kramer, 'New British Painter Dazzles', *The New York Times*, 28.10.77.

Gerrit Henry, *Art News*, January 1978.

Hilton Kramer, 'The Work of William Wilkins – Miniaturist of Light', *The New York Times*, 19.10.79.

Elizabeth Dipple, 'The Work of William Wilkins', Robert Schoelkopf Gallery, 1981.

Hilton Kramer, *The New York Times*, 9.10.81.

John Russell Taylor, *The Times*, 24.05.83.

Eric Rowan, 'Painting in Wales 1850-1980', University of Wales Press.

Rosalind Roberts, 'Radiating the Otherness', *Status*, April 1987.

Charles Jencks, 'The Classical Sensibility', *Art and Design*, August 1987.

Sean Kelly/Edward Lucie-Smith, 'The Self-Portrait – A Modern View', Serena Press 1987.

Charles Jencks, 'Post Modernism', Academy Editions, 1988.

Marina Vaizey, Critics Choice, *The Sunday Times*, 31.01.88.

William Wilkins, 'The True Expression of the Subject', *Art and Design*, June 1988.

Edward Lucie-Smith, 'Themes and Variations', Glynn Vivian Art Gallery, 1989.

John Petts, 'The New Wales' 1991.

David Fraser Jenkins, 'Presence and Absence,' Martin Tinney Gallery 2011.

Biographies

David Fraser Jenkins

David Fraser Jenkins studied at the Warburg Institue, London University, and was curator at the National Museum of Wales, Cardiff, and at the Tate Gallery. He has written on modern British art, including the Slade School artists, Gwen and Augustus John, the Camden Town Group, James Pryde, J.S. Sargent, Orpen and William Nicholson. He has also written on art appreciation, on museums, also on Cézanne, Rodin, Lipchitz, Hopper, Moore and Hepworth. David has written on Welsh artists including Merlyn Evans, Ceri Richards, Heinz Koppel, Evan Charlton and Arthur Giardelli. He recently curated an exhibition of Paul Nash at Dulwich Picture Gallery and has curated several of John Piper and is publishing a monograph on his art.

David Moore

David Moore has worked as a curator in Welsh public museums and art galleries and is currently a consultant who writes mainly about art from Wales since the mid twentieth-century. *A Taste of the Avant-Garde: 56 Group Wales, 56 Years* is his concise illustrated history of an exhibiting group of professional artists strongly influenced by international movements in art.

Geraint Talfan Davies

Geraint Talfan Davies is Chairman of Welsh National Opera. He was Controller of BBC Wales from 1990-2000. He has been deeply involved in the arts in Wales, and is a past Chairman of the Arts Council of Wales. He has been a member of the Radio Authority and, in the arts, chairman of CBAT, the Arts and Regeneration Agency, a board member of the Artes Mundi International Visual Arts Prize and Wales Millennium Centre and a Governor of the Royal Welsh College of Music and Drama.

Credits

Published by Graffeg Limited October 2014
ISBN 9781905582891

Graffeg Limited, 24 Stradey Park Business Centre, Mwrwg Road, Llangennech, Llanelli, Carmarthenshire SA14 8YP Wales UK
Tel 01554 824000 www.graffeg.com

Graffeg are hereby identified as the authors of this work in accordance with section 77 of the Copyrights, Designs and Patents Act 1988.

William Wilkins
Introduction text © Geraint Talfan Davies
The Paintings of William Wilkins text
© David Fraser Jenkins
William Wilkins: Professional Artist and Creator of Gardens text © David Moore

Designed and produced by Graffeg
www.graffeg.com

Images © William Wilkins
Photographs by Prudence Cuming Associates, Graham Matthews, Martha McGuire, Mike Roberts and Ken Dickinson.

Distributed by the Welsh Books Council
www.cllc.org.uk castellbrychan@cllc.org.uk

A CIP Catalogue record for this book is available from the British Library.

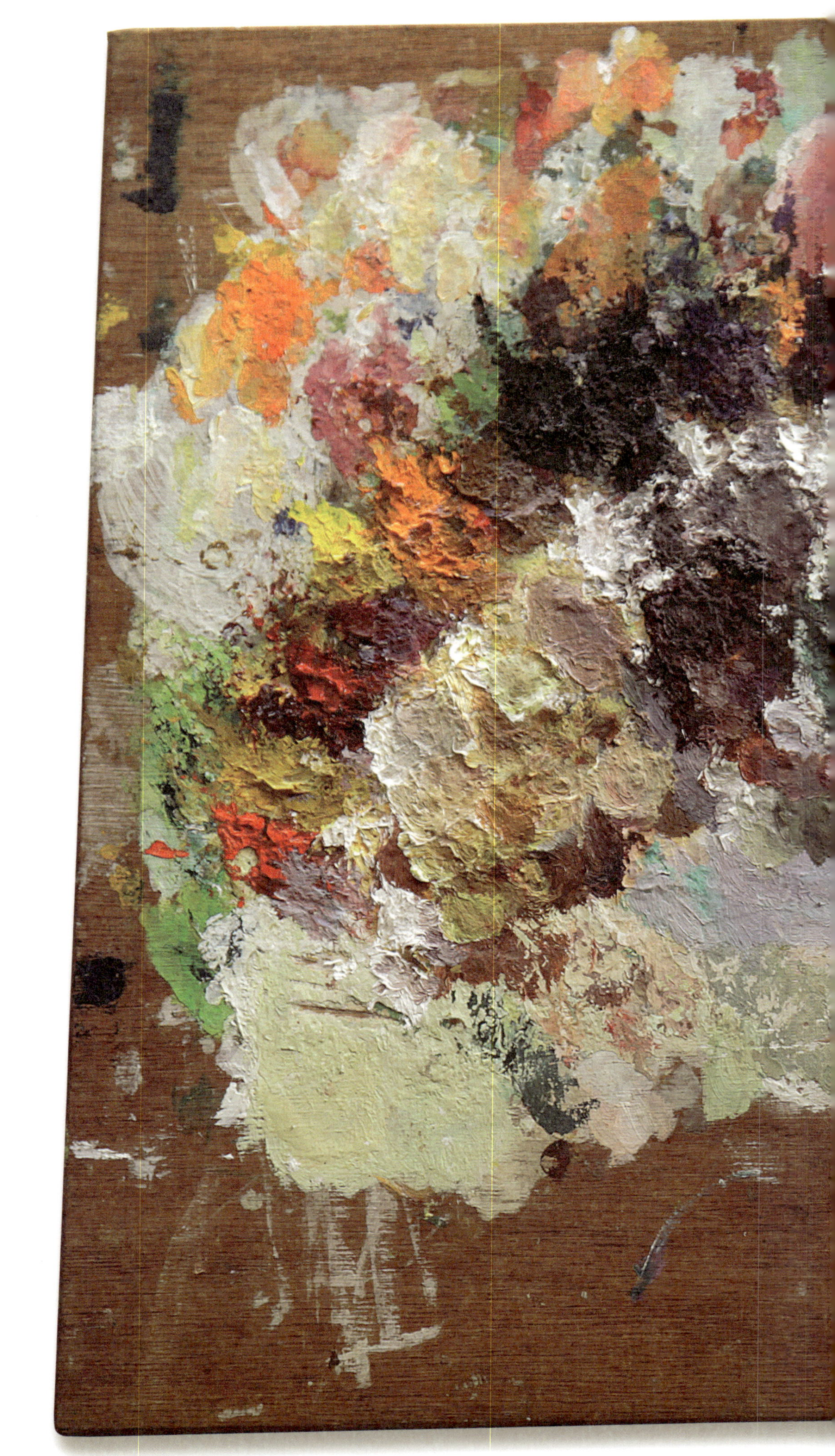